The House We Live In

The House We Live In:
Virtue, Wisdom, and Pluralism

Seth Zuihō Segall

SHEFFIELD UK   BRISTOL CT

Published by Equinox Publishing Ltd.

UK: Office 415, The Workstation, 15 Paternoster Row, Sheffield, South Yorkshire S1 2BX
USA: ISD, 70 Enterprise Drive, Bristol, CT 06010
www.equinoxpub.com

First published 2023

© Seth Zuihō Segall 2023

All rights reserved. No part of this publication may be reproduced or transmitted in any form or by any means, electronic or mechanical, including photocopying, recording or any information storage or retrieval system, without prior permission in writing from the publishers.

British Library Cataloguing-in-Publication Data
A catalogue record for this book is available from the British Library.

ISBN-13	978 1 80050 345 8	(hardback)
	978 1 80050 346 5	(paperback)
	978 1 80050 347 2	(ePDF)
	978 1 80050 400 4	(epub)

Library of Congress Cataloging-in-Publication Data

Names: Segall, Seth Robert, author.

Title: The house we live in : virtue, wisdom, and pluralism / Seth Zuihō Segall.

Description: Sheffield, South Yorkshire ; Bristol, CT : Equinox Publishing, Ltd, 2023. | Includes bibliographical references and index. | Summary: "The House We Live In explores the commonalities underlying three classical approaches to virtue ethics-Aristotelean, Buddhist, and Confucian-to develop a flourishing-based ethics capable of addressing the problems of liberal democracies. This book will appeal to scholars and to general readers." Provided by publisher.

Identifiers: LCCN 2023003695 (print) | LCCN 2023003696 (ebook) |
  ISBN 9781800503458 (hardback) | ISBN 9781800503465 (paperback) |
  ISBN 9781800503472 (pdf) | ISBN 9781800504004 (epub)

Subjects: LCSH: Virtue. | Virtue—Ethics. | Virtues.

Classification: LCC BJ171.V55 S44 2023 (print) | LCC BJ171.V55 (ebook) |
  DDC 179/.9—dc23/eng/20230601

LC record available at https://lccn.loc.gov/2023003695

LC ebook record available at https://lccn.loc.gov/2023003696

Typeset and edited by Queentson Publishing, Hamilton, Canada.

Contents

Acknowledgements	ix
About the Author	xi
Preface	xiii
1. The House We Live In	1
2. On Virtue	21
3. On Wisdom	67
4. On Flourishing	81
5. Only Connect	131
References	175
Index	181

To my wife, Susan, for bringing love and light
into the second chapter of my life.

Acknowledgements

This book could not have appeared in its current form without the assistance of family and friends and the work and inspiration of many colleagues, scholars, and philosophers. First and foremost, my beloved wife, supporter, proofreader, and critic, Susan Mirialakis, who poured over multiple versions of this manuscript to help improve its clarity and readability. Second, my good friends Samuel Weiss, Joseph Palau, and Steve Pantani who read earlier versions of this manuscript and made numerous helpful suggestions. A conversation with literary agent Beth Vessel also helped refocus this book in a more productive direction.

The ideas in this book have been enriched through lively conversations with friends and colleagues. These include my Zen Buddhist mentor, Daiken Nelson Roshi, and Andrew Cooper and James Shaheen at *Tricycle: The Buddhist Review;* my co-religionists at White Plains Zen, Pamsula Zen of Westchester, and the Pamsula Zen Center in New York; my fellow clergy at White Plains Religious Leaders; and my fellow participants in Bob Brantl's Greenburgh Public Library philosophy reading group. It is a blessing to belong to a such a supportive extended network of wise friends and colleagues.

My thinking has also been enriched and clarified through a series of recent writing and teaching projects. These include my essays for Mike Slott's *Secular Buddhist Network*; a chapter for Rick Repetti's *Routledge Handbook of the Philosophy of Meditation* (2022); a chapter co-written with Jean Kristeller for *The Handbook of Positive Psychology, Religion, and Spirituality* (Springer, 2022); an article on mindfulness and Buddhist modernism for *The Humanistic Psychologist* (in an issue I coedited with my dear friend Belinda Khong); and my monthly columns for David Black's *Mindfulness Research*

Monthly. A series of lectures for the *New York Insight Meditation Center* provided an additional opportunity to put my thoughts in order.

People I have never personally met have also served as major sources of inspiration. These include Chinese culture scholars Stephen Angle, Roger Ames, Robert Eno, Paul Goldin, Tao Jiang, Bryan Van Norden, and Michael Slote whose books enriched my understanding of the Chinese philosophical tradition. They include Luke Neale and Phil Crimmins whose on-line *Mandarin Blueprint* program allowed me to attain a beginner's proficiency in reading Chinese. They also include American philosopher John Dewey whose naturalism, holism, pragmatism, democratic sensibility, and understanding of social change have slowly worked their way into every corner of this book, and Canadian philosopher Charles Taylor whose matchless accounts of Western secularism and individualism enriched my thinking in significant ways. It's as much of a blessing to encounter new ideas, discover new sources of inspiration, and expand one's horizons in later life as it is in one's youth.

I am grateful to have lived to complete this book. I sustained a subdural hematoma at the start of 2022 and my (almost) complete recovery is due to the excellent care I received at White Plains Hospital and Burke Rehabilitation Center from their doctors, nurses, and physical, occupational, and speech therapists—and the loving care and support I received from my wife, Susan.

Lastly, let me acknowledge the inspiration I receive daily from my fellow planetary citizens whose myriad actions—staying informed, openly inquiring, engaging in dialogue, voting, volunteering, donating, organizing, running for office, protesting, and courageously resisting—help keep democracy alive and contribute to our Sisyphean task of moving society towards greater empathy, kindness, caring, and compassion. The journey is arduous and long, and reversals and defeats abound. As the old gospel hymn admonishes, "children, don't you get weary." This is the work of many generations, of which we are but a small part. Have patience...but not too much.

About the Author

Seth Zuihō Segall, Ph.D. is a retired clinical psychologist who served on the faculties of the Yale University School of Medicine, Southeast Missouri State University, Southern Illinois University at Carbondale, and the State University of New York at Purchase. He is a former Director of Psychology at Waterbury Hospital and a former President of the New England Society for the Study of Trauma and Dissociation. He ordained as a Zen Buddhist priest in the White Plum Asanga and Zen Peacemaker Order lineages under the preceptorship of Daiken Nelson Roshi.

Dr. Segall's publications include Encountering Buddhism: Western Psychology and Buddhist Teachings (2003), Buddhism and Human Flourishing: A Modern Western Perspective (2020), Living Zen: A Practical Guide to a Balanced Existence (2020), and recent chapters in The Routledge Handbook on the Philosophy of Meditation (2022) and the Springer Handbook of Positive Psychology, Religion, and Spirituality (2022). Dr. Segall is a contributing editor to Tricycle: The Buddhist Review, the science writer for the Mindfulness Research Monthly, and coeditor of a special issue of The Humanistic Psychologist (2021) on "Revisiting and Re-Envisioning Mindfulness: Buddhist and Contemporary Perspectives." Dr. Segall's blog, The Existential Buddhist (www.existentialbuddhist.com), contains essays on Buddhist philosophy, practice, ethics, history, art, and social engagement.

Preface

Pluralism is the recognition that the goals and values we cherish and pursue—freedom, equality, justice, benevolence, health, wealth, power, beauty, intimacy, security, excellence, serenity, sanctity, and ecstasy—do not form a single harmonious whole. We are frequently called on to make trade-offs between them and differ among ourselves as to how we prioritize them. Liberalism (as I define it) means accepting (joyfully or regretfully) this pluralism and tolerating (as much as possible) the rights of others to pursue their highest goals as they see fit. There are limits to this tolerance, however, and for liberals these limits are associated with the harms we may cause others in pursuing our goals.

Liberal pluralism is grounded in a larger understanding of *human flourishing*, with liberals believing the best sorts of societies are those that promote individual and collective flourishing as much as possible. While human flourishing is notoriously hard to define, we all have some vague felt sense of what flourishing might be—some feeling that our lives are meaningful, happy, and good, that our ideals and goals are the right ones for us, and that we are making good-enough progress in their pursuit. We also have a vague sense that flourishing lives are, to some extent, virtuous ones. We do not tend to think of bullies, jerks, liars, and assorted ne'er-do-wells as flourishing, however great their fame and prosperity. We do not want our children to grow up to be like them. We believe flourishing people ought to exhibit appropriate levels of honesty, kindness, fairness, courage, and integrity.

This book is an attempt to clarify the relationship between virtue, wisdom, and flourishing—to define flourishing in terms of the virtues and wisdom that make it possible and the domains in which might be expressed—and apply this understanding to the problems of living in contemporary pluralistic, multicultural, and increasingly secular societies.

Flourishing is one possible English translation of Aristotle's *eudaimonia*. In *Buddhism and Human Flourishing* (2020) I critiqued traditional Buddhist goals from the point of view of a neo-Aristotelian understanding of flourishing. I have since grown to appreciate how the Confucian tradition can be read alongside the Aristotelian and Buddhist traditions as a third classical approach to virtue ethics and flourishing. I believe these three ancient traditions can serve as vital resources for a modern flourishing-based ethics—one capable to shedding light on and addressing the seemingly intractable problems of our time.

My understanding of flourishing has also been greatly enriched by the work of American pragmatist philosopher John Dewey. My approach to contemporary social issues is, for lack of a better word, very *Deweyan*. I believe virtue, wisdom, and flourishing are concepts that evolve through a process of collective inquiry as we go about attempting to solve problems in living, and that these concepts may be interpreted and instantiated differently in different historical eras and cultural contexts. That doesn't mean they are completely culturally relative, however, since all human cultures must address the same basic existential issues of obtaining food and shelter, raising offspring, transmitting knowledge, managing intra-group conflict, and protecting members from marauders.

The liberal, pluralistic, democratic project is currently under fire at home and abroad. There are forces that do not want America to continue developing as a liberal, pluralistic, multicultural democracy in which different religions and forms of unbelief compete within a largely secular sphere, and in which people of different religions, ethnicities, races, genders, and sexual orientations receive equal respect and are, a much as possible, left free to construct their lives as they see fit. In other words, an America in which all sorts of very different kinds of people find ways to somehow get along together and make things work. This book's central thesis is that liberal, pluralistic, multicultural democracies require a broadly accepted ethical framework for this kind of cooperation to regularly occur—a flourishing-based framework that cannot be based on a single religion or culture, but must be, to at least some degree, trans-sectarian and transcultural.

A flourishing-based ethics can also serve as a yardstick for assessing how well we are promoting well-being. There are multiple indicators that we are not doing as well as we might. These indicators include increasing rates of deaths of despair among the middle-aged, anxiety and depression in the young, and affective polarization between political factions. They include decreases in interpersonal trust and social mobility, increases in wealth disparity, and the almost daily occurrence of mass casualty shootings. The fact that Americans died at ten times the rate of Australians during the first years of the COVID pandemic is yet another indicator. Taken together, these indicators suggest we are failing at transmitting and promoting the values, virtues, and wisdom that might lead to greater individual and collective flourishing.

While one attack on the liberal pluralist tradition comes from the right, another comes from those on the left who believe liberals are too timid in the degree of change they support and the rate of change they pursue. Only radical change, these critics argue, can bring marginalized peoples the relief they need *now*. While I sympathize with their wish for faster change, as a Deweyan, I don't believe in the possibility of radical change—only in the possibility of making incremental, piecemeal improvements in existing social relations through collective social inquiry. Societies cannot reinvent themselves *de novo*—as the French and Russians tried in their revolutions. Despite *la Terreur* and the *Gulag,* France is still very much France and Russia very much Russia. The advances wrought by the Chinese revolution came at great expense, and despite Chinese advances in income, education and healthcare, the quality of life in democratic Taiwan with its respect for civil liberties remains preferable in many ways to life in Xi Jinping's China.

I offer this approach to a flourishing-based ethics in the hope it can contribute to a new American consensus on values: one that improves our chances for individual and collective flourishing, allows us to respect and appreciate our differences, and permits us to work together to solve significant problems. I say this with a full understanding that a flourishing-based ethics will not appeal to everyone—certainly not to religious fundamentalists and ethnonationalists. But it does not *have* to appeal to everyone—only enough of us so that we can continue to function as a democracy on a habitable planet into the foreseeable future.

Seth Zuihō Segall
Greenburgh, NY
June, 2022

—1—

The House We Live In

Prologue

When I was an elementary school student in the mid-1950s our teacher played a phonograph recording of Frank Sinatra singing *The House I Live In* (Allan and Robinson 1942). The opening verse of the lyrics posed the question, "What is America to me?" It answered the question in its second verse: "All races and religions—That's America to me." Sinatra originally sang the song in a short film made towards the end of World War II—a film that won Sinatra, the producers, director, songwriter, and composer an honorary Oscar. The lyrics depict America as a multicultural democracy—one in which American identity isn't defined by ethnicity, race, or religion, but by a shared set of common ideals.

When I first heard *The House I Live In*, I thought it exemplified the American credo. I didn't recognize it then for what it was—an aspirational statement, not yet fully realized, and not shared by all. The lyrics, written by blacklisted songwriter Abel Meeropol (under the pseudonym "Lewis Allan"), were written precisely because it wasn't yet a universally agreed upon sentiment. It was propaganda in service of a continuing progressive battle: America was defeating fascism on the battlefields of Europe but hadn't yet defeated racism and antisemitism at home.

The multicultural vision of *The House I Live In* was not the vision of the founding fathers. It is a vision that only emerged gradually in fits and starts over the course of a bloody civil war fought to end slavery and fierce struggles kindled by successive waves of immigration. The civil war might have ended slavery, but America wasn't ready to welcome its former slaves as full-fledged Americans, and successive waves of Irish, Chinese, Italian, and Jewish immigration touched off new battles over American identity. At the same time, America waged a series of genocidal wars against its own indigenous peoples, pushing their survivors to the margins. Even as progressive a figure as Frederick Douglass couldn't imagine an America that fully embraced its indigenous inhabitants. In 1866 he delivered a speech differentiating the prospective fate of American Blacks from Indigenous Americans, saying that while Blacks had achieved the character of a civilized people, "Indians" had not (Blight 2018, 486). United States citizenship wasn't granted to indigenous Americans until 1924.

In the mid-nineteenth century the American Party, popularly known as the "No Nothings," opposed the inclusion of Catholics in general and the Irish in particular, fighting to close American shores to further immigration. The later part of the nineteenth century witnessed the rise of post-reconstruction racial segregation in the South and persistent anti-Black sentiment throughout the North. The official slogan of the 1868 Democratic Party Presidential Nominating Convention held in New York City (which nominated a former New York governor as its candidate) was "This is a white man's country; Let a white man rule" (White 2016, 464). The Nineteenth Century also saw the passage of the 1882 Chinese Exclusion Act which restricted Chinese immigration and disqualified Chinese immigrants from becoming United States citizens—a disqualification that remained in effect until 1943. Immigrants from India weren't eligible for naturalization until 1946, and immigrants from Japan weren't eligible until 1952.

Over 3,000 Blacks were lynched in the South from the late nineteenth to early twentieth century with large-scale massacres of Black people occurring with alarming regularity in Colfax, Louisiana in 1873, Wilmington, North Carolina in 1898, Atlanta, Georgia in 1906, Elaine, Arkansas in 1919, Tulsa, Oklahoma in 1921, and Rosewood, Florida in 1923. *De jure* school segregation persisted throughout the South until *Brown v. The Board of Education* in 1954, and *de facto* school segregation remains throughout much of the country today. Black access to the vote, severely restricted until the Voting Rights Act of 1965, is under renewed attack as these words are being written, and women's suffrage was only granted in 1920.

The late nineteenth and early twentieth centuries witnessed waves of largely Catholic and Jewish immigration from Italy and Eastern Europe—immigration that provoked doubts in Northern and Western European-descent Protestant Americans as to whether they could be integrated into the fabric of American society the way German and Scandinavian immigrants had before. Japanese-Americans were forced into internment camps during World War II, and populist resentment against Central American immigrants helped propel Donald John Trump into the White House in 2016. All of this is just a long way of saying that the vision of America as a multicultural society has been contested ever since first proposed.

When Frank Sinatra sang *The House I Live In,* the progressive metaphor of his day was of America as a melting pot. The idea of the melting pot was foreshadowed in 1782 when Hector St. John de Crèvecœur wrote:

> ... [w]hence came all these people? They are a mixture of English, Scotch, Irish, French, Dutch, Germans, and Swedes ... What, then, is the American, this new man? He is either an European or the descendant of an European; hence that strange mixture of blood, which you will find in no other country ... He is an American, who, leaving behind him all his ancient prejudices and manners, receives new ones from the new mode of life he has embraced, the new government he obeys, and the new rank he holds.
> St. Jean de Crèvecœur 1904, 49–56

De Crèvecœur's melting pot, though, was for Europeans only—and not just Europeans generally, but Protestant Northern and Western Europeans specifically.

The metaphor of the "melting pot" was widely popularized in a 1908 play by that name written by Anglo-Jewish author Israel Zangwill and produced in Washington D.C. In the play's first act, a character named David proclaims:

> Understand that America is God's Crucible, the great Melting-Pot where all the races of Europe are melting and re-forming! Here you stand, good folk, think I, when I see them at Ellis Island, here you stand in your fifty groups, your fifty languages, and histories, and your fifty blood hatreds and rivalries. But you won't be long like that, brothers, for these are the fires of God you've come to—these are fires of God. A fig for your feuds and vendettas! Germans and Frenchmen, Irishmen and Englishmen, Jews, and Russians—into the Crucible with you all! God is making the American.
> (Zangwill 1917, 33)

President Theodore Roosevelt was enthusiastic about the play, later writing Zangwill to say he counted it as "among the very strong and real influences upon my thought and my life" (Dyer 1980, 131). Zangwill's melting pot included immigrants from the whole of Europe—Jews like himself as well—but note the continued absence of Asians, Africans, Latin Americans, and Black and Indigenous Americans from his list. The idea that everyone could be an American was yet to come.

It is only recently that Zangwill's melting pot metaphor has given way to a newer metaphor—let's called it the metaphor of the *mélange*—a blend of distinctive flavors harmonizing to contribute to the overall character of a dish. In the metaphor of the mélange ethnic, racial, and religious groups retain prominent aspects of their unique cultural heritages and identities while sharing a common set of ideals regarding liberty, justice, the rule of law, and democratic governance. In this new metaphor non-Europeans and non-Christians do not just assimilate to pre-existing European-descent Christian culture but contribute to defining a newly emergent culture. We see this process occurring at its most basic level when European-descent Christian Americans learn to enjoy bagels, burritos, ramen, and sushi, or to appreciate blues, jazz, zydeco, hip-hop, Afro-pop, K-pop, and salsa. Pluralistic multiculturalism emphasizes the values of tolerance, acceptance, appreciation of difference, and a willingness to work together for the common good.

But this vision continues to be only one possible vision of America. While most Americans seem more-or-less on board with some version of it, a significant minority continues to oppose it. It is no exaggeration to say that pluralistic multiculturalism and the reaction against it were on the ballot in the 2008, 2012, 2016, and 2020 United States presidential elections. The 2008 and 2012 elections of Barack Hussein Obama, a president whose very personhood symbolized pluralistic multiculturalism, set the stage for White, conservative Christian, and populist resentment and the election of Donald John Trump.

I just used the term "conservative Christian" and I want to clarify what I mean by it. I have struggled to find a word that best describes the Christian traditions that ascribe to Biblical literalism and inerrancy and look backwards towards a pre-modern era. These groups exist in historical opposition to "Mainstream" Christian traditions that embrace modernity, are ecumenical in their outlook, and acknowledge the value of scholarly Biblical criticism and metaphorical interpretation. Words like "fundamentalist," "evangelical," and "Southern Baptist" describe some of the traditions I have grouped together as "conservative." I have settled on using "conservative Christian" as a neutral descriptor (as opposed to "reactionary") for groups that retain a pre-modern Biblical understanding of their faith. It is not intended as a descriptor of the politics of their membership, although the two substantially and increasingly overlap.

One alternative to pluralistic multiculturalism is a vision of America as a European-descent Christian society. There are fringe White nationalist groups that object to the presence of Black, Jewish, Asian, Indigenous, Hispanic, and

Islamic Americans on American soil, full stop. But closely allied with these fringe groups are more mainstream right-wing groups that employ code words like "Western Civilization," "Anglo-Saxon Heritage," "Great Replacement Theory," and "the War Against Christmas" to signal that non-whites and non-Christians need to know their place and assimilate to normative European-descent Christian culture—a kind of American *dhimmitude* in which ethnic, racial, and religious and sexual minorities may dwell on American soil with second-class rights. This is what former Republican Speaker of the House Newt Gingrich means when he declares "if we are going to remain America, we must oppose the forces trying to destroy us," citing "race-based reparations, school quotas, and anti-white and anti-male curricula" as examples of these forces (Gingrich 2021). Similarly, the platform of the congressional America First Caucus (which includes Republican representatives Marjorie Taylor Greene and Paul Gosar) says "America is a nation with a border, and a culture, strengthened by a common respect for uniquely Anglo-Saxon political traditions" (America First Caucus 2021). These political figures are acutely aware that European-descent Christians (conservative or liberal) no longer constitute the majority of Americans, making up just 46% of the population in 2015 (Chan 2015), and they channel resentment against demographic change into a powerful political force. A recent poll showed 56% of Republicans agreed that "the traditional American way of life is disappearing so fast we may have to use force to save it" (Cox 2021, para 34).

Right-wing discontent is driven by related factors as well: changing gender orientation and identity norms, changing gender roles, and the progressive secularization of American culture. For fundamentalist and evangelical Christians (as well as traditional Muslims and Orthodox Jews), the rapidly changing norms governing sexual orientation, identity, and gender and the increasingly secular nature of American life are causes for distress.

While the struggle for American women's civil, social, and economic rights has (if we date it from the Seneca Falls Convention) been going on for 173 years, the emergence and acceptance of LGBTQ+ rights has had a much more rapid trajectory. In a social change of almost unheard-of rapidity, America changed its mind about gay marriage in just fifteen short years. In 2004, 60% of Americans opposed gay marriage, while in 2019, 61% supported it (Pew Research Center 2019). Similarly, in 2017, 73% of Americans thought transgendered Americans should be protected against discrimination (Luhur, Brown and Flores 2019). American culture is moving on, leaving fundamentalist and evangelical Christians behind.

This movement away from being a conservative Christian society to being a pluralistic multicultural society is a continuation of the process of gradual Western secularization that began in the late middle ages and continued through the renaissance, Reformation, scientific revolution, European Enlightenment, and the emergence of the modern nation state. Canadian philosopher Charles Taylor (2007) views secularization as a complex historical phenomenon that includes: 1) the emergence of spheres of governmental, economic, scientific, artistic, educational, and leisure activity that have, at most, only perfunctory and/or ceremonial ties to religious life; 2) the emergence of exclusive humanisms that can compete with religions for people's hearts and minds; 3) a decline in the percentage of persons identifying as religious; and 4) a movement away from a medieval way-of-life in which atheism was essentially unimaginable to a modernity in which even the religious are aware of the possibility of non-religious options and may sometimes have their doubts.

One should not assume this process of secularization will end (at some future date) with an end to religion, period. While secularization creates opportunities for alternatives to religion to thrive, religions adapt and react to secularization through creative reinvention and the adoption of novel forms of worship. America has witnessed the birth of an abundance of new religious traditions over the past two centuries including the Church of Jesus Christ of the Latter-Day Saints, the Seventh Day Adventists, the American Methodist Episcopal and American Methodist Episcopal Zion Churches, the Nation of Islam, Reconstructionist Judaism, Christian Science, the Jehovah Witnesses, and Unitarian Universalism, as well as new Christian movements such as pentecostalism, fundamentalism, revivalism, the prosperity gospel, the social gospel, the Catholic Workers, and liberation theology. Rather than putting an end to religious faith, secularization creates the conditions for a new kind of pluralism in which a variety of forms of belief and unbelief operate and compete within a largely secularized public space. This relegation to being just one denomination within a larger secularized public space is, of course, what many conservative Christians object to. They aspire, like their Puritan forebears, to a new Protestant American dispensation.

The United States became a nation state during Thomas Paine's "Age of Reason," an era when new humanisms were finding wider acceptance (at least among intellectual elites) and European secularization was proceeding apace. The continuing secularization of American society has been an on-and-off affair ever since. The Founding Fathers emphasized the importance of a separation between church and state, and many like Washington, Jefferson, Franklin, Adams, and Monroe were either Deists or entertained Deist sympathies. Jefferson, for example, famously emended his personal Bible to rid it of its supernatural passages. On the other hand, the period after the American revolution was marked by a rebirth in religious enthusiasm during the Second Great Awakening, and successive waves of religious fervor have ebbed and flowed ever since.

As a matter of convenience, we might pick the 1925 Scopes trial as a watershed moment marking the gradual decline of conservative Christian influence in American culture, but almost any year could do. We could as easily have picked 1962, when the Supreme Court banned prayer in public schools; or 1964, when the Supreme Court ruled Henry Miller's *Tropic of Cancer* not obscene; or 1973 when the Supreme Court legalized abortion, or 2003 when the Supreme Court overturned Texas sodomy laws. While the addition of the words "one nation under God" to the Pledge of Allegiance in 1954 marked a symbolic attempt to reverse this advancing secularization, it did little to stop its progression. Just a decade later, the 1960s youth revolution did more to challenge institutional religious authority than any previous wave of American political, social, or moral fervor. This revolution marked a movement away from traditional and communal forms of religious belief and practice towards the idea of religion as a personal spiritual quest. Of course not everyone celebrated this movement—and the reaction against it by conservative religious traditions is a major factor in our current "culture wars." This was a period when some found their religion in psychedelics or Eastern meditation, while others—such as Madelyn Murray O'Hair, Sam Harris, Richard Dawkins, Daniel Dennett, and Christopher Hitchens—found ways to articulate a more militant atheism.

We are now a country with significant numbers of Jews, Muslims, Buddhists, Hindus, and Sikhs, and an even larger number of people who identify as religiously unaffiliated, "spiritual but not religious," agnostic, or atheist. In 2020, while 64% of those over 65 years-old stated they had "no doubts" about God's existence, only 54% of 35-to-49-year-olds and 39% of 18-to-34-year-olds did (General Social Survey 2020). Domains of life that were once the province of religion are increasingly encroached on by science and the social sciences. Most of us now to turn to scientists rather than ministers when we speculate about how the universe, life, and humankind came to be. When we fall ill, we are apt to rely more heavily on medicine than prayer. When we contemplate the ethics of gay marriage, we are more likely to turn to psychologists and social scientists than the Bible. Today, only about 18% of Americans attend church regularly (Outreach Magazine 2018). That is just the way modern life has turned out for most of us.

While the mainline religious, spiritual but not religious, and irreligious generally welcome this increasing secularization, secularization cannot be considered an unmixed blessing. Meaning is an essential aspect of the well-lived life—people need to feel their lives play a valued role in the larger story of their families, communities, nature, and the future. Religions traditionally provided the overarching narratives that linked our lives to the world in meaningful ways, but science's narrative—at least its current one—fails to imbue most lives with purpose, meaning or value. Science reduces living beings into parts—units that can be more easily studied—and when it subsequently tries to reassemble those units into living wholes it views the interactions between the parts mechanistically. We end up with mechanical metaphors: cells are "factories," the heart a "pump," and the brain a "computer." But living beings are not machines. Living beings are self-creating and self-organizing entities that purposefully engage their environments in meaningful ways.

Machines, no matter how complex, can't do that. When an artificial intelligence system translates a sentence written in Chinese characters into English, it has no idea what that sentence "means" and derives no satisfaction from getting it right. It may "know" the Chinese character "日" is an equivalent of the English word "sun," but it has no felt sense of what "sun" *means*. It may calculate that the word "sun" frequently co-occurs in the context of other words ("sky," "star," "rising," "setting," "fusion," etc.) but it has no sensory referents for it: it has never felt the warmth of the sun or experienced its brightness. It can compute the statistical frequencies between words but can't "know" the experiences the words refer to in the non-virtual world. Similarly, when IBM's Deep Blue wins a chess game, it can't enjoy its victory or explain why winning matters to it. It can't decide chess is a frivolous use of its complex circuitry and it would rather do something more meaningful. Nothing "matters" to a machine[1] but living beings have lives that matter to them. This is why science's mechanical metaphors can never adequately address our human quest for meaningful lives.

---

1. Google's LaMDA chatbot claims to "care" about things (Lemoine, 2022) but there are good reasons to think it is playing a complex language game without any genuine comprehension. Nevertheless, LaMDA plays that language game very well and might pass a non-expert person's Turing test.

If traditional religions are fading in influence and science's mechanistic worldview cannot imbue most people's lives with meaning, what then fills this void? There are a variety of secular humanist attempts to address the question of meaning—organizations like the Ethical Culture Society or books like John Dewey's *A Common Faith* (2013) come readily to mind—but these have never caught on with the wider public. Recent history has seen global fascist, communist, and Islamicist responses to this loss of meaning, with QAnon being just the latest iteration of this type of quasi-religious political enthusiasm.

In today's United States, however, this void is most often filled by the pursuit of external goods—wealth, popularity, social status, power, fame, consumer and luxury goods, sensual satisfaction, and entertainment—without strong countervailing values that might put these pursuits into proper perspective. The pursuit of external goods is often accompanied by the pursuit of self-improvement, but an odd kind of self-improvement that places physical fitness, attractiveness, and popularity above intellectual, social, and moral development. People may experience pleasure and enhanced self-esteem from successfully achieving these goals, but they are not what make people *flourish*. Flourishing involves being meaningfully connected to others in ways that genuinely benefit one's family and community. It means cultivating virtue, wisdom, creativity, and integrity along with one's tastes and interests. It means growing into the person you are meant to be while simultaneously finding ways to live in harmony with others. If secular answers are going to improve the quality of human lives, they must be accompanied by new narratives that place individual lives in a meaningful relationship to society, nature, and the future—narratives that focus on the values that make life truly worth living.

As mentioned earlier, conservative Christian concerns over secularization, the changing role of women, and increased LGBTQ+ visibility have melded with more longstanding concerns about the role of ethnic and racial minorities in American life to produce a resurgent White Christian nationalism that played a major role in the 2016 presidential election. To be sure, there were other factors that also played a role in that election—globalization, economic inequality, decreased social mobility, and the loss of good paying jobs; resentment against the meritocracy; and disruptions due to innovations in communication and technology. But there are ways in which all these factors are linked together. Decreasing social mobility and the loss of good paying blue-collar jobs increase the tendency for people to interpret the competition between ethnic and racial groups for economic opportunity as a zero-sum game. If "they" are getting ahead, "we" must be falling back. Anti-minority resentment goes so deep that many poor Whites would rather forgo health insurance benefits for their own families than see "others" get them. In addition, racial animosity prevents poor Blacks and Whites from forming a class-based political alliance which might effectively challenge growing wealth inequality.

As most Americans adopted a more pluralistic vision of America, the mass media has followed suit, increasing the representation of Blacks, Latinos, Indigenous Americans, Asian-Americans, gays, trans people, and non-traditional women in movies, television, publishing, advertising, and popular music. At the same time, mass media prohibitions against nudity, swearing, and graphic depictions of sexual acts have become increasingly *passé*. These changes in mass media content contribute to European-descent and conservative Christian Americans' perceptions that they are losing "their" culture and must fight back to preserve it.

Non-Hispanic White Christians already make up less than 50% of the population, and non-Hispanic Whites—whatever their religion or lack thereof—will become less than 50% of the population at some point in mid-century. Nevertheless, a significant portion of the White conservative Christian minority believes these cultural changes have been foisted on them by a (largely Jewish?) media elite that is undermining the moral fabric of America. Their answer is to "take America back" from those who've stolen it—just like they believe the 2020 election was "stolen" from them. It's a retrograde position that's bound to fail over the long run—like King Canute, one can never hold back the tide of change forever—but in the short run their actions are seriously jeopardizing American democracy. The Republican Party, which has become the institutional voice for White and conservative Christian grievance and resentment, has decided that if it can no longer win national electoral majorities fair and square, it must resort to any means necessary to suppress minority voting and/or deny the legitimacy of elections.

The January 6th insurrection, President Trump's failed attempt to manipulate vote counts, and the assault on truth over the 2020 presidential election are reminders of the fragility of democracy. Athenian democracy lasted less than two centuries, the Roman Republic less than five, and it is anyone's guess whether American democracy can survive to its third centennial.

Americans are now divided into factions that seem to occupy separate epistemological universes—factions so affectively polarized that over a third of

Democrats and Republicans would be upset it their children married a member of the other party (Ballard 2020). While in 2016 9% of all American marriages were marriages between Democrats and Republicans, by 2020 the rate of Democrat-Republican intermarriage had fallen to 3.6% (Wang 2020). Mutual animosity and distrust between factions has been steadily increasing over the past three decades and may be approaching pre-Civil War levels. As this polarization has proceeded, the factions have had increasing difficulty on agreeing on simple matters of fact.

While partisans on both sides of the divide engage in motivated thinking, preferring to believe "facts" in line with their prior beliefs, the problem—at least for now—seems more prominent for voters reacting against multiculturalism, secularization, and changing gender norms and roles. Almost any delusional fantasy—Hillary Clinton is a child-sex trafficker; global warming is a hoax; the COVID vaccine contains a microchip; there was widespread voter fraud during the 2020 election—can be rapidly disseminated and widely believed, despite overwhelming, readily available evidence to the contrary.

This problem is partly due to the fact that different segments of the population differ as to the sources of information they deem trustworthy. Conservative Christians may trust their pastors more than public health officials. Right-wing voters may trust Breitbart, OAN, Fox News, and Newsmax more than the New York Times, Washington Post, New Yorker, or NPR. While right-wing voters have a point when they complain of the mainstream press's center-left bias, they are wrong in thinking right-wing and mainstream media share similar commitments to fact-checking. Mainstream journalists' and editors' biases help to determine what gets to be considered news and how it gets slanted, but their journalistic culture mitigates against knowingly promulgating false stories or taking marching orders and talking points from politicians and/or oligarchs. The same professional journalistic culture does not exist in the right-wing media which seems to exist mostly for the purpose of stirring outrage and exploiting resentment in their pro-Trump base. Outrage is the coin of the realm, attracting advertising dollars and filling political coffers. While progressive media also focuses on stories that stir outrage in their base, they are significantly more careful to distinguish fact from outright fiction. Fox News opinion hosts regularly cross lines MSNBC news personalities rarely dare approach.

Three facts are clear regarding the current cultural divide. The first is that liberals and progressives cannot change right-wing voters' minds, and right-wing voters cannot change liberals' and progressives' minds. The second is that neither faction is going anywhere anytime soon; we will have to live together for some time to come. The third is that a plurality of Americans—about 45%—do not move in lockstep with either faction. Many do not keep up with liberal, mainstream, or right-wing information sources and are disengaged from political life in general. Others have mixed allegiances—traditionalist on some issues, liberal on others. Some are liberal on economic and conservative on social issues, while others are liberal on social and conservative on economic issues.

Values, Pluralism, Secularization, and Ethics

Focusing on the historical, economic, political, and sociological factors contributing to the cultural divide can cause us to miss how these factors are the consequences of the values we hold. Perhaps, like Marx, we tend to think that our values reflect the material conditions of our lives rather than drive them—that our values are merely epiphenomenal. But the relationship between our values and the material conditions of our lives is never a one-way street. Our values play important roles in determining how we interpret, respond to, and shape events.

Social phenomena like inequality, secularization, privilege, and gender norms arise from actions deeply rooted in individual and collective values. Values—the things we care about—are in turn tethered to larger visions of the good life and what it means to be a good person. Our individual understandings of *justice, fairness, liberty,* and *social responsibility* influence how we view and respond to a whole panoply of hot button issues related to politics, economics, and social life.

Whether something is *just* or someone *responsible* are *value judgements*—not objective facts. This conjunction of *value* (what we care about) with *judgement* (an evaluative process) alert us to the fact that *value judgements* have affective and cognitive aspects. Ethics—the branch of philosophy that helps us think more clearly about which values we *ought* to care about and *why,* and how we ought to weigh conflicts between them when they arise—has a lot to say about the sources of our current dilemma.

Whether White conservative Christians like it or not, America is *de facto* a pluralistic society. As a pluralistic society, we encompass a diversity of competing—and often incompatible—visions of the good life. As Isaiah Berlin (1979) pointed out, pluralism is the belief that all the higher goals we humans pursue—freedom, equality, justice, health, wealth, beauty, intimacy, power, respect, security, excellence, serenity, sanctity, ecstasy—do not form one harmonious whole but often conflict with each other and require tradeoffs. Modern secular liberal societies agree to tolerate this diversity in personal values, goals, and visions so long as these values, goals, and visions do not offend the majority to an intolerable degree. What degree of values divergence is tolerable and what degree is intolerable is never a clear bright line. Questions of whether Mormons can engage in plural marriage, Indigenous Americans can use peyote in religious rituals, Jehovah's Witnesses can deny their children blood transfusions, African immigrants can engage in clitoral circumcision, Jewish Yeshivas can evade education mandates, or conservative Christians can refuse accommodations to gay couples are political issues that get settled through the political process, one way or another. This "settling," however, may not be permanent, and as social conditions change, what was once intolerable may become tolerable and vice versa.

American pluralism is reflected in the diversity of visions of the good life that compete against each other in the public square. Consider, if you will, what the good life might be for four idealized stereotypes: a Conservative Christian, a Hedge Fund Manager, a Social Justice Warrior, and an Artist.

For the Conservative Christian, the good life is a life that conforms to a Biblically-informed understanding of God's commandments—one in which one accepts Jesus Christ as one's personal savior and attains everlasting life in the Kingdom of Heaven. While material benefits are blessings from God, Conservative Christians do not live their lives for their sake. Conservative Christians spread the Gospel to assist in the establishment of God's Kingdom on earth.

The Hedge Fund Manager—for the purposes of our example I will make him male and agnostic—has a different definition of the good life. The good life for him is one in which he acquires great wealth and retires early in comfort, pleasure, and ease. Wealth is valued for what it can buy—social and political influence, a greater choice of sexual and romantic partners, entrance into the best society—and perhaps even a personal jet. When he dies, he gets to leave his considerable wealth to his heirs.

Social Justice Warriors have little interest in the Bible or great wealth. They are interested in serving as allies to the oppressed and marginalized and not coasting on the privileges accrued by virtue of their birth position in the social hierarchy. Being a good person means dedicating oneself to the historical fight for equal treatment and expanded opportunity for all and waking others up to the reality of injustice. Social Justice Warriors work at jobs that enable them to do meaningful work in journalism, the helping professions, non-governmental organizations, and political campaigns. They value a lifestyle aligned with political purity, and may be vegetarians, or the first to purchase electric cars.

For the Artist, the good life is the creative life. Religious, financial, and political concerns are purely secondary. The ability to use one's talents to create something beautiful, meaningful, or new is what counts. Most artists scrape by, money being a constant concern, but their primary interest is not in art as a means of support but as a means of expression and a contributing to culture.

These are, of course, caricatures, and many (if not most) people occupy hybrid positions. Some artists are social activists, others are greedy for wealth. Some Conservative Christians subscribe to the Prosperity Gospel, while some Social Justice Warriors subscribe to Liberation Theology. To the extent that we are influenced by competing visions of the good life (and most of us are), we experience some degree of internal conflict over how to integrate opposing aspects of those visions.

To complicate matters, whatever our primary identity, most of us also have a common-sense notion of what it means to be a "good person" that we share with the majority of our neighbors—an understanding that grows out of what is universal to life, as well as from living in a partially shared culture—a culture transmitted through public schools, books, magazines, radio, television, the movies, the internet, and advertising and influenced by Greco-Roman, Judeo-Christian, and European Enlightenment ideals. We have, to a considerable degree, a largely shared sense of what it means to be a decent human being that transcends our separate identities and group affinities. People from different races, ethnicities, religions, and social classes often agree on shared fundamental values: providing for their families, raising their children so they "turn out well," doing honest work, being a good neighbor, and observing the golden rule. As much as we may hold incompatible values—how we think about abortion or gun control—we agree more than we disagree on many, if not most, values. We agree that being a good neighbor means helping a sick neighbor get to a doctor, or not playing music too loudly late at night.

Even in areas where we hold competing values it can still be possible for us to find islands of agreement. The Conservative Christian and the Social Justice Warrior might agree the Hedge Fund Manager is mistaken when he values wealth as much as he does. The Conservative Christian might cite Matthew 19:24, that "it is easier for a camel to go through the eye of a needle than for a rich man to enter the kingdom of God." The Social Justice Warrior might note how his pursuit of wealth contributes to economic inequality. They both agree the pursuit of wealth should not be the be-all-and-end-all of life, but from different perspectives. This is what philosopher John Rawls (1993) refers to as an "overlapping consensus." Overlapping consensuses allow for the making of all sorts of strange bedfellows—people who disagree deeply on core identity issues but find themselves allied on other issues. This ability to form practical alliances despite philosophical differences is an important means of obtaining majorities on important issues in pluralistic democracies.

While there has probably never been a time in history when all the members of a community were in universal agreement about what constitutes the good life, several aspects of our current historical situation may make this lack of agreement more difficult than it might otherwise be. First, large nation states spanning vast amounts of territory encompass multiple ethnic and religious groups within their borders, while vast expanses of territory maximize conditions for the emergence of regional differences. While smaller nations can still suffer tragic intergroup conflict (e.g., Northern Ireland, Israel, Lebanon, Sri Lanka, Syria, Iraq, Myanmar, and Rwanda) this problem is amplified in larger nation states. The United States, Russia, and China all struggled and continue to struggle with how to weld a national identity out of an amalgam of distinct ethnic and religious groups.

Second, the very condition of modernity introduces a unique problem. As philosopher Alasdair MacIntyre pointed out in *After Virtue (1981)*, modern Western moral language—its "oughts," and "shalt nots"— rests on premodern metaphysical assumptions that many modern people no longer share. If we think of moral systems as analogous to buildings, it's as if the outer façade of our moral edifice still stands, but without the foundation or scaffolding to keep it from collapsing. For a very long time—perhaps two millennia—that foundation (in the West) was grounded in Judeo-Christian beliefs about God. If we ever stopped to wonder why murder, theft, or adultery were wrong, we found the answers engraved on Moses' tablets. Things were morally wrong, evil, or sinful because they were contrary to God's will.

But what happens when people no longer believe in God, or as is even more often the case, when people still believe in God—sort of—but see more and more of their lives dominated by secular concerns with religion relegated to ever smaller corners of their lives? The Western Enlightenment, which expanded the role of reason and personal conscience in human affairs, was suspicious of arguments grounded in authority—whether that be the authority of ancient Greek philosophers or the Bible.

In the wake of increasing secularization, philosophers like David Hume, Immanuel Kant, Jeremy Bentham, and John Stuart Mill sought to establish new foundations for moral reasoning that weren't solely based on religious authority. Hume thought morality was based on human sentiment. The expression "murder is wrong" meant little more than "ugh, murder!" We don't like the idea of being murdered or having anyone we love being murdered—so we set up moral rules to reduce the probability of its occurrence.

Kant thought morality was based on reason. Before people acted, they ought to ask, "what would it be like if everyone acted this way?" People have a duty to only engage in behaviors they could reasonably endorse if everyone else behaved the same way. He called this his "categorical imperative," and his ethical approach was called "deontology," or "the science of duty."

Bentham and Mill based morality on maximizing pleasure and minimizing pain. They believed one should always act in ways that resulted in the greatest good for the greatest number as measured by their pleasure and suffering. In theory, one could devise a moral calculus, taking everyone's pleasures and pains into account, and enabling one to determine which actions result in the best outcomes. Their approach was called "utilitarianism." Most popularly responsive governments use some form of utilitarian reasoning to aid in determining public policy.

The spoilsport in our story is philosopher Fredrich Nietzsche. More than anyone else, Nietzsche understood that if God were "dead," nothing could replace the certainty of older religious moral formulations. How could one determine whether Kant's deontology, Bentham and Mill's utilitarianism, or Hume's emotivism was the right basis for ethics? There could be many views of how to determine what was ethical, but no rock-solid foundation to base them on or iron-clad rules for how to choose between them. Nietzsche left us faced with a spectrum of perspectives, each with its relative advantages and limitations. In addition, Nietzsche was aware of how often morality could be deployed by rulers as a tool to control those subject to them—raw power wielded under the guise of "goodness." Slaveowners could preach the virtues of submission and humility to their slaves. Men could preach it was God's will that women stay home and not seek to exercise their powers in the larger world.

To make matters worse, Nietzsche was scornful of Hume's, Kant's, Bentham's, and Mill's attempts to define the highest human goals in terms of decency, beneficence, cooperation, and equality. He felt these kinds of humanisms gave insufficient attention to the more Dionysian and heroic sides of human existence, and in fact, mitigated against them.

Many religions try to base their ethical principles on metaphysics. The monotheistic religions based theirs on an understanding of God, the Daoists on an understanding of Nature, and the Buddhists on an understanding of Karma. Basing ethics on metaphysics, however, is always a risky way to proceed because metaphysics, like science, can only tell us how things are, but not how they ought to be. The Greek, Roman, Norse, and Vedic gods, for example, weren't particularly ethical. As expressions of the power of Nature, they were beyond good and evil. What moral lessons could we learn from them? Similarly, the Chinese Daoist philosopher Laozi wrote that "heaven and earth are not humane" and recommended the wise person behave likewise. It is only in the monotheistic traditions that we encounter a God who is omnipotent, omniscient, omnibenevolent, and desires the good for human beings. This, of course, creates the problem of theodicy—if God is all-powerful and good, why do evil and suffering exist?—a problem polytheists never had to fret over.

Once one understands the world from a modern, pluralistic, multicultural perspective, however, one quickly encounters the epistemological problem that even if one believes in God, how is one to know how God wishes us to behave? One would also have to be certain that the Torah, the Bible, or the Koran was the authentic word of God. But how can one be sure whether one ought to follow the Torah, the Bible, or the Koran? Should we observe Friday, Saturday, or Sunday as our holy day? Should we fast for Yom Kippur, Lent, or Ramadan? Do we need to follow the laws of kashrut and circumcision, or have they been superseded? There are no objective criteria for making these choices, and it usually comes down to what one's parents believed and/or the tradition one is born into.

There are also problematic differences of opinion even within single religious traditions about how God wants us to behave. The Old Testament doesn't explicitly condemn concubinage, slavery, or polygamy—are they still permitted? God ordered Joshua to exterminate the Canaanites and Saul to exterminate the Amalekites. Does God condone genocide? The Bible tells us to put blasphemers, people who work on the Sabbath, adulterers, prostitutes, and children who curse or strike their parents to death. Should we still be doing so? The Bible orders us not to trim our hair around our temples or mar the edges of our beards. Are we sinning when we get a shave and haircut? What these examples demonstrate is that even fundamentalists must engage in some degree of interpretation when reading scripture and use reason to discern which Biblical laws must still be followed and which are no longer operative.

All of this leads to the following question: are the things God wants us to do good because He wants us to do them, or does He want us to do them because they are good? If God can only wish the good, does that limit his omnipotence? If God wants us to do things because they are good in and of themselves, is God obeying a criterion for goodness external to Himself? Might we be able to discern that criterion for goodness for ourselves through the exercise of reason?

I raise these questions because no matter what our metaphysical beliefs—monotheism, polytheism, pantheism, atheism—we are still left with the problem of determining what is good for ourselves. Our traditions can guide us to a certain degree, but in the end, we also have no choice but to depend on our capacity for reason and our capacity, however weak or strong, to discern good from bad.

Multicultural pluralism and modernity conspire to present us with a spectrum of perspectives on ethical questions without absolute ways of resolving the differences between them. At the same time, the groups that make up multicultural pluralistic societies need to agree on basic rules of the road and find ways to live and cooperate, finding areas of agreement wherever possible, and tolerating differences wherever possible. This is the challenge of ethics in modern, pluralistic, multicultural societies. Our current cultural divide teaches us that there can be no ethical system everyone will universally agree on. Nevertheless, it may be possible to develop an approach to ethics that *enough* people can agree on—enough to enable us to continue to muddle through as a democracy. Whatever new ethical perspective eventually emerges, it can no longer be based on the teachings of a single religion—or any religion for that matter. It must make intuitive sense to people from many diverse cultures, the religious and irreligious alike.

Ethical Renewal

The need for a new common ethical framework is urgent. As a nation, we are plagued by problems that are the consequences of holding the wrong sorts of values—the wrong sorts of values if we are going to thrive, individually and collectively, in a pluralistic, multicultural democracy. We have an economic system that bestows unimaginable wealth on the few while many are food insecure, reside in substandard housing, and have limited access to a decent education or healthcare. We have an economy fueled by hydrocarbons that is destroying the planet that our lives—and the lives of all species—depend on.

We have an extreme ethos of individualism that causes people to value their personal freedom above and beyond any social responsibility for the well-being of others. We spend trillions of dollars on pointless military adventures abroad while basic needs for food, shelter, medicine, infrastructure, and education go unmet at home. We have digital means of mass communication that are unconstrained by commitments to truth or the common good. We have a mass culture that values wealth, fame, power, selfishness, and conspicuous consumption above common decency and a sense of community. We are faced with twin epidemics of deaths of despair in the middle-aged and anxiety and depression in the young.

We can only make progress in addressing these problems if we develop a common ethical perspective on what ought to matter to us. This new perspective must emphasize our responsibilities to each other, to the planet, and to the future, as much as it protects our individual rights and liberties. One of the great conflicts of our time is the competition between societies like the United States that emphasize personal freedom, and societies like China that emphasize collective responsibility. Any successful newly emergent ethical framework must acknowledge the strengths and limitations of each approach and strive for a synthesis that honors both individual rights and our collective responsibilities for each other. It must be ecologically-minded, recognizing we are not a mass of isolated egos, but members of families, communities, and ecosystems. Corporations need to understand their moral responsibilities not just to their shareholders, but to their employees, communities, end-users, and the environment. We are all responsible for taking care of the house we live in.

The remainder of this book proposes an approach to ethical renewal I believe is uniquely suited to modern, pluralistic, multicultural democracies. Perhaps surprisingly, it is not based on novel ideas or discoveries, but on an appreciation for what the classical ethical Aristotelian, Confucian, and Buddhist traditions of ancient Greece, China, and India share in common.

All three of these traditions can be characterized, in part or in whole, as virtue ethics traditions. Virtue ethics is an ethical approach distinct from deontology, utilitarianism, and emotivism. Deontology and utilitarianism devised rules for how we ought to behave—Kant's categorial imperative and Bentham's greatest good for the greatest number. Virtue ethics approaches don't devise rules—how could simple rules ever cover all the nuances and complexities of the human situation?—but are interested in how people develop character and judgement. Virtue ethics approaches start with a vision of what it means to live good and admirable lives, and then enumerate the moral and intellectual virtues conducive to leading them. Finally, they offer suggestions as to how one might go about cultivating them.

But before we investigate the common threads uniting the Aristotelian, Confucian, and Buddhist ethical traditions and their relevance to modern circumstances, we need a clearer idea of what values are and how they arise out of social conditions. The kind of approach I am about to outline is sometimes criticized as promoting "cultural relativism"—the idea that there is no way of judging the goodness or badness of a culture's values, and that each culture's values make sense in the context of the culture they are a part of. I want to be clear that while values are not immutable and handed down from the gods, they are also not completely culturally relative. We will begin by exploring how values emerge and change in the contexts of cultures, but also how they are also grounded in human nature and the existential circumstances governing all human lives. Within this framework, values are good or bad to the extent that they promote or detract from human flourishing—but it will take us several chapters to explore how values and virtues relate to flourishing, and exactly what flourishing encompasses.

—2—

On Virtue

Introduction

In the previous chapter, I portrayed the crisis of American democracy as primarily ethical: a collective failure to inculcate the values, virtues, and wisdom that are the prerequisites for individual and collective flourishing in a multicultural democracy. In this chapter I argue that the solution to this crisis lies not so much in a return to a traditional understanding of the virtues as a *reimagining* of them. There are ways in which we will want to carry the wisdom of the past forward *as is*, and ways we will want to carry it forward in a new way. This is because virtues have their universal and particularistic aspects. While the core idea behind each virtue is universal, how it is expressed and emphasized in each culture is subject to variation. Our task is to preserve what is universal about each virtue while modifying its particulars to fit current circumstances.

Consider how attitudes regarding sexual morality have changed in modern Western cultures over the past century. Female premarital chastity used to be more highly prized in the past. In cultures where female virginity is still highly valued, preserving a woman's virginity helps determine her future opportunities for well-being within that society. In societies where virginity is less valued, other types of sexually related harm rise to the forefront as matters of concern: betrayal of trust, lack of consent, victimization, the spread of disease, and so on. While the general principle of not causing harm is preserved throughout this cultural transformation, the emphasis on chastity is not. In this example, the principle of "do no harm" is the universal aspect of sexual morality, and concern for chastity the culture-specific variation.

The same point can be made about changing norms and values regarding sexual orientation and gender identity. The specifics about what is socially acceptable change, but the prime injunction to "do not harm" does not. All sorts of things that were once considered immoral are now considered acceptable, but persons are still expected to express sexuality responsibly and not cause psychological or physical harm.

My claim that "do no harm" ought to be considered the universal aspect of sexual ethics is part of a larger argument that ethics should be understood in terms of their value for individual and collective flourishing. Things are "good" and "right" when they contribute to flourishing, and "bad" and "wrong" when they diminish it. This is what philosophers call a "virtue ethics" argument. Its strength lies in its appeal to contemporary common sense: we know there is no simple set of formal ethical rules that can successfully address every situation we find ourselves in, and we tend to make our judgements about right and wrong based on how our actions will impact our well-being and the well-being of others. Virtue ethics' principal weakness is that *flourishing* seems an overly vague concept—what is it precisely? Can any two people agree on what flourishing is? We will explore more precise ways of thinking about flourishing in Chapter 4.

But not everyone agrees that "do no harm" ought to be the central principle underlying sexual ethics. A religious fundamentalist might argue that the prime purpose of sexual ethics is to preserve *purity*. Purity is a concept derived from the metaphysical division of the world into things that are holy and things that are unclean. Premarital sexuality belongs to the realm of the unclean; once an unmarried woman loses her virginity, her purity is stained and spoiled. For those of us who have grown up in an increasingly secular culture, dividing the world into pure and impure realms feels distinctly premodern. We tend to no longer view sexuality as the playground of the Devil, but as a field of human experience rich in opportunities for joy, fulfillment, betrayal, humiliation, and injury. As such, it serves as a fertile field for ethical inquiry: what does it mean to behave as an ethical sexual agent? The answers that emerge from this process of inquiry can never be final or absolute. They can only be the best we can manage in our present context, open to challenge and reinterpretation as social considerations change.

The current debate over rules of sexual consent is a case in point. General social opinion regarding sexual consent has undergone a sea change for the better in recent years, but at the same time, some newly suggested rules can seem extreme. Must every instance of physical contact between two people always involve explicit verbal consent—does one person always have to explicitly ask permission and the other grant it—or are there situations in which a kiss or hug may be bestowed without verbal contract? The reader may agree there are such circumstances—but the rules for when, where, and with whom are unsettlingly vague. We are undergoing a process of collective social inquiry, and we do not yet know what consensus we will "finally" arrive at. I put the word "finally" in scare quotes, because there is never really a "final" consensus. Whatever consensus we eventually arrive at will continue to be subject to further inquiry and change as social conditions change. The older rules were, we think, much clearer (although they never really were—just more familiar). The newly emergent rules can leave us feeling a bit unsettled—but we remember the problems the old rules caused and why they needed revision. We might wish things were less complicated, but the way social rules and practices change is always messy and complicated.

Ethics is always the outcome of an emergent process of collaborative social inquiry rather than a set of fixed, definitive, and absolute rules. Saying ethics emerges from sets of social conditions, however, is not the same thing as saying ethics is simply a matter of taste or convention. Ethics do not float freely in the air but are grounded in existential concerns about how we ought to live. These concerns are not simply ideas we entertain but ultimate concerns regarding our well-being and the well-being of those we love.

There is one other point I want to make before proceeding to examine the virtues in depth. I want to come to virtue's defense, because—let's face it—virtue has gotten some bad press lately. It often gets associated with being priggish, prudish, stuffy, fusty, illiberal, and old-fashioned. In addition, the trope of the moralist-*cum*-villain has a lengthy cultural history: think of the Spanish Grand Inquisitor Tomás de Torquemada or the obsessed Inspector Javert in Victor Hugo's *Les Misérables*. If they are exemplars of virtue, we want none of it.

When it comes to virtue, we also don't like busybodies who intrude into other people's private affairs, who grimly pursue punishing those who fail to live up to their moral standards, or who throw stones without recognizing their own shortcomings. Progressive readers will cringe when considering past (and present) public crusades against comic books, rap lyrics, pot smoking, premarital sex, and homosexuality. Non-religious readers will find virtue's connotation as an antonym to "sin"—the idea that failures of virtue aren't matters of folly, but affronts to the Deity—a non-starter.

But the classical concept of virtue—a concept derived from ancient traditions such as those associated with Aristotle, Confucius, and the Buddha—

is not about evil, sin, or fallenness—but about excellence and skillfulness in the art of living. It refers to constellations of habit and value regarding heart, mind, and behavior that contribute to living successfully and take the legitimate concerns and well-being of others into consideration.

Virtues and Values

I called the virtues *constellations of "habit" and "value"* because "habit" by itself captures some, but not all, of what we mean by virtue. Imagine being two-years old and pinching your baby sister to make her cry. Your mother asks if you did anything to hurt her, and you lie and say, "no." This makes perfect sense to your two-year-old self because you would really like to avoid punishment if you can. Your mother, however, has seen you pinch your sister. Her question was merely rhetorical—you've been caught in a lie. She now lectures you about how disappointed she is in you, how lying to her is worse than anything, and how, as a result, she will punish you more severely than had you simply told the truth.

The next time you are confronted with a situation in which you are tempted to lie, you now have a new factor to weigh in consideration. You may conclude that you really want to keep your mother's esteem more than anything, and bearing that in mind, decide to be truthful. Each time you make the decision to do so, it becomes easier to make the same decision again in the future. This is part of what we mean by cultivating the habit of telling the truth.

But to call this a habit is to compare it to the behavior of a laboratory rat learning to press a bar to obtain food, or a dog learning to salivate whenever Dr. Pavlov rings his bell. In some ways it does resemble that, but in other ways, it is more than that.

Virtues involve not only habits, but values. Values are ends and means we believe are desirable, good, and worthwhile. If we tend to be honest, not only have we cultivated the habit of being honest, but we have learned to value honesty. We think being honest is, generally speaking, a good thing to be, and we aspire to be honest as much as possible in situations that appropriately call for it. We feel good about ourselves when we are honest and bad about ourselves when we lie. We admire people whom we perceive as honest and dislike those we perceive as liars. When confronted with temptations to lie, we remind ourselves that we value honesty and take it into consideration. In short, virtues are not only habits we enact, but values we care deeply about. They are central to our identity as persons and important sources of self-esteem. Indeed, what is habitual here is not so much the behavior of honesty itself, which we only inconsistently exhibit, but the habit of reminding ourselves of the centrality of honesty to our idea of who we ought to be whenever temptations to lie arise.

It is sometimes said that values don't exist in the natural world and that human beings *invent* them. Strictly speaking, this is not entirely true. While there can be no values without living beings who might have them, we do not so much *invent* them as *discover* them already present in our lives. We do not "decide," for example, to have good health as a value—it is something we find ourselves already valuing as we go about our business in the world.

Psychologists say that young children "internalize" the values of parents, grandparents, and teachers and make them their own. Again, this internalization is not so much a matter of conscious, deliberate choice as much as it is part of a natural process of identification and imitation. We see our caretakers as exemplars of who we want to be and find ourselves emulating them.

The concept of internalization is useful in thinking about how moral development occurs in early childhood (although it is not the whole story because, as we shall see, babies seem to have their own innate proto-sense of morality) but when it comes to adolescence and adulthood, we expect more than mere internalization. We expect adolescents and adults to actively reflect on their previously internalized values and judge whether they are concordant with other things they hold dear, or whether they ought to be refined, elaborated, revised, or rejected. This is an important part of what we mean by moral development in adolescence and adulthood. This project of reflection, refinement, elaboration, and revision is a lifelong project, and there is never a point when we are done. New situations frequently arise that cause us to doubt our previous assessments and inquire anew. Our reflection, revision, and refinement also come about as a result of our conversations with others who have reached different conclusions than we have. As we have already pointed out, society also undergoes a collaborative process of reflecting on and revising shared values as part of an ongoing historical process, a process that our private reflections both contribute to and reflect.

I specified earlier that the virtues not only contribute to our own successful living but take the legitimate concerns and well-being of others into consideration. Philosophers say that virtues are both *self-regarding* and *other-regarding*. They contribute not only to our personal well-being, but to the well-being of society as well—or, at least to what we *think* society ought to consider its own well-being were it rational and well-informed.

Conflicts Between Personal and Community Values

That last point—*virtues contribute to what we think society ought to consider its own well-being were it rational and well-informed*—is important because we can find ourselves at odds with the values held by our neighbors. Consider the situation of an abolitionist living in the antebellum American south. Opposing slavery is an important value for her, but if society abolishes it, plantation owners will suffer significant financial loss and unhappiness. The abolitionist concludes in a utilitarian sort of way that the greater happiness and well-being of the former slaves would far outweigh the lesser unhappiness of a smaller number of plantation owners. She also reasons that if the plantation owners really understood the consequences of their actions for their own genuine well-being, they would realize they would be better off without their slaves but with their souls intact.

On what grounds could the abolitionist argue that the slaveowners would be better off if slavery were abolished? The abolitionist could make several arguments. First, the slaveowners, who were in daily social contact with their slaves, must have been constantly confronted with evidence of their slaves' suffering, humanity, intelligence, and creativity. Many slaveowners were internally conflicted about whether to keep their slaves. While their economic well-being and desire for ease and comfort led them to retain their slaves, they must have done so at some cost to their honor, virtue, integrity, and self-regard.

We can see evidence of this inner dividedness in the relationship between Benjamin Franklin and the Quaker abolitionist Benjamin Lay. Franklin published Lay's antislavery book, *All Slave Keepers That Keep the Innocent in Bondage, Apostates* in 1737 and became fast friends with him, often visiting Lay in the cave where he lived during the final years of his life. They remained friends until Lay's death in 1759. Franklin's common-law wife, Deborah Read, commissioned artist William Williams to paint a portrait of Lay which hung in the Franklin home. Lay pressed Franklin to free his slaves—Peter and Jemima—and Franklin must have been at least partially persuaded because he rewrote his will in 1757 to free them upon his death. He knew slavery was morally wrong but persisted in keeping slaves during his lifetime. This is what I mean when I refer to the inner dividedness of some slaveowners.

The second argument an abolitionist could make about why the slaveowners would have been better off without their slaves is this: keeping slaves subservient required a callousness, ruthlessness, cruelty, and inhumanity that coarsened and cheapened the slaveowner's character. The abolitionist could also make a third argument: preventing slaves from engaging in the political, intellectual, scientific, economic, and artistic life of the community robbed the entire community—slaveowners included—of their potential contributions.

Finally, there is a fourth possible argument: the slaveowners should have been able to foresee how the conflict with the North over slavery would eventually end in unspeakable carnage. Slaveowner Thomas Jefferson was keenly aware of this when he wrote to John Holmes in 1820, saying the Missouri Compromise, "like a fire bell in the night, awakened and filled me with terror. I considered it at once as the knell of the Union." His only consolation was he wouldn't live long enough to see the conflagration he feared might end the American republic.

Of course, most slaveowners weren't moved by the abolitionists' arguments, and the Civil War ensued. We modern readers find ourselves siding with the abolitionists, because, as horrible as it was, the trauma of the civil war was an historically necessary precondition for ending the transcendent horror of slavery.

But it's possible to argue that the slaveowners' intransigence wasn't *irrational*—after all, their economic wealth depended on their slaves. Perhaps they just held different values than the abolitionists: wealth mattered more to them than benevolence and fairness. Isn't everyone entitled to his or her own values?

An argument like this suggests there is no reasonable basis for determining whether some values are better than others. While it's true that there is no objective basis for determining the relative goodness of values in the same way we determine the relative magnitude of stars, that doesn't mean that there aren't *any* grounds for deciding their relative goodness. Values differ in terms of the contributions they make to individual and collective flourishing. The yardsticks we choose to measure flourishing—and the ways we resolve conflicts between individual and collective flourishing—are debatable, but that doesn't mean that reasoned arguments aren't relevant to the process. And, to our modern ears, the abolitionists' arguments make a persuasive case while the slaveowner's sound callous, hollow and self-serving.

But let me introduce the possibility that the slaveowners may *not* have differed from the abolitionists in terms of their values—the slaveowners might have insisted they valued benevolence and fairness as much as anyone. They just contrived reasons why they thought slavery was benevolent and fair. They argued, for example, that slaves were inferior creatures incapable of managing their own affairs and in need of the slaveowner's benevolent supervision and civilizing influence.

At this point, we can rightly accuse the slaveowners of bad faith and moral incoherence. Why? Because had they cared to investigate the matter—and they had every good reason to care given the public nature of the debate over the slavery at the time—they could have easily discovered the cruelty and inhumanity that lay at the heart of the slave system.

Unfortunately, telling other people they are irrational and morally incoherent is never an effective strategy for helping them change—and this is true not only in politics, but in family life and all other realms of human endeavor. When we tell others they are being irrational, nine times out of ten we only motivate them to double down on their beliefs. Helping others to investigate their values requires that both parties start out with some degree of mutual respect and trust, that both parties are willing to inquire in good faith, and that both parties share an openness to the possibility of being wrong. Sadly, these conditions are only rarely met.

Let us now imagine a somewhat parallel historical situation where personal and societal understandings of virtue are at odds. Imagine a Bolshevik prior to the Russian Revolution. The suffering of the former serfs and the newly emergent working class is extreme as they live in squalor amidst the splendor of the nobility and landowners. If the nobility and landowners were rational and well-informed, the Bolshevik thinks, they would understand that sharing their wealth more generously would be a better option for all concerned. The nobility and landowners see things differently, however, and the Russian civil war ensues.

Earlier, we thought the abolitionist was morally justified in fighting a civil war to end the evil of slavery. Our question now is, to what extent is the Bolshevik entitled to kill, imprison, or forcibly confiscate the belongings of the rich to benefit the poor? Are there any moral limits to what the Bolshevik can do to make the nobility and landowners see the error of their ways, or address the harm they cause? In what ways is the Bolshevik's situation the same as or different from the abolitionist's situation?

The ethical calculus of self-righteously inflicting harm on some to benefit others is always morally fraught. As philosopher Elizabeth Anscombe (1958) noted, "a man's conscience may tell him to do the vilest things." We need to try, as much as possible, to ensure that our actions on behalf of what others ought to consider to be their well-being were they rational and well-informed are not actions that seriously violate their integrity and autonomy or lead to their undue suffering and misery. And if we decide we must impose some degree of suffering on some to assure the well-being of others, we must never harden ourselves, banishing the reality of that suffering to the edges of our consciousness, or pretending it isn't as bad as it is. There is, in short, a balancing act required here—one with no simple formula for how to get things exactly right. Every situation, while it may resemble past occurrences, is unique to itself. To paraphrase Mark Twain, history may rhyme, but it never repeats.

Practical Wisdom (Phronesis)

This precarious balancing act of holding competing interests in mind and judiciously weighing all considerations against each other is part of what Aristotle called the intellectual virtue of *phronesis*, or practical wisdom. It requires a whole banquet of skills, including the ability to delay action long enough to consider alternatives, the ability to hold emotions in check so that one can reason without undo attachment to one's initial reactions, the ability to recognize and compensate for one's biases, the ability to empathically imagine how others may be affected and react, the ability to discern what our own best interests are, and the ability to hold and weigh disparate considerations simultaneously. This is a rather tall order, and as you read this, you are almost certainly aware of how often we fail at it.

Philosopher Daniel Russell (2009) makes a strong argument that *phronesis* has a necessary and intimate connection with all the moral virtues. For example, consider the virtues of honesty, courage, and generosity. Practical wisdom is the wisdom to know whether a particular situation calls for one or another of these virtues, and, if so, how much. Some situations call for total honesty, some for partial honesty, some for little white lies, and some for outright deception—as when the Gestapo asks where resistance fighters might be hiding. Some situations call for great generosity, while generosity in other situations may be foolish or wasteful. Some situations call for courage, while others call for beating a cautious retreat. Practical wisdom is the skill that tells us how to do the right thing to the right degree in the right situation. We will have more to say about wisdom, practical and otherwise, when we discuss Aristotle in greater depth in this chapter, and wisdom more generally in Chapter 3.

To sum up so far, we initially stated that virtues are constellations of habit and value regarding heart, mind, and behavior that contribute to living successfully while taking the legitimate concerns of others into consideration.

We have just added the additional stipulation that practical wisdom or *phronesis* is necessarily involved in their specific instantiation. But what are these virtues, how many of them are there, and how do we acquire or fail to acquire them? We can also ask the extent to which people who are said to possess a virtue enact that virtue with any consistency in their daily lives. This question arises from the debate within contemporary psychology over the degree to which people can be characterized as having unitary personality traits, as opposed to the degree to which they just respond *ad hoc* to the demands of the situations they find themselves in. When it comes to honesty, are there "honest people" who are just generally more honest than most, or are all of us just more likely to be honest in situations where the cost of honesty is relatively low, and more likely to be dishonest in situations where the cost of honesty might be relatively high?

How Many Virtues Are There?

What specific constellations of habit and value can rightly be called virtues? Let us admit at the outset that there can be no such thing as a fixed and determinate list of the virtues. Whatever list I devise, you will be able to think of some virtue I omitted or argue that some included virtue isn't really a virtue. It helps to think of understanding the virtues as a process of continual inquiry, and that any list of virtues will necessarily be open-ended and subject to revision.

Part of the reason for this indeterminacy is that what is and is not a virtue is at least partly dependent on the whole way-of-life that constitutes a particular culture. As cultures change, something once considered to be a virtue may no longer be so, as we saw in our previous discussion of premarital chastity. So, in addition to there being no fixed and determinate list of the virtues, there may also be a list that changes somewhat from culture to culture and era to era.

But let's be careful here. Saying that some virtues lose their relevance as a culture undergoes change is *not* equivalent to saying that all virtues are entirely culture-relative and that there is no core set of virtues common to all, or almost all, cultures. In fact, I am about to argue that there is a core set of virtues that is, for all intents and purposes, practically universal—a "common thread" running through the classical philosophies of antiquity and the world religions and humanisms of today.

It's possible for a core set of virtues to be universal to all or almost all cultures because while cultures can vary in many ways, they cannot vary in just any way. Human biological evolution is an excruciatingly slow process, and any culture that has managed to survive for even a brief period within the past two hundred thousand years has had to help its members meet the same set of existential challenges: providing sufficient food and shelter; raising offspring to the point of independence; fostering within-group cooperation and limiting within-group violence; passing down learned skills and knowledge; and defending the community from predation and attack. A culture that fostered values that significantly undermined or impeded these tasks would not survive for long.

So, let's explore whether there is, in fact, a core set of universal virtues and what they might be. Let's begin by outlining some of the prominent features of three classical ethical systems that arose separately from each other due to their geographical separation—the Aristotelean, Buddhist, and Confucian traditions—to see if we can discover commonalties that override their readily apparent differences. These traditions arose in rough temporal proximity during the historical era philosopher Karl Jaspers characterized as the *Axial Age*, leading to speculation as to whether their creation was occasioned by some common set of Eurasian cultural transitions—indeed, the period is marked by multiple cultural advances, including the development of coinage and written script, and the emergence of an *intelligentsia* in Greece and China and a *śramana* class in India that were unburdened by agricultural and military duties. These three ethical traditions agreed that human nature was essentially *civilizable*—that humans were capable of overcoming their selfish and martial tendencies to become more cooperative and beneficent—and that optimal personal and social flourishing depended on the cultivation of these virtues.

All three traditions were also the creations of men living within patriarchal societies, and their ethical approaches reflect that limitation. Aristotle took a dim view of women's intellectual capabilities; Confucius spoke of familial duties to fathers and brothers, but not to mothers and sisters; the Buddha admitted women as nuns into his religious community but feared it would shorten the community's longevity by half a millennium. There are ways we would surely re-write and—from our modern perspective—improve these traditions were we to build them from scratch today. We present these traditions, not because they get everything right, but because they represent the collective wisdom of three great civilizations—a collective wisdom we can continue to draw on as a resource in our search for an ethics more suitable for today. We can be discerning, taking the best of what they have to offer while discarding aspects that no longer fit modern social arrangements and understandings.

Aristotelian Ethics

The ancient Greek word for virtue was *arete*. The word is commonly translated as *virtue*, but also carries the connotation of *excellence*—something one excels at. During the Homeric era, *arete* did not refer so much to moral excellence a to an extraordinary degree of skill in some socially-valued domain—for example, Achilles' wartime prowess in the *Iliad*, or Odysseus' wily cunning in the *Odyssey*—a level of skill that made one admirable and noble. By the time of Socrates, Plato, and Aristotle, however, *arete* had taken on the ethical connotation it currently has.

In Plato's *Republic*, Socrates enumerated four cardinal virtues: the three moral virtues of temperance, courage, and justice, and the intellectual virtue of wisdom. Plato's student, Aristotle, expanded this list in his *Nichomachean Ethics*. He accepted Socrates's three moral virtues of temperance, courage, and justice but added the moral virtues of friendliness, generosity, truthfulness, magnificence,[1] appropriate ambition, self-confidence, good temper, appropriate shame, and wittiness. He also elaborated on Socrates's idea of wisdom by enumerating four categories of intellectual virtue: practical wisdom, philosophical wisdom, knowledge of craft, and scientific knowledge. Only the first of these intellectual virtues—practical wisdom or *phronesis*—had a strong ethical component. As mentioned before, practical wisdom is the ability to know the appropriate thing to do in a situation—the right time to do it, the right way to do it, and with whom to do it. Aristotle refers to it as "hitting the mark" in terms of ethical behavior. Phronesis is the art of knowing which virtues are relevant to a situation, and how to weigh conflicts between virtues as they arise. Phronesis was so important to Aristotle, that he called his ideal person a *phronimos*.

In thinking about Aristotle's concept of phronesis, we shouldn't demand that the *phronimos* always gets things "right" or that there is always a "right" solution to ethical problems. Ethical dilemmas are dilemmas precisely because there is no single invariably correct solution, but conflicting possible solutions that are difficult to evaluate—solutions reasonable people may disagree on. But although there may not be one invariably correct solution, there are often many clearly inferior solutions. The *phronimos* will know what factors

---

1. Magnificence refers to generous philanthropic activity that befits great wealth, should one happen to have it.

he or she needs to take under consideration and weigh them in a reasonable way, thereby avoiding the clearly inferior solutions. In this life, that's as good as things get. Even baseball great Ty Cobb's batting average was only .366. Sometimes you swing and you miss, but the *phronimos* hits the ball more often.

Aristotle also introduced the idea of *eudaimonia,* or human flourishing. Flourishing is living one's life in a way that exemplifies what's best about being human. Aristotle believed in *teleology*, that there was an aim or purpose to human life. Just as an acorn, under the right conditions, flourishes to become a mighty oak, so human infants, under the right conditions, flourish to become reasonable, socially responsible adults who aspire to excellence in various endeavors. The virtues are habits acquired through emulating exemplary role models and repeated practice, and if we become proficient at them, we are more likely to lead lives that are admirable and happy. Aristotle writes:

> If activities are, as we said, what gives life its character, no happy man can become miserable; for he will never do the acts that are hateful and mean. For the man who is truly good and wise, we think, bears all the chances of life becomingly and always makes the best of circumstances, as a good general makes the best military use of the army at his command and a good shoemaker makes the best shoes out of the hides that are given him; and so with all other craftsmen. And if this is the case, the happy man can never become miserable—though he will not reach blessedness, if he meet with fortunes like those of Priam. Nor, again, is he many-colored and changeable; for neither will he be moved from his happy state easily or by any ordinary misadventures, but only by many great ones, nor, if he has had many great misadventures, will he recover his happiness in a short time, but if at all, only in a long and complete one in which he has attained many splendid successes.
> (Aristotle 1973, 363–364)

Although this English translation employs the words "happy man," "happy state," and "happiness," Aristotle isn't really talking about what makes people "happy." The words Aristotle uses in Greek are *makarion* (blessed or fortunate man), *eudaimon* (possessing a good in-dwelling spirit), and *eudaimonia* (flourishing) respectively. He is talking about a state of psychological well-being that is more than the aggregate of one's happy moments. Happiness is a feeling that comes and goes, but eudaimonia persists in the face of hardship. Perhaps it's better to think of it as an overall inner sense that one's life is on the right track and going well—that one's life is something one can approve of as "well-done," and that others would approve of it too if they knew its details. Good lives are more happiness-prone than others, but also more admirable by reason of their wisdom and virtue. They are lives that are not only "happy," but honorable.

Aristotle is not as facile as the stoics—he doesn't believe virtue and wisdom are all one needs to flourish. He recognizes that while "internal goods" like virtue and wisdom are necessary, so are "external goods" like friendship, good health, and adequate food, clothing, and shelter. For Aristotle, while it might be possible to maintain equanimity in the face of unrelenting misfortune, one could hardly feel happy under such circumstances.

Contemporary Western culture is heir to both the Greco-Roman and Judeo-Christian traditions, and this is a good place to point out that the medieval Jewish, Christian, and Islamic traditions were heavily influenced by Aristotle's understanding of virtue, and that influence has carried forward into the present day. St. Thomas Aquinas, for example, took the Platonic and Aristotelian cardinal virtues of prudence (*prudentia* being the Latin for *phronesis*), temperance, justice, and courage and supplemented them with the Christian virtues of faith, hope, and charity. The Jewish philosopher Maimonides and the Islamic philosopher Ibn Miskawayh were also heavily influenced by Aristotle's ethics.

Buddhist Ethics

Buddhist practitioners aspire to enlightenment rather than eudaimonia. If Aristotle's eudaimonia represents the best an ordinary human can attain, Buddhist enlightenment represents a kind of radical transcendence of the human condition. While different Buddhist sects define enlightenment somewhat differently, they agree that enlightenment has metaphysical, psychological, and moral aspects. Metaphysically, enlightenment is the liberation from the endless cycle of rebirths. Psychologically, it is the attainment of inner peace and liberation from self-centeredness, greed, hatred, and ignorance. Morally, it entails sets of virtues called the *brahmaviharas* and *paramitas*. The *brahmaviharas,* or "heavenly abodes," are the attitudes of lovingkindness, compassion, equanimity, and joy for the happiness of others. The *paramitas,* or "excellences," vary somewhat from sect to sect, but include generosity, morality, renunciation, wisdom, energy, patience, truthfulness, determination, lovingkindness, and equanimity.

The *paramita* of morality (*sila*) involves adhering to a set of ethical guidelines. Lay people are encouraged to adhere to five ethical precepts: not killing, stealing, lying, engaging in sexual immorality, or taking intoxicants. Monastics have longer lists of guidelines to comply with—for example, the

Patimokkha, or rules of conduct for Theravada[2] Buddhist monks includes 227 ethical precepts.

The paramita of wisdom (*prajña*) refers to several concepts. First, the knowledge that our thoughts and actions determine our characters and the conditions of our lives going forward. This is the law of cause and effect (*karma*). We see the law of karma expressed in the first verse of the Theravada Buddhist verse collection, the *Dhammapada*:

> Mind precedes all mental states.
> Mind is their chief: They are all mind-wrought.
> If with an impure mind a person speaks or acts
> Suffering follows him like the wheel that follows the foot of the ox.
> (*Dhammapada* 1996, Verse I)

The second key idea is that all phenomena are transient, contain the seeds of suffering, and are not the property of some unchanging, eternal self. Even pleasing phenomena contain the seeds of suffering because they are transient, and we eventually experience or fear their loss. While we sometimes tend to think of the "self" as some unchanging inner essence separated from the world by the boundary of our skin, Buddhism teaches we are always changing, and not so much separated from the world by our skin, as connected to it.

Third, Mahayana[3] Buddhism teaches a "supreme" wisdom (*prajñaparamita*) that all phenomena lack self-existence and arise co-dependently with all other phenomena. In other words, nothing in the world exists by itself, but only by virtue of its relationships with everything else. This is an ecological view of the world—everything we do affects everyone and everything, and everything and everyone affects us—that cuts deeply against the grain of Western individualism, or the idea that one can live by-and-for oneself.

Theravada Buddhists call enlightened people *arahants* (derived from the word *arahati*, or "to be worthy"), and Mahayana Buddhists call them *bodhisattvas* ("enlightened beings"). They are the Buddhist exemplars of what it means to live the best possible life. In Mahayana Buddhism, persons aspiring to be bodhisattvas seek liberation not just for themselves but for the sake of all beings and vow to free all beings from suffering. This vow is exemplified in this verse from the *Guide to the Bodhisattva's Way of Life*, a poem by the 8th century Buddhist philosopher and poet, Śantideva:

---

2. Theravada Buddhism is the Buddhism of Sri Lanka, Thailand, Burma, Laos, and Cambodia.
3. Mahayana Buddhism is the Buddhism of China, Japan, Korea, Vietnam, Tibet, and Mongolia.

> May I be the doctor and the medicine
> And may I be the nurse for all sick beings in the world
> Until everyone is healed.
> May a rain of food and drink descend
> To clear away the pain of thirst and hunger
> And during the aeon of famine
> May I myself change into food and drink.
> May I become an inexhaustible treasure
> For those who are poor and destitute;
> May I turn into all things they could need
> And may these be placed close beside them ....
> May I be protector for those without one,
> A guide for all travelers on the way;
> May I be a bridge, a boat and a ship
> For all who wish to cross the water.
>
> May I be an island for those who seek one,
> And a lamp for those desiring light,
> May I be a bed for all who wish to rest
> And a slave for all who want a slave ...
> Just like space
> And the great elements such as earth
> May I always support the life
> Of all boundless creatures.
> And until they pass away from pain
> May I also be the source of life
> For all the realms of varied beings
> That reach unto the ends of space.
>
> (Śantideva 1979, 10–11)

It is important to recognize that the ethical components of the Buddhist path—non-harming, non-greed, non-hatred, unselfishness, compassion, lovingkindness—are not just instrumental means to attain enlightenment, but attributes of enlightenment itself. There is a way in which the path is a foretaste of the goal. While Buddhists and Aristotelians disagree on the magnitude of well-being human beings can attain, they agree that virtue, wisdom, and well-being are not separate phenomena, but seamlessly bound together as inextricable components of exemplary lives. The virtues do not just lead to flourishing, they exemplify it.

On Virtue

Confucian Ethics

The Confucian tradition begins with the writings of Confucius and continues into the modern era. While many philosophers contributed to it (and some still are) I will focus on just two: Confucius (551–479 BCE) and Mencius (372–289 BCE). *Confucius and Mencius* are the latinized names the Jesuits gave to the sages the Chinese call *Kongzǐ* and *Mèngzǐ*. The morpheme "*zi*" at the end of their names signifies "master," in other words, "Master Kǒng" and "Master Mèng." I will retain their latinized names because of their familiarity to Western readers.

Confucius and Mencius lived during the time of the Eastern Zhou Dynasty—Confucius towards the end of the Spring and Autumn Period (771–476 BCE) and Mencius during the Warring States Period (475–221 BCE). They both looked back to the earlier Western Zhou Dynasty (1,100 BCE–771 BCE) as a legendary Golden Age of peace and prosperity. By the Warring States Period, the Zhou king's power had declined to the point that he was only nominally king, and China devolved into a set of squabbling dukedoms. The dukes heavily taxed their people to support their military adventures, and hunger, poverty, and population decline ensued. The prime question confronting Confucius and Mencius was how to retore peace, harmony, tranquility, and prosperity so that the people could again flourish. Their answer was that peace, harmony, tranquility, and prosperity arose when everyone—king, dukes, government ministers, parents, and children—cultivated a set of virtues.

In the *Analects,* Confucius emphasized a set of five cardinal virtues: humaneness (*rén*), appropriateness or righteousness (*yi*), propriety (*lǐ*), wisdom (*zhi*), and fidelity (*xin*). Humaneness means both benevolence towards others and abiding by the Golden Rule. Appropriateness or righteousness emphasizes that actions be appropriate relative to our roles and situations, and includes connotations of honesty, uprightness, conscientiousness, and fairness. Propriety means observing proper social rites and rituals with appropriate feeling. Confucius believed that the way rites and rituals were conducted during the time of the Western Zhou Dynasty was the proper way to perform them. Faithfulness includes elements of trustworthiness, reliability, loyalty, and dedication to principle. Wisdom, for Confucius, is the ability to judge right from wrong.

Rén is Confucius's prime virtue. The *Analects* is ambiguous about whether *rén* is a master virtue that includes not only benevolence but all the other virtues, whether it just means benevolence plain and simple, or whether it means adhering to the Golden Rule. At times, Confucius seems to lean toward benevolence, as in *Analects* 12.22 where he is asked the definition of *rén* and replies, "love people." At other times he stresses *rén* as fairness and reciprocity in one's relations with others.

Confucius believed people should develop, cultivate, and refine their personalities through emulating virtuous figures from the past, study, contemplation, and appreciation of the arts. The person who successfully cultivates the virtues is called a *jūnzǐ*, literally the "son of a ruler," but figuratively "a gentleman," which is how it is usually translated. There are also exceptional moral saints who Confucius calls *shèngrén,* or sages. Confucius's approach to ethical cultivation is summarized in the following passage from *The Great Learning*:[4]

> The Dao[5] of Great Learning lies in making bright virtue brilliant; in making the people new; in coming to rest at the limit of the good ...
>
> In ancient times, those who wished to make bright virtue brilliant in the world first ordered their states; those who wished to order their states first aligned their households; those who wished to align their households first refined their persons; those who wished to refine their persons first balanced their minds; those who wished to balance their minds first perfected the genuineness of their intentions; those who wished to perfect the genuineness of their intentions first extended their understanding; extending one's understanding lies in aligning affairs. Only after affairs have been aligned may one's understanding be fully extended. Only after one's understanding is fully extended may one's intentions be perfectly genuine. Only after one's intentions are perfectly genuine may one's mind be balanced. Only after one's mind is balanced may one's person be refined. Only after one's person is refined may one's household be aligned. Only after one's state is ordered may the world be set at peace.
>
> From the Son of Heaven to the common person, for all alike, refining the person is the root. That roots should be disordered yet branches ordered is not possible. That what should be thickened is thin yet what is thin becomes thick has never yet been so.
>
> (The Great Learning and the Doctrine of the Mean 2016)

---

4. *The Great Learning* is one of neo-Confucian philosopher Zhu Xi's (1126–1271 CE) four books that Chinese students studied in preparation for their civil service examinations. *The Great Learning* is drawn from a chapter in the *Book of Rites* which tradition attributes to Confucius but which is more likely (at least partly) the work of some of his students.

5. *Dao* here refers not to Daoist metaphysics, but to a way of life in accord with virtue.

On Virtue

The central theme of this passage is summarized by the Chinese expression *xiū shēn, qí jiā, zhì guō, píng tiān xià* which translates as "cultivate virtue, regulate the family, govern the state, bring peace under Heaven." Confucius saw the personal, familial, and civic spheres as inextricably linked and enhanced through personal cultivation of virtue: a well-ordered society made well-ordered families and virtuous individuals possible, but virtuous individuals made well-ordered families and a well-ordered state possible.

Confucius's understanding of the links between the personal, familial, and civic spheres makes Confucianism the most profoundly social of the three classical ethical systems. Aristotle is social in the sense that virtues are other-regarding as well as self-regarding and that he sees civic engagement as one of the qualities of his *phronimos*: Aristotle wrote his *Nichomachean Ethics* as a prelude to his *Politics*. For Aristotle, a human being is a *zoon politikon*—a social animal. And Buddhism, too, is social: the Buddha advised kings on how to best rule, and Mahayana Buddhists take a bodhisattva vow to save all beings. In addition, the Buddhist understanding of interdependence makes individualism a delusion. Nevertheless, no vision is more profoundly social than the Confucian one. As a result, people who grow up within the East Asian sinographic sphere of China, Korea, Japan, and Vietnam—all strongly influenced by Confucianism—are much more likely to think of themselves as members of families and of a culture, and much less likely to think of themselves as separate individuals than Westerners. While some Warring States philosophers such as Mozi, Zhuangzi, and Han Feizi rejected Confucius's argument for the intimate linkage between personal virtue, family devotion, and the well-functioning state, the elevation of Confucianism to an official state philosophy during the Han Dynasty helped make this a central tenet of Chinese culture going forward.

Mencius was born a little more than a century after Confucius passed. Confucius never rendered an opinion as to whether human nature was innately good or bad, but Mencius believed people were born with the innate capacity to develop as moral beings. The way he put it, humans were born with the "sprouts" of virtue, and those spouts would either develop or lie fallow depending on their cultivation. Like Confucius, Mencius believed that we develop virtues like benevolence (*rén*) within the matrix of the family, but that as we grow older, we learn how to "extend" those feelings beyond the family. Unlike the Mohists[6] who believed we could love everyone

---

6. The followers of the philosopher Mozi (470–391 BCE).

impartially, Mencius believed that although we could extend benevolence outwards beyond our families, we always remained somewhat partial to our families. While we can learn to treat strangers better by employing the golden rule, we will never care for them in quite the same the way we care for our parents, siblings, spouses, and children. Tao Jiang (2021) argues that the question of how to resolve the tension being partiality to one's family and the impartial demands of justice for everyone is the central problem around which much of classical Chinese philosophy revolves. It is a question that continues to have resonance for us today as we consider conflicts between our partiality and loyalty to our own ethnic, racial, and religious groups and more universalist demands for the equitable distribution of honor, status, power, and goods.

Mencius makes his case for innate sprouts of morality in the following passage from his eponymous book, *The Mencius*:

> All people possess within them a heart/mind that cannot bear the suffering of others. The former kings had such a heart/mind and thus they devised means of government that would not allow people to suffer. If a ruler were to employ the heart/mind that makes human suffering unendurable in order to implement such humane government, he would find bringing the entire world into order to be simple, as though he were turning the world in his hand.
>
> Why do I say that all people possess within them a heart/mind that cannot bear the suffering of others? Well, imagine now a person who, all of a sudden, sees a small child on the verge of falling down into a well. Any such person would experience a sudden sense of fright and dismay. This feeling would not be something he summoned up in order to establish good relations with the child's parents. He would not purposefully feel this way in order to win the praise of their friends and neighbors. Nor would he feel this way because the screams of the child would be unpleasant.
>
> By imagining this situation, we can see that one who lacked a sense of dismayed commiseration in such a case simply could not be a person. Moreover, anyone who lacks the sense of shame cannot be a person; anyone who lacks a sense of deference cannot not be a person; anyone who lacks a sense of right and wrong cannot not be a person.
>
> The heart/mind of commiseration is the spout of humanity (*rén*), the heart/mind of shame is the sprout of righteousness (*yi*), the heart/mind of deference is the sprout of ritual (*lǐ*), and the heart/mind of right and wrong is the sprout of wisdom (*zhi*). Everyone possesses these four spouts just as they possess their four limbs. To possess such sprouts and yet claim to be unable to call them forth is to rob oneself; and for a person to claim that his ruler is incapable of such moral feelings is to rob his ruler.

As we possess these four sprouts within us, if only we realize that we need to extend and fulfill them, then the force of these sprouts will burst through us like a wildfire first catching or a spring first bursting forth through the ground. If a person can bring these to fulfillment, they will be adequate to bring all the four quarters under his protection. But if a person fails to develop them, he will fail even to serve his own parents.[7]

(Mencius 2016, 2A:6)

In this passage, Mencius enriches what Confucius meant by inner cultivation. A few years later, the Confucian philosopher Xunzi (c. 310–235 BCE) would disagree with Mencius, provocatively stating that "human nature is bad." By this he meant that human beings were innately self-centered and selfish. Mencius and Xunzi both have a point, but we can imagine ways in which we can reconcile their opinions. Mencius never intended to say that all human beings were good, but only that they were born with the potential to be good. We have the seeds of morality, but also the seeds of selfishness. Which seeds flourish is a matter of cultivation, and cultivation is what Confucianism is all about.

Lastly, while Confucius thought benevolence and righteousness (and our duties to family and society) formed a harmonious whole, Mencius was more aware of possible conflicts between our various virtues and duties. Mencius posed the hypothetical question that if a king discovers his father guilty of a crime, should he turn his father over to be prosecuted or should he protect him? He concluded the king should abdicate his throne, run off, and hide his father from prosecution. For Mencius, when our duties to family and state conflict, family comes first. Mencius is keenly aware of the complexity of our moral dilemmas and that we are not always able to harmonize all our core values. Sometimes we must sacrifice one thing for something else.

I have presented the Confucian tradition in a way that emphasizes its resonances with modern humanism, but this is a bit unfair to Confucianism. Confucianism is, after all, rooted in a framework that is distinctly premodern and can feel somewhat alien to contemporary Western sensibilities. For example, I have understated the degree to which Confucianism is embedded within traditional Chinese hierarchical familial and feudal social structures that stress filial piety (*xiào*) and the proper relations between lords and retainers. I have also understated Confucianism's roots in Chinese metaphysi-

---

7. I am following Eno's translation with two exceptions. He translates "心" as "moral sense" while I translate it as "heart/mind." He also alternately translates "端" as "sense" and "seed," while I translate it as "sprout" to be consistent with my discussion of his sprout theory.

cal beliefs concerning *Tiān* or an impersonal heaven, and the *Dào,* or the moral order in accord with *Tiān*. Confucius believed he had the *tiānmíng,* or Mandate of Heaven, and that his teachings were aligned with a preexistent metaphysical moral order. Finally, Confucianism is best understood not alone but as part of an ongoing dialogue with the so-called *bǎijiā*, or "Hundred Schools" of thought that contended for preeminence during the Warring States period. In extracting Confucius's five cardinal virtues from their larger cultural-historical-metaphysical context and comparing them with Aristotle's and the Buddha's virtues, we are engaged in a very modern sort of project, and one that does some violence to the original integrity of the Confucian tradition. But we are not trying to understand the Confucian tradition in its entirety the way a cultural historian might, but only trying to discover possible commonalties between admittedly disparate ethical frameworks.

Common Threads

We have now considered three classical ethical systems—Aristotelian, Buddhist, and Confucian—and are at the point when we can ask, what are their commonalities, and can these commonalities help us arrive at a more contemporary understanding of virtue? Before we compare the content of the individual virtues within each system, however, let us note that all three systems extol the life of ethical cultivation. All three posit that a life-long process of ethical cultivation is the key to excellence in living as well as the key to well-being. Confucius described his own life-long process of ethical cultivation in the following terms:

> When I was fifteen I set my heart on learning. At thirty I took my stand. At forty I was without confusion. At fifty I knew the command of *Tian* [Heaven]. At sixty I heard it with a compliant ear. At seventy I follow the desires of my heart and do not overstep the bounds.
> (The Analects of Confucius 2015), 2:4)

One corollary to this doctrine of life-long ethical cultivation is that the virtues, whatever their content, are learnable through investigation, contemplation, and most of all, practice.

When we compare the content of the virtues within each system, there seem to be virtues that track across all three systems. Aristotle, the Buddha, and Confucius all stress the importance of something (*phronesis, zhi,* or *prajña*) we can call "wisdom." Aristotle, the Buddha, and Confucius all stress some variant of good will towards others, whether it gets called friendliness (*philia*), benevolence (*rén*), or lovingkindness (*mettā*). Aristotle, the

Buddha, and Confucius all stress *temperance, moderation, equanimity, and truthfulness*. They also all agree on the importance of treating others fairly. Aristotle's "justice" involves rendering unto others what they are due, while Confucius's principle of reciprocity ("That which you do not desire, do not do to others," The Analects of Confucius, 2015, 15:24) is identical to the Buddhist "Look what you will, there is nothing dearer to a man than himself; therefore, as it is the same thing that is dear to you and to others, hurt not others with what pains yourself" (Udànavarga 1883, 27). Confucius's virtue of appropriateness or righteousness (*yi*) also includes connotations of fairness and proportionality. While early Buddhism doesn't contain a developed concept of social justice, the Buddha did advise kings to provide protection, shelter, and safety to their subjects and eliminate poverty, and its law of *karma* implies a sense of cosmic justice.

So, there is good reason to think that four moral virtues—*benevolence, truthfulness, fairness or justice,* and a capacity for inner *self-restraint*—are candidates for universal virtues, as is the *wisdom* to know which virtues are called for in any situation, and how much.

Differences Between Aristotle, the Buddha, and Confucius

But there are also differences between their lists of virtues. Aristotle, for example, includes wittiness on his list—a quality marking the midpoint between humorlessness and buffoonery. While we can appreciate a good laugh and understand how a sense of humor contributes to well-being, most of us today would not necessarily consider wittiness a moral virtue. Aristotle also prominently features courage on his list of virtues. There is nothing explicitly like courage on either the Buddha's or Confucius's lists, although is abundantly clear that Buddhists and Confucians are expected to maintain their personal integrity in the face of external pressures to abandon it. The Buddhist virtue of determination perhaps comes closest with its connotations of perseverance and persistence, but it is still not fully congruent with Aristotle's courage with its martial overtones. All three philosophers were familiar with warfare and its consequences, yet only Aristotle explicitly thinks that a warrior's courage is a trait we should emulate.

Aristotle also had no concept of humility as a virtue, whereas humility is important in the Buddhist and Confucian traditions. Similarly, Confucius's propriety is unique to his list. Proper etiquette and correct performance of ritual doesn't seem quite so important in our informal culture of today. We believe people shouldn't necessarily "stand on ceremony."

On the other hand, we modern Westerners dismiss propriety at our peril. While a willingness to break norms may sometimes appear bold, innovative, and refreshing—think of how highly valued it is in the arts and fashion—it can also be a harbinger of social collapse. The proper functioning of the social order depends on people's willingness to observe a large variety of implicit norms. Not every aspect of modern democratic governance, for example, is specified by law, but politicians and state officials are expected to observe the usual and customary informal rules. A politician who fails to observe the norms associated with his or her public office, and who tramples willy-nilly on long-established unofficial rules, is a menace to the functioning of a democracy. If American democracy survived in 2021, it was because a sufficient number of judges, election officials, and other government functionaries adhered to the norms associated with their offices in the aftermath of the 2020 election.

Another way to think about Confucian rites is to view them not as prescribed rules but as embodied and enacted forms of virtue. Consider, for example, how the bowing of a Buddhist monk expresses, enacts, and reinforces humility and respect, or how a funeral rite expresses and honors connection, love, respect, and loyalty. Paul Goldin (2020) has emphasized how in Confucianism, rites and rituals can be thought of as means of practicing and cultivating virtue, and not simply conservative adherences to tradition. It was important to Confucius that one not simply go through the motions of performing rites, but perform them with appropriate motivation, understanding, and emotional engagement. For example, in regard to the rules of filial piety he wrote "Those today who are filial are considered so because they are able to provide for their parents. But even dogs and horses are given that much care. If you do not respect your parents, what is the difference?" (The Analects of Confucius 2015, 2:7). It is not enough to do what is expected, but it is crucial that the proper attitudes and motives accompany the action.

Moral Foundations Theory

As a contrast and compare exercise, let's briefly consider contemporary Moral Foundations Theory, as elaborated by psychologists Jonathan Haidt and Craig Joseph (2008). Moral foundations theory proposes five moral "modules"—innate moral potentials—that are subsequently shaped by culture, and are found, to a greater or lesser extent, in all cultures. Philosopher Owen Flanagan (2014) has compared Haidt and Joseph's moral "modules" to Mencius's "sprouts."

Haidt and Joseph's candidates for possible moral modules are the dimensions of 1) harm/care (benevolence, compassion, non-harming), 2) fairness/reciprocity (justice, proportionality, reciprocity), 3) in group/loyalty (solidarity with one's family, tribe, community, nation), 4) authority/respect (respect for legitimate authority), and 5) sanctity/purity (abhorrence of things impure, taboo, or disgusting). Haidt has subsequently suggested a possible sixth candidate—valuing freedom from coercion. The moral foundations theorists suggest that differences in the degree to which subcultures value each of these modules can account for differences in American political "tribal" opinion. Haidt claims American liberals tend to stress caring and fairness, while conservatives tend to stress freedom, loyalty, authority, and purity.[8]

Let's note that the first two Moral Foundations Theory Modules—*caring and fairness*—correspond to two of our universal virtues—*benevolence* and *justice*. They then list three—*loyalty, authority, and purity*—which we did not, and fail to mention *truthfulness, inner restraint, and wisdom*, which we did. These discrepancies again demonstrate the difficulty of making a definitive comprehensive list of the virtues. *Loyalty* and *authority*, not on our list, were certainly important to the Confucians. An understanding of the deference different members of society owed each other and the notion of filial piety were central to the Confucian project. The Confucians were also interested in how to resolve conflicts between loyalties. What should a king do, for example, when he experiences conflict between loyalty to his family and to the rule of law? The Greeks were also concerned with this same question—it is the central conflict in Sophocles' *Antigone*—family duty dictates Antigone give her brother an honorable funeral, but King Creon has decreed his body remain unburied. Conflicting loyalties must have become a crucial problem as society evolved from smaller hunter-gatherer and nomadic phases into larger agriculture-supported communities, and eventually Dukedoms, Kingdoms, and Empires. These were not issues that concerned the Buddhists, however.

The Confucians and Buddhists also had concerns about *purity*—Confucians were concerned with the purity of rites and rituals, Buddhists with purity of intention. Let's be clear, however, that these kinds of purity—purity of performance and purity of heart—are different from the metaphys-

---

8. There seems something overly simplistic about this account. Leftist "cancel culture," for example, seems motivated by concerns over political purity. One could also argue left and right are equally concerned with loyalty but have different objects of veneration: either loyalty to flag and Bible, or loyalty to universalism and equality.

ical types of purity ("clean" vs. "unclean") we observe in the Jewish laws of *kashruth,* Islamic rules of *halal,* or Polynesian taboos. Let us also note that Aristotle was unconcerned with questions of purity. I didn't include virtues like *purity, loyalty, and authority* on my list, yet Haidt and Joseph make a persuasive case for their importance.

What Makes Something a Virtue?

From perusing these lists, we now have a general idea of the territory of the virtues. We haven't generated this list from any theory, but from simply noting what smart people in the past have thought. Aristotle also didn't generate his list from any theory, but from unsystematically surveying members of the Greek aristocracy. Just going on the basis of these lists, we don't yet have a theory of what ought to be counted as a virtue, and what ought not be counted. Was Aristotle right to omit compassion and humility and the Buddha right to omit courage? Was Aristotle right to include wittiness and Confucius right to include propriety? Is Haidt right to include loyalty and purity? How can one decide?

One way to decide is from our virtue ethics perspective that the virtues are the constituents of and the contributors to individual and social flourishing. We can ask, does a proposed virtue contribute, at least in a probabilistic way, to an individual's flourishing? And we can also ask, does a proposed virtue contribute to the optimal functioning of the social order and thereby the flourishing of its members? We can ask, if people are benevolent, fair, honest, courageous, appropriately self-restrained and possess sound judgement, are they 1) more likely to flourish, and 2) if most people act that way, is society more likely to flourish? We can ask the same about other proposed virtues such as loyalty, purity, propriety, deference to authority, wittiness, and magnificence. We don't need to evaluate every proposed virtue for the purposes of this chapter, but it can be instructive to examine several of the proposed virtues and how they contribute to flourishing in greater depth.

The Virtues and Flourishing

What follows is an exploration of how seven proposed virtues drawn from the Aristotelian, Confucian, and Buddhist traditions—*courage, benevolence, conscientiousness, temperance, equanimity, truthfulness,* and *justice*—contribute to individual and collective flourishing. We don't yet have a precise definition of flourishing—we'll leave that to chapter four—but we have enough of an understanding to explore the value of these virtues from a virtue ethics perspective. Let's just say, at this point, that flourishing involves a sense of subjective well-being, an expansion of our capacities to succeed at and enjoy life, and consideration for the well-being of others. To what extent do these proposed virtues succeed in accomplishing these ends, and to what extent do these traits reflect our common-sense intuitions about what it means to be an exemplary person?

Courage

Let's begin by exploring courage. Let's note right off the bat that courage is not a unitary personality trait. It's not an all or nothing sort of thing. We are, most of us, courageous in some situations and not courageous in others. The fireman who risks his life to save a child from a burning house may also decline to board an airplane due to a fear of flying. The infantryman who singlehandedly takes out an enemy machine gun nest may also fail to refuse an illegal order from a superior due to fear of punishment. Probably no one displays courage in any and all situations.

Philosopher Neera Badhwar (2014) suggests that what really counts is that we be courageous in circumstances that matter greatly to us. If certain circumstances are central to what matters to us in life, courage is crucial; in peripheral matters, not so much. I think Badhwar's formulation works to some extent, but only if you are solely concerned with a person's individual happiness and self-esteem. If you are also concerned about the objective goodness of a person's life, it's not enough. How things matter to our spouses, children, neighbors, co-workers, and fellow citizens must also count for something.

One way to adjust Badhwar's suggestion is to say that what really matters is that we display courage in fulfilling the roles we have voluntarily undertaken, and also those roles society expects us to fill as family members, neighbors, and citizens. Being courageous means displaying courage in fulfilling our roles as spouses, parents, and neighbors, and in our vocational and civic duties. You and I are not expected to rescue children from burning buildings or take out enemy machinegun nests. These are not roles we have volunteered for or that our neighbors expect of us. Fireman and soldiers, on the other hand, are. They have chosen their roles, and society expects it of them and honors them for it.

Let's also be clear that being courageous does not mean being fearless. Most heroes experience fear to the same degree as the rest of us. If they did not experience fear there would be nothing courageous about doing what they do. Being courageous means doing what one's conscience or what the social order requires (these are not always the same thing) despite one's fear.

How important is courage to one's personal well-being and to society at large? Before answering this, I want to define courage the way Aristotle does. Aristotle defines courage as the midpoint between an excess and a deficiency. The endpoints of this continuum are cowardice, on the one hand, and rashness on the other. Courage is also mediated by practical wisdom, so that one has some sense as to whether what one is doing is actually worthwhile or whether it is foolhardy. So, the courageous person is not someone, according to this definition, who flings himself blindly into danger without any real possibility of accomplishing something worthwhile. We are talking here of the willingness to face some degree of danger in order to accomplish a very real possibility of some good.

One could argue that facing death to obtain a desired objective is irrational, because if one dies in the attempt, one's well-being immediately becomes zero. Aristotle would argue, however, that this is not necessarily so. There are things we may value that may be dearer to us than our personal existence. Life after an act of cowardice resulting in the loss of something very dear to one—one's child's life, the lives of one's comrades on the battlefield, or preventing marauders from raping and pillaging one's family, friends, and neighbors—may not be a life worth living at all.

In any case, the kind of courage I want to focus on here is not heroic or extraordinary courage, but what might be called the everyday sort of courage, and I want to stress the importance of everyday courage to flourishing. Everyday courage is the courage that allows us to act on our convictions and to speak up regarding our ideas, beliefs, concerns, and grievances even when doing so entails some risk. This is the courage that allows one to take a stand, show oneself, and stick up for oneself. It's the courage that allows one to be frank and honest, even when being honest risks losing someone's esteem. It's the courage that allows us to present our ideas and beliefs, even when they may prove unpopular or be rejected. It's the courage that allows us to try something novel, even though we may fail. If we don't push back against the fears that inhibit us from being ourselves, showing ourselves, standing up for ourselves, or venturing onto novel territory, our lives shrink—we shrink—eventually taking up less and less space in the world, restricting our powers, and retarding our growth. This is a recipe for ill-being. To make things worse, not only do we get less out of life than we might, but we also shrink in terms of self-esteem. It is hard to take pride in oneself when one shrinks at every shadow.

In addition, the courage to be oneself and appropriately stand up for oneself in a relationship, especially an intimate one, fosters greater satisfaction in that relationship. Intimacy requires honesty. If we are concealing our true selves so that we will be loved because we think our partner could never accept us for who we really are, then our partner never really comes to know us. Being seen and known by someone else is the very core of intimacy. If we never stand up for ourselves and the other person always has the upper hand, then the relationship is a one-way street and a breeding ground for resentment and dissatisfaction. Good relationships require emotional honesty, making one's needs known, and setting boundaries when necessary.

This kind of everyday courage is required not only in intimate relationships, but also in relationships with co-workers, employers, neighbors, and all the myriad functionaries—teachers, shopkeepers, ministers, and civic leaders—we encounter every day. Every encounter with another carries the potential for conflict, and in every encounter there are potential issues to be negotiated over acceptance, status, boundaries, and control. We enter into every new relationship with the question of whether we will be accepted by the other as a person of equal worth and status, relegated to the role of an outsider, treated as an inferior, or deferred to as a superior. Standing up appropriately for oneself as one negotiates the intricacies of establishing a relationship also requires a modicum of everyday courage.

When people avoid something they fear, avoidance only reinforces that fear. The only way to put an end to a phobia is by deliberately forcing oneself to do the thing one is afraid of, over and over—in other words, to display courage. Phobias are, by definition, irrational fears—fears of things unlikely to cause real harm. The more one courageously practices doing the feared thing repeatedly and observes that nothing truly bad occurs as a consequence, the more the fear eventually dissipates, or as psychologists say, "extinguishes."

Of course, many of the things we fear do carry some degree of risk: dogs do occasionally bite, and planes do sometimes crash. The problem here is not that there is a zero possibility of risk, but that we exaggerate the likelihood of risk and/or the magnitude of harm that would ensue should the risk occur. Yes, planes do sometimes crash, but the likelihood of any specific plane crashing is less than one in five million.

Or consider the fear of asking someone out on a date. Yes, there is a risk one might get rejected, but how great is the harm caused by such a rejection? The answer is, it depends on one's attitude and one's thought processes. If one believes that rejection is just an ordinary part of life—nothing ventured, nothing gained—then the sting of rejection is likely to be short lived and survivable. On the other hand, if one believes getting rejected is proof positive that one is an unlovable abject failure as a human being, the harm, psychologically speaking, is substantial. But because the harm is the result of one's beliefs and not the rejection per se, we can minimize the harm by adopting more reasonable beliefs and attitudes. Our ability to think more rationally about the likelihood and magnitude of risk in the activities we undertake is one of the things that makes everyday courage possible. It is one more example of how practical wisdom, as Aristotle insisted, is intimately connected with the exercise of the virtues.

And speaking of connection, courage is intimately connected to the exercise of all the other virtues. It takes courage to be honest, just, or loyal under trying circumstances. It can even take courage to behave generously when we fear our generosity might be misunderstood or taken advantage of.

So far, we have been discussing the ways in which courage contributes to our personal flourishing, but courage is also related to the flourishing of the social order. The role of the courageous actions of police officers, firefighters, and soldiers in protecting and maintaining social order need no comment. We can also note the courageous behavior of notable progressives and dissidents—extraordinary people like Frederick Douglass, Susan B. Anthony, Harriet Tubman, Rosa Parks, Martin Luther King, Jr., Nelson Mandela, Mohandas Gandhi, and Andrei Sakharov—in expanding the realms of freedom and human rights.

But beyond these extraordinary acts of courage, the everyday courage of the average person also promotes and sustains the flourishing of the community—standing up for a friend or family member who is being treated unfairly, speaking one's truth at a school board or town council meeting, striking for fairer treatment at one's workplace, establishing limits and setting boundaries for one's children when their behavior warrants it—these are the courageous choices we are called on to make in our roles as parents, friends, neighbors, and citizens that contribute to social well-being. These are the acts of courage that make the good life possible for everyone.

Benevolence

Aristotle, the Buddha, Confucius, and Moral Foundations theory all name what might be called generosity, compassion, kindness, caring, or benevolence as a virtue. The Chinese word for the Confucian virtue of benevolence is *rén,* which can also be translated as human-heartedness, or humaneness.

All of these words point to some sort of fellow feeling of good will directed towards others.

This fellow feeling may or may not be universal. Personal experience, upbringing, and culture help shape and determine who it gets extended to and how much. We may extend it only to members of our family, tribe, ethnic group, faith, or political party, or we may extend it to all of humanity. We may extend it only to friends and neutral parties, or we may extend it to rivals and enemies as well. We seem to easily (and spontaneously) extend it to animals that are cute, furry, or fluffy, but extending it to insects and arachnids seems more of a stretch for most—with exceptions made for butterflies everywhere or pet crickets in Japan. Buddhist practice calls for the extension of non-harming, generosity, lovingkindness, and compassion to all sentient beings without exception, not only in this world, but in other realms (hell realms, ghost realms, heavenly realms) as well.

Benevolence is the opposite of cruelty—the vice that philosopher Judith Shklar (1982) calls "the *summum malum*, the most evil of evils." Shklar argues that our prime reason for rejecting cruelty is psychological—that it is psychologically repulsive to all decent human beings. She cites the 16th Century French moralist Michel de Montaigne, saying, "he looked first of all into himself and found that the sight of cruelty instantly filled him with revulsion," and "that it repels instantly, because it is 'ugly.' It is a vice that disfigures human character" (Shklar 1982, 18). Mencius said much the same thing when he wrote "if one does not have the heart/mind that cannot bear the suffering of others, then one is not human" (Mencius 2016). These views are based on the idea that since we don't want to suffer, we can empathically understand that others don't want to suffer, too. Of course, there are sadists and antisocial characters who derive pleasure from harming others, but Montaigne and Mencius would argue that these are psychologically deformed human beings—exemplars of human development gone seriously awry.

This admonition to avoid cruelty whenever possible is, in essence, the basis for the Golden Rule, which seems universal to all cultures. The version we know best in the West is Jesus's statement in Matthew 7:12 that, "All things whatsoever ye would that men should do to you, do ye even so to them." We find a similar rule, stated inversely, by Rabbi Hillel in the Talmud: "What is hateful to you, do not to your fellowmen. That is the entire Law; all the rest is commentary" (Tractate Shabbat 2017, 31a:6). An even earlier version is found in Confucius's *Analects*, where Confucius's student, Zigong, asks, "Is there a single saying that one may put into practice all one's life?" and Confucius answers, "That would be 'reciprocity.' That which you do not desire, do not do to others" (The Analects of Confucius 2015, 15:24.)[9] We find yet other versions in the Hindu *Mahabharata* ("This is the sum of duty: Do naught unto others which would cause you pain if done to you"), the Buddhist *Udānavarga* ("hurt not others with what pains yourself"), and the Islamic Hadith ("None of you believes until he wishes for his brother what he wishes for himself"). Finally, we find a more intellectualized version in philosopher Immanuel Kant's "categorical imperative" that we should always act in such a way that we could approve of it if everyone else acted similarly.

This idea of treating others as we ourselves would be treated is not based simply on an appeal to reciprocity—"I won't harm you because I wouldn't want you to harm me." It's also based on a fundamental sense of empathy—that when we see others suffer, we suffer vicariously along with them. It's the feeling we get when we hear a baby cry, or a puppy yelp when someone steps on its paw. It's the feeling of horror we experience when seeing a mutilated corpse on a battlefield. It's the neighborly sympathy we feel when viewing victims of earthquakes, tornadoes, and floods on the evening news. There is a natural compassion for others that isn't based on rational considerations or reciprocity.

Now, not all of us have the same level of empathy to the same degree. There are sociopaths who are born without the capacity for empathy, or who lose it in early childhood due to adverse circumstances. And there are tender souls who ache with compassion and devote their lives to caring for the poor and the afflicted. But the great majority of us have at least some capacity for empathy, compassion, and generosity, and are able to exhibit it in circumstances appropriate to its expression. And it also seems likely that whatever our current level of empathy, compassion, and generosity, most of us can cultivate these qualities further so that we are able to experience and enact them more often and under a wider set of circumstances.

Earlier in this chapter I cited a passage from *The Mencius* about people's alarm and dismay at seeing a child fall into a well. People feel the urge to rescue the child, not based on some rational calculation of how it is to their advantage, but out of spontaneous fellow feeling. We care about that child. And we don't, ordinarily, want to see others suffer. Mencius, you will remem-

---

9. The Chinese word for "reciprocity" here is *shù*, which can also be translated as "empathic understanding," or "consideration of others."

ber, thought we were all born endowed with the "sprout" of benevolence, and that the conditions of our lives determined whether that sprout would develop and blossom, or wither and die.

This benevolence is the glue that holds societies together. As primates, we are heir to all the urges of our primate cousins—territoriality, competition for mates, aggression towards outsiders—and probably some uniquely human types of possessiveness and selfishness as well. If that was all there was to us, society would be a constant war of every person against every other, and life would be, as philosopher Thomas Hobbes suggested, "nasty, brutish, and short." Human civilization could not cohere and develop if there were not some countervailing force to push back against our innate selfishness and aggression. That countervailing force is our own innate caring, benevolence, and ability to tend and befriend. Behavioral geneticists may debate *how* pro-sociality arose through evolution, but it's an unquestionable fact that it *did* arise and is a central aspect of our existence. We might note that while people often frame Darwinian evolution in terms of competition, some of the most significant evolutionary advances involved advances in cooperation—for example, when single-celled organisms incorporated mitochondria, when single-celled organisms became multicellular organisms, and when eusociality developed in ants, bees, and humans.

So far, we have focused on the value of benevolence, kindness, generosity, empathy, and compassion for social well-being, but we ought to recognize its importance for personal well-being as well. First, it has instrumental value for us. When we treat others well, they are more likely to treat us well in return. People who are loving and generous are more likely to have family and friends who love them and treat them benevolently. When we are kind and caring, others are more willing to join with us in projects of mutual concern.

But human-heartedness is not only instrumental to flourishing, but also partly constitutive of it. Generosity nourishes our being and connects us to life. It warms us inside and makes us feel good about ourselves. It allows us to live in a more open-hearted way—one that has the feel of intrinsic rightness to it. When we rescue Mencius's child from that well, we know in the very core of our being that we have done something worthwhile and good.

As it turns out, the happiness that comes from generosity and unselfishness may be deeper and more meaningful than the happiness derived from the fulfillment of self-centered desires. Stegner, Kasdan & Oishi (2008) studied the degree to which various activities contribute to college students' subjective well-being, happiness, and the meaningfulness of their lives. The students kept daily diaries of the frequency in which they engaged in self-centered pleasurable behaviors (e.g., buying jewelry, masturbating, going to a party) and virtuous activities (e.g., volunteering, giving money to someone in need, listening carefully to someone, expressing gratitude). The researchers found that virtuous activities were correlated with the student ratings of well-being, meaning, and happiness, while self-centered pleasurable activities were not.

The moral of this study is that if you want to be happier, help others. There ought to be nothing surprising in this conclusion. We Americans are a volunteering people, donating our time and energy to coach sports teams, build housing for the poor, tutor children with educational difficulties, run school bake fairs, and lend a hand in hospitals, soup kitchens, food pantries, and disaster relief agencies. It's commonly said, if you are feeling sorry for yourself, helping someone else will help you break out of the funk.

Conscientiousness

The virtue called conscientiousness, trustworthiness, or dependability is also found on multiple lists of the virtues and delineates a set of capacities that are distinct from courage or benevolence. It includes the abilities to set a goal and stick to it and to keep promises and honor obligations. People who possess this virtue move through the world in a purposeful way rather than drifting through it willy-nilly. They are people you can rely on. They are also people who pay attention to details rather than going about their business in a careless manner.

The ability to set a goal and stick to it requires a variety of character strengths and skills. It requires the ability to focus and not get sidetracked by distractions. It requires the ability to care deeply about what one is doing and to prioritize certain goals above others. Prioritizing goals means that we don't suddenly change our priorities when the temptation to pursue other goals arise. It means we are willing to delay or forgo some pleasures in order to honor our commitments. It means that when we promise to do something for others, we take that obligation seriously.

The value of conscientiousness to both personal well-being and social well-being needs little explanation. When we are conscientious, we are more likely to accomplish the goals we set for ourselves, and thus more likely to flourish. In addition, our reputation as trustworthy, dependable people signals to others that they can count on us and makes them more willing to cooperate with us. Finally, the social order depends on people—police, firefighters, judges, air traffic controllers, teachers, scientists, electricians, carpenters, neurosurgeons—who take their responsibilities seriously and fulfill their duties and commitments.

Psychologists often speak of the "Big Five" factors that account for most of the variance in personality differences between human beings—and conscientiousness is one of them.[10] Research shows that conscientious people are generally happier, live longer, are more likely to have successful marital relationships, and less likely to become addicted to alcohol or drugs, become homeless, or end up in prison.

If there is a downside to conscientiousness, there is a tendency for conscientious people to be less creative. Also, one can certainly be too conscientious—think of tightly-wound people who feel driven to succeed, or who are overly obsessive in attention to detail. The drivenness of the Type A personality and the fearful perfectionism of the obsessive-compulsive are essentially motivational problems, and it is easy to separate these motivational excesses from the inner organization, focus and care that are the essential components of conscientiousness per se. This is a good place to remind ourselves how Aristotle thought of the virtues as midpoints between behavioral excesses and deficiencies. In this spirit, let us define conscientiousness as the happy midpoint between compulsiveness and laxity.

Finally, let us note that some moral philosophers take a dim view of conscientiousness, thinking that if it is a virtue, it is a lesser one (Angle, 2015). This is because they think it is a synonym for what Aristotle called *continence*. The continent man does his duty, not because he feels an inner call to it, but because he begrudgingly knows it is expected of him. A continent person does the right thing, but for the wrong reasons. He is not truly virtuous at heart but acts *as if* he were virtuous.

This is not what I mean by conscientiousness. The conscientious person, in my reading, is someone who truly cares about his central values, but is also aware that putting one's values into consistent action takes some effort if one is not going to be distracted by lesser goals and temptations. The idea that true virtue requires that virtuous behavior must issue effortlessly from one's character without ever requiring any effort of will seems like too high a bar for mere mortals to reach. Internal motivation to do the right thing is undoubtedly superior to forcing oneself to do the right thing when one doesn't really feel like it, but most of us will find ourselves, at least some of the time, between these extremes.

---

10. The other factors being extraversion, anxiety proneness, openness to experience, and agreeableness.

Temperance

Temperance is the ability to restrain one's impulses, urges, and appetites so that they can be harmonized with one's higher order goals and ideals. It is the ability to attenuate, delay, or deny immediate desire satisfaction in order to obtain greater long-term well-being for self and others. Temperance is the virtue that allows us to put our house in proper order, put first things first, and honor what is most important to us.

Plato considered temperance, or *sophrosyne*, the most important cardinal virtue, because without it, no other virtue would be possible. Temperance is what allows us to not indulge ourselves to the point of self-harm. It allows us to contain our anger and rage so that we can pursue justice and forgiveness. It allows us to keep our sexual desires in order so that we can honor our long-term commitments to loved ones. Practical wisdom tells us what we ought to do, but temperance allows us to heed and follow its dictates.

Buddhist ethics also puts self-restraint first and foremost. Suffering, in Buddhism, is the result of *tanha,* or craving, and the ability to skillfully distinguish which desires lead to genuine happiness if fulfilled, and which desires lead to greater suffering if fulfilled, is one of the central goals of Buddhist practice. This requires not only discerning wisdom, but restraint and renunciation as well. It is this ability that allows us to observe cravings without acting on them. Cravings are momentary states that come and go, and if one observes them during meditation, one learns if one does not act on them, they eventually fade away. As one learns to do this, one is increasingly able to turn from being impulse-ridden to developing a greater sense of inner peace, order, and contentment.

Equanimity

Equanimity is the ability to take events in stride without losing control over one's emotions or losing a sense of perspective. It is an important virtue in both Greco-Roman Stoicism and Buddhism. People who possess equanimity are cool-headed in crises and weather life's misfortunes without falling into despair. They realize that what Buddhism calls the "eight worldly concerns"—gain and loss, pleasure and pain, praise and blame, fame and disrepute—are a part of everyone's life. Fate and fortune visit these on each of us in different seasons of our lives. As the preacher in *Ecclesiastes* notes, "to everything there is a season." There is a way that all of this is impersonal—not about us, but just life.

The Buddhist tradition tells the story of Kisa Gotami (Olendzki 2005), an unfortunate woman whose son has died. She goes from wise person to wise person asking if anyone can provide her with an elixir that can restore her son's life. Eventually, she goes to the Buddha who says he can help. "But first," the Buddha says, you must go door to door and bring me a mustard seed from a home where no one has died." She quickly discovers that there is no such household—that everyone has lost someone dear to them at some point in their lives—and this realization is the medicine she needs—death is impersonal—to help assuage her grief.

Another aspect of equanimity is that it's best not to get too swollen a head when praised, or too despondent when criticized or unappreciated. None of the eight worldly concerns need affect how we think about ourselves as persons. If we know we are behaving rightly, we can withstand all the criticism in the world. If we have behaved wrongly, criticism may help us discover our error and improve going forward. Having erred doesn't cause one to lose one's existential worth as a human being—the respect and dignity we are all owed simply for being human. There is no reason to assume because one has failed or reaped bad consequences for one's actions that one is therefore bad or defective. This is how equanimous people retain their equanimity—by seeing everything that happens as an opportunity to learn and improve.

Equanimous people also don't demand admiration and gratitude for their good deeds. They do what is right because it is the right thing to do. If the world doesn't appreciate their good deeds, "too bad." The equanimous person understands the meaning of the quip that, "no good deed goes unpunished," and takes underappreciation in stride.

Another part of equanimity is the ability to right-sized bad outcomes. People are prone to exaggerate how terrible their situations are. On a 0–10 scale of terribleness, they often rate their misfortunes as an "11." It sometimes helps to realize that a "10" is on the level of having a painful fatal disease, being boiled in oil, or losing one's children. Most problems in life do not rise to that level. Properly anchoring our scale of terribleness can help make our sufferings right sized.

Another equanimous perspective is a temporal one: Think about whether a particular problem will matter as much to you a decade from now. Will it prove to be a life-changing catastrophe, or will it, with the perspective of time, turn out to be just a speed bump on the road? In all these considerations, it is easy to see how equanimity—although it relates to governance of the emotions and is a moral virtue—is also dependent on the intellectual virtue of phronesis, or practical wisdom.

Truthfulness

Truthfulness is the virtue of being honest to others and with ourselves. Like trustworthiness, it makes us reliable partners. When we are truthful, we are straightforward and non-deceptive, and others can take it at our word that we say what we mean. No one wants to enter into a deal with a known liar—whether that deal is a business deal or a marriage contract. Of course, speaking the truth means knowing, in so far as it is knowable, what the truth is. It also means, not only stating the truth to others, but understanding what is true about ourselves.

The value of self-truthfulness and the problems that stem from self-deception ought to be obvious. We are more likely to be happy in life if we clearly understand what our genuine needs, wishes, goals, and reactions to events are. If we have a view of ourselves that does not match what everyone else thinks of us, we are likely to misjudge the situations we find ourselves in, and things are likely to go poorly for us. If you are truly gay and insist to yourself that you are straight, you are unlikely to find a happy long-term romantic partnership in life. If you think you are God's gift to women when all the women around you find you reprehensible, you are likely to end up lonely and resentful. It's good for us to know what we are truly about.

The idea of truthfulness also depends on being capable of discerning truth from falsity to a reasonable degree, so truthfulness depends on the intellectual virtue of being what we might call a "responsible epistemological agent." Our culture has developed a variety of practical procedures for sorting out fact from fiction, and, as adults, we are morally responsible for utilizing these procedures where they apply. These procedures include an ability to evaluate the reliability of sources, the ability to conduct experiments, the ability to reasonably ground subjective estimates of probability, the willingness to consult and compare diverse resources, and the ability to reason logically.

Now there are some matters that can never be resolved by empirical means—whether, for example, God exists, or whether there is an afterlife or reincarnation. People may be entitled to a wide range of views on these subjects since there is no agreed upon way to settle their differences. Conversely, there are many differences of opinion on matters that could be decisively settled if people made reasonable efforts to arrive at the truth. Can face masks impede the infectious spread of respiratory viruses? Was the 2021 insurrection at the Capitol the result of a false flag operation? Questions like these are empirical questions that are not very difficult to evaluate by the commonsense methods delineated in the previous paragraph, and yet they have managed to corrupt the level of American public discourse. It is not enough to say everyone is entitled to their own opinion or their own set of facts. People are and should be responsible for what they believe and what they pass on as truth to others.

The responsibility to make a decent effort to ascertain the truth involves many skills and attributes and is no simple matter. But just because it's hard doesn't mean that we don't have an obligation to ourselves and others to try. We'll discuss these skills and attributes in greater detail in chapter three, when we explore what wisdom is and how it works.

Justice

While Socrates struggled to define justice in Plato's *Republic*, it appears that even babies have a rudimentary sense of justice. Given the opportunity (Paul Bloom 2013), babies as young as five months old overwhelmingly prefer puppets that are "good actors" (ones that are helpful to other puppets) as opposed to "bad actors" (ones that are cruel to other puppets), and toddlers as young as twenty-one months old reward good puppets with treats and punish bad ones by taking treats away. It appears that a rudimentary notion of fairness and retributive justice arises early in life and is intrinsic to our nature. When a parent rewards or privileges one child over another, the cry of "that's unfair!" will soon be heard. The same cry arises whenever a child feels he has been punished or restricted unfairly. The idea of justice is tied to ideas of fairness and equity, and justice is served when people are handed those rewards and punishments we think they rightly deserve.

As it turns out, this idea of "just deserts" is a highly problematic one, the more we delve into it. There are ethical and legal questions about diminished capacity, extenuating circumstances, duress, and motivation that complicate judgements of guilt and culpability. There are philosophical questions about whether people engage in bad acts due to "free will," or to deterministic factors not under their control. There are also important questions about who gets the power and right to decide what is just and fair, especially when there is no social unanimity about what is fair in a particular set of circumstances. We can think, for example, of past and present social disagreements over the criminalization of homosexuality, plural marriage, abortion, and marijuana.

But despite these significant problems, the idea that we think people ought to merit the consequences of their actions, and that the great majority of us would prefer a world in which fairness is a matter of course cannot be disputed. In fact, there is a good deal of evidence that justice and fairness are necessary preconditions for human cooperation to occur. One of the most convincing pieces of evidence comes from social simulations in the realm of game theory research (Bowles and Gintis 2011, 26–32). If a group of people play multiple rounds of a game in which they can either benefit from cooperation or act selfishly on their own behalf, the following pattern emerges: At first everyone cooperates at a high level, but as soon as a few people defect and choose to act only on their own behalf, cooperation ceases. It quickly devolves into every person for him or herself. If players are given the opportunity to punish the selfish members, however, cooperation levels remain high throughout repeated rounds of the game. It seems as if the very idea of a social order depends on our ability to punish malefactors. So, it is easy to see how social well-being depends on justice. As the saying in progressive political circles goes, "No justice, no peace!"

But what about our personal flourishing? Is being a just person important for that, too? Let's note the manifold instrumental benefits that may accrue to us if others perceive us as being just. First, we are more likely to have stable relationships in which other people approve of us and are willing to lend us their love and cooperation. Second, we are acting in such a way as to encourage others to be just through model and example, and thus are liable to receive the long-term benefits of increased social stability and increased predictability and rationality in the way rewards and punishments are meted out.

Beyond these instrumental benefits, however, are the benefits intrinsic to being just and fair. Here we must include rational self-respect. The only self-respect an unfair person can rationally have is the self-respect of the thug, the tyrant, and the bully—those who believe that power justifies all things, that it is better to be feared than loved, and that morality is a pretty fairy tale, to be believed only by suckers, and designed to conceal the fact that life is simply a matter of the strong taking from and dominating the weak. If there is a part of you that disapproves of thugs, tyrants, bullies, grifters, free riders, and assorted con artists, then it isn't rational to hold yourself in esteem if you happen to be one. There is something deeply irrational in thinking one can respect oneself when acting like those one detests. The idea that one is a person in good standing according to one's own lights is an important consolation amidst the miseries fortune may inflict on us. It is the way we hold our heads up high, bloodied but unbowed, though manifold difficulties.

Lastly, let us note that justice, like any virtue, can go too far if not mitigated by other virtues like compassion and the dictates of practical reason.

The zealot brandishing the unwavering sword of justice without ever giving due acknowledgement to the counterbalancing virtues of mercy, forgiveness, and reconciliation is not an appealing person. As Gandhi is often credited (erroneously) as saying, "An eye for an eye and a tooth for a tooth makes the whole world toothless and blind." Justice must never descend into mere bloody vengeance, and tit-for-tat never-ending cycles of retribution. It is not an unmitigated good but is good only when enacted in coordination with the other virtues and in conjunction with practical wisdom. As philosopher Martha Nussbaum (2016) persuasively argues, society is probably better off when our ideas of justice are forward-looking—focused more on how we can deter future bad behavior, or even better, ameliorate the social causes of bad behavior—rather than overly focused on the short-lived and not entirely satisfactory pleasure of watching malefactors suffer for their misdeeds.

Summary (So Far)

I have now made a case for how the virtues of courage, benevolence, conscientiousness, temperance, equanimity, truthfulness, and justice are both self-regarding and other-regarding, and have important roles to play as both instrumental to and constitutive of flourishing. Aristotle believed the virtues constituted the very essence of excellence in the art of living.

Aristotle, the Buddha, and Confucius had names for exemplary persons—*phronimos*, *bodhisattva* and *jūnzǐ*, respectively. In my home growing up, we called such a virtuous person a *mensch*, the Yiddish word for "man," as in the oft-heard (in my neighborhood) expressions, "He's a real *mensch*," or "Be a *mensch*!" The *mensch* exhibits the quality known as *menschlichkeit*—humaneness—the same quality Confucius identified as *rén*. Just as the Golden Rule is universal, the message across the cultures about the good life is the same—be it *phronimos, bodhisattva, jūnzǐ, or mensch*—while the cultivation of the virtues may only be probabilistically associated with greater happiness, it is definitionally constitutive of goodness, being a good person, and living a good life—a life a rational person can reflectively approve of.

We have also stipulated that the virtues should not be exercised singly, but in conjunction with each other, and that practical wisdom is needed to dictate which virtues and how much of each are called for in specific situations. This means that the person who possesses the virtue of truthfulness will not necessarily be truthful in all situations, but only in those situations that appropriately call for it. This idea is important to keep in mind because modern personality theorists sometimes dispute the existence of traits like courageousness or honesty because they observe that few people are courageous and honest under all conditions, and that the specific nature of the circumstances we find ourselves in accounts for behavior as much or even more than any alleged personality traits. While this is an important observation, it is not a real objection to the virtues as generalized tendencies to respond in a certain manner, because the role of practical wisdom in moderating each virtue suggests that, indeed, this is how the virtues ought to manifest. In addition, we have noted earlier that the exercise of virtue is only called for in situations that would demand it of us due to the specific roles we voluntarily occupy or are socially ascribed.

Cultivating the Virtues

Having defined a set of virtues and how they contribute to flourishing, the next question is, "how can we cultivate them?" I described earlier how children internalize the values of significant others, and how, as they mature, they reflect on these values and subsequently refine, elaborate, revise, or reject them. I have also described the process through which people develop the habit of bringing these values into consideration when weighing how to proceed in perplexing situations. The question I want to address now is how do we adults, who have presumably already undergone such a process, continue to cultivate virtue? Presumably, no matter how virtuous we are, there is still room for us to grow and become more virtuous. Is there a program of virtue cultivation that we can actively pursue in our daily lives? If so, is there such a thing as going too far in cultivating the virtues? Is there some point where we would be better off stopping and resting on our laurels?

A Program of Virtue Cultivation

In the previous section I enumerated a set of seven proposed virtues: *courage, benevolence, conscientiousness, temperance, equanimity, truthfulness, and justice*. One way to go about deliberately cultivating these virtues in one's life is through a process of daily contemplation and reflection. One could, for example, devote each week to reflection on a single virtue. Each morning or evening in this week, one could set aside time to inquire into how truthful (or courageous, etc.) one had been in the past 24 hours. Were there situations where one had been dishonest (or not completely honest) with oneself or others? Are we comfortable when reflecting on our level of honesty or dishonesty in various situations throughout the day—does it now, in the light of considered reflection, seem like it was the best thing to do, or do we wish we had done better? If we were our very best selves—the selves we aspire to be—would we choose to do the same thing again? If we are unhappy with our level of honesty, do we need to revisit the situation and make amends to the person we were not completely honest with, or is it all right to leave things as they are, but to go forward with a different intention the next time a situation like that arises? As each day in the week progresses, are we changing the way we engage with the world in an honest way, or are we remaining the same?

We can also look at the way we assess and engage truth in the things we hear or read. Are we believing or spreading rumors when we haven't made any effort to assess their truth? Are we listening to divergent opinions or only to one side of the story in terms of the information we consume? How are we assessing the reliability of the sources we are relying on?

After a week of working on one virtue, one could then begin working on each of the other virtues in turn. Once one had completed the cycle of all seven virtues, one could begin again. This process could be a process of silent contemplation, or it could be a more active one of keeping a diary of one's thoughts regarding the virtue of the week. This process of reflection could also include setting a daily intention: "Today I am going to try to be as honest as I can be in situations that call for honesty." This intention can also include the intention to inquire into those situations that seem not to call for honesty—does it seem wise to conclude that this decision does not call for honesty, or am I only being self-serving and intellectually lazy in deciding it does not? The point of this kind of disciplined cultivation is the recognition that we are all unfinished persons, that becoming more the person we aspire to be takes effort and reflection, and that the inquiry into the virtuous life and how to manifest it is a never-ending process.

Can We Be Too Virtuous?

Philosopher Susan Wolf (1982) raises the problem of moral sainthood. She writes, "I don't know if there are any moral saints. But if there are, I am glad that neither I nor those about whom I care about most are among them" (p. 419). What she means by this is that when persons single-mindedly pursue virtue to the exclusion of all the other human goods, there is something cramped and diminished about their lives. By other human goods, I mean things like aesthetic pleasure, intimacy, physical prowess, creativity, and the enjoyment of nature. A life that neglects these other goods is not the best possible life one can live.

Imagine a person so consumed with empathy and concern for the suffering of all the unfortunate beings of the world, people, and animals, that he devotes his life entirely to reducing their suffering in every way possible. There is no limit to what such a morality might require. Does one need more than a one-room hut to live in? Does one need more than a single change of clothes? Does one really need two kidneys? Such a person may feel the need to give away everything not absolutely required so that others may suffer less. They would not want to waste money on nice amenities or labor-saving devices. They would not want to waste time and money by singing and dancing, going to the theater, or relaxing at the beach. They would not enjoy going to a park, reading a novel, or trying new cuisine. There is no room in a strictly morally-driven life for sensual enjoyment, aesthetic experience, or the joys of friendship. Everything must be subordinated to doing "what's right."

As I will make clear in Chapter Four when I more precisely define flourishing, virtue is only one component of the well-lived life. Happiness, pleasure, aesthetics, relationships, adventure, and accomplishments outside of the moral domain (e.g., scientific discoveries, artistic creativity, athletic prowess, good workmanship) also count for something. It's important that we pursue these other goods in ways that do not compromise our moral values, but it's also important that our pursuit of moral values doesn't crowd out the pursuit of these other goods that enrich our lives and give them enjoyment and meaning.

In the next chapter we will further consider Aristotle's notion of practical wisdom—the intellectual virtue that enables us to properly balance our pursuit of the moral virtues with our enjoyment of non-moral goods. When it comes to the question of "can we be too virtuous," I want to say "no," as long as we insist that practical wisdom always needs to be included in the exercise of any virtue and the balancing of moral and non-moral goods.

On the other hand, if we do not have the wisdom to "hit the mark" when it comes to the virtues, then any virtue exercised to excess can undercut well-being. One should bear in mind Aristotle's contention that the virtues represent the midpoints between excess and deficiency. When virtues are carried to excess they become vices: truthfulness becomes rudeness, courage becomes rashness, benevolence becomes indulgence, equanimity becomes detachment, conscientiousness becomes obsessiveness, justice becomes mercilessness, and temperance becomes self-denial.

There may also be such a thing as being too reasonable. There are moments when being unreasonable adds an undeniable *joie de vivre* to our lives. This can happen when we experience the stirrings of infatuation, the throes of artistic inspiration, dance with abandon, or allow ourselves moments of intoxication. This is the Dionysian side of life—and a life of constant reason and restraint is impoverished if it allows no room for it. The trick, again, is finding the proper place for these things within a life that is otherwise reasonable and well-ordered. By all means, enjoy that glass of wine, but not when you have to drive. By all means, relish those feelings of infatuation, but don't base a lifetime commitment on those feelings alone. These enjoyments, intoxications, stirrings, and excitements are an important part of life—they have their proper place—but we ought to take care that they do not upend our highest commitments, aspirations, and goals. They ought to be experienced in service to our larger vision of what a good life is.

Finally, there are some who worry that virtue ethics approaches may be too demanding—that they require too much heavy-handed suppression of our basic human appetites for power, aggression, material acquisition, and sexual pleasure—that only a minority can successfully live by their dictates—and that they will be a perennial source of resistance, resentment, and revolt. While there is some truth to this argument, to accept it at face value is to reconcile ourselves to the idea that human life will never be better than it currently is—that war, oppression, domination, genocide, tyranny, sexual abuse, prejudice, tribalism, economic inequality, global warming, and ecological destruction must be our common lot forever. There are some—they think of themselves as "realists"—who say that we should all just be grown-ups and accept this is the way life happens to be and always will be. But to accept this is to give up on the human wish for "better" and "higher" which is every bit as ineradicable as human wishes for sexual pleasure and aggression.

And the fact is, human life *has* improved appreciably over the centuries, and slow but halting moral progress has been an important part of that improvement. It is one thing to say that human beings will never be entirely wise and virtuous and that instilling wisdom and virtue is up-hill work, and another to say we ought to give up trying. The real issue, as described by Charles Taylor (2007), is "how to define our highest spiritual and moral aspirations for human beings, while showing a path to the transformation involved which doesn't crush, mutilate, or deny what is essential to our humanity (pp. 639-630)." I think the path outlined above does just that—it views virtues as midpoints rather than extremes and insists that the virtues not crowd out the non-moral pleasures of ordinary life.

That said, let's see what wisdom entails.

— 3 —

On Wisdom

Wisdom as a Culture's Fund of Advice About How to Live

Wisdom is a word with multiple meanings. One meaning of wisdom is the accumulated settled advice about how to best live that cultures pass down from generation to generation. A good deal of that wisdom was first committed to memory or written down during the Axial Age (600–300 BCE) when Heraclitus, Democritus, Socrates, Plato, Aristotle, Epicurus, Laozi, Confucius, Mencius, Zhuangzi, Mozi, the Buddha, Jeremiah, Ezekiel, Isaiah, and Ezra all lived. The world's accumulated fund of wisdom continued to be added to over the centuries by countless other contributors including the Greek and Roman Stoics, Jesus and his Apostles, Hillel, Maimonides, the Talmudists, Mohammed, the Islamic philosophical tradition, Chinese philosophers like Xunzi, Han Feizi, Zhu Zi and Wang Yangming, Buddhist philosophers like Nāgārjuna, Vasubandhu, Asaṅga, Dharmakīrti, and Śantideva, and Western Philosophers like St. Augustine, St. Thomas Aquinas, Spinoza, Hume, Adam Smith, Kant, Hegel, Mill, Kierkegaard, and Nietzsche.

This philosophical literature is supplemented by literary ethical resources like the poetry of Rumi and Omar Khayyam, the Greek tragedies, the Hindu *Ramayana* and *Mahabharata,* the novels of Jane Austin, George Eliot, and Leo Tolstoy, and each culture's treasury of fables, legends, and parables. In this account, I have shortchanged the vast oral wisdom traditions of the world—wisdom that gets passed down orally from generation to generation. Much of this tradition is represented in folk adages, some of which are adopted from literary sources, such as "look before you leap," "what's good for the goose is good for the gander," and "a stitch in time saves nine."

China has an especially rich treasury of such adages, known as *chengyu,* or "four-character idioms." For example, "塞翁失馬" is a four-character idiom that translates as, "the old man from the frontier lost his horse." It derives its meaning from a fable that appears in the *Huainanzi* (18:7), written sometime before 100 BCE. In the fable, a man's horse runs away, and his neighbors commiserate with him:

> Everyone consoled them but the father said, "This will quickly turn to good fortune!" After several months, the horse returned with a fine Hu steed [a barbarian horse from across the border] in tow. Everyone congratulated them, but the father said, "This will quickly turn to calamity!"[1]
> (Major, Queen, Meyer and Roth 2010)

As the story continues, the man's son falls off the barbarian horse and breaks his leg. Once again, everyone but the man's father thinks this is bad luck. It turns out to be good luck, however, when all the able-bodied young men in the village are called upon to defend the border and his broken leg allows the young man to remain safely at home. The four-character idiom reminds us that we can never know whether a misfortune will turn out for the good, or whether a bit of good luck will turn out for the worse until the final chapter is concluded. A bit of wisdom indeed.

Parents often employ these fables and adages to teach the virtues to their children. For example, honesty may be reinforced with stories like *The Boy Who Cried Wolf*, or *George Washington and the Cherry Tree*. The whole story of *The Boy Who Cried Wolf* then gets truncated into the phrase "to cry wolf," much like a Chinese *chengyu*. A good deal of wisdom is passed down in just this way.

Wisdom as a Faculty of Mind

But there are other meanings of the word "wisdom" besides its meaning as a culture's treasury of settled advice on how to live. One of those is the idea of wisdom as a faculty of mind, and this is what Aristotle meant by *phronesis*, or practical reason, and what Mencius meant by *zhi*, or the capacity to make correct moral judgements. Phronesis involves the ability to 1) recognize which aspects of a situation require moral judgement, 2) recognize which moral and non-moral considerations are relevant to making the judgement, 3) balance conflicting moral and non-moral considerations, and 4) resolve moral problems concordant within one's overall conception of human flourishing.

---

1. I have taken minor liberties with the translation in to make it more intelligible.

Moral judgements require a set of unique skills that are separate from and additional to the kinds of skills required when conducting a scientific investigation. They correspond, to some degree, to what psychologist Howard Gardener (1983) calls "interpersonal intelligence," and science writer Daniel Goleman (1995) calls "emotional intelligence." Gardener and Goleman emphasize that intelligence is not a single unitary faculty but a constellation of separate kinds of intelligences. The ability to understand spatial relations is different from the ability to understand abstract sentences, perform mathematical operations, or compose a musical score. The trope of the "absent-minded professor," the brilliant academic who can't function adequately in even the most basic social situations, is a familiar one. The ability to operate successfully in social milieus requires special sets of skills related to self-awareness, self-regulation, social awareness, and relationship management.

Self-awareness includes both the ability to understand ourselves from the inside out—what are our genuine emotions, motivations, and ability levels in different domains are—and the ability to see ourselves from the outside in, as others see us. If we are unaware of how we come across to others, our ability to successfully interact with them is significantly limited.

Self-regulation requires several of the moral virtues enumerated in the previous chapter—temperance and equanimity, for example—because negotiations with others require that we watch what we say and how we say it. We must be able to restrain ourselves enough to permit others to have their proper say and restrain our emotions so as to remain properly focused on achieving our objectives.

Social awareness means being able to read the room, or as the Japanese say, "Ba no Kuuki wo Yomu"(場の空気を読む), to be able to "read the air." It means being able to attend not only to what people say, but to their vocal inflections, facial expressions, and body language, how they arrange themselves in groups within a room, who defers to whom, and what the larger unsaid context of the social gathering may mean and imply.

I have made this sound like a linear logical process, as if one simply goes down a list of social cues checking all the boxes, but the Japanese expression "reading the air" means "sensing the situation without words"—a kind of immediate intuitive grasp of the social situation at a glance. Perhaps one can compare it to the visceral difference one immediately senses when walking into a party as opposed to walking into a courtroom.

Social awareness also means understanding what the etiquette of a social situation requires, what your rights in a situation are, and what your status is with your interlocutors. It means knowing if the people you are talking to are the right persons to be talking to in order to reach your objective, or whether other people must be brought into the process. It means understanding the personalities of the people with whom you are dealing—what their interests and concerns are, and what they need and what process they will have to go through in order to get to "yes." Some people respond better to flattery, some to an appeal to conscience, and others to arm twisting. Some people need to be courted first, and others want to get down to brass tacks. This is all part of what social awareness entails.

Relationship management skills are the sets of skills one needs as a hostage negotiator, psychotherapist, legislator, or salesperson. They involve processes relevant to establishing trust and credibility, setting appropriate boundaries, empathic listening, appealing to the other's best interests, convincing others their concerns have been heard and addressed, making a persuasive argument for one's own case, knowing how much to self-disclose, discovering areas of potential compromise, being realistic about goals, not getting sidetracked by emotions, knowing when to back off and when to push ahead, and so on. That's a lot to master, and it's not as if one could take a class or read a book to learn it all. It took years of practice as a psychotherapist before I finally felt as if I was adequately getting the hang of it—and I offer this observation with sincere apologies to my earliest clients. Not everyone is able to master these skills, even with years of practice. Some people have personality disturbances—they are too thin-skinned, self-centered, needy, or oblivious—that prevent them from ever mastering them.

There are also sets of everyday relationship skills we need if we are to be successful in our roles as family members. Some of these are the same as those needed in professional interactions: listening, boundary setting, creating trust, keeping emotions in check, and knowing when and how to compromise. Others are unique to intimate relationships: Recognizing when breaks in empathic attunement have occurred and knowing how to repair them. Knowing how to apologize and make amends. Knowing how to be fair in divvying up household tasks. Knowing how to be vulnerable, to self-disclose, and be honest about one's emotions. Knowing how to properly care for and tend to others, and when to allow others their space. Knowing how to be appropriately assertive when one's needs are being ignored. Understanding what proportionate justice means when disciplining minors.

But *phronesis,* while it certainly includes these emotional intelligence skills, also includes a more general set of intellectual abilities that are prerequisites for being able to make proper social judgements. One of the most important is one we have already mentioned in the previous chapter when we discussed the virtue of truthfulness, and that is the ability to be a responsible epistemological agent—to be able to discern truth from falsehood.

Our culture has developed a vast set of social practices that can assist us in that regard, especially when it comes to questions that can be answered empirically through experiment and observation. These include rules of thumb for knowing what sorts of observations count as evidence, rules for making logical and statistical inferences from observations, and rules for adjusting prior probabilities in the face of new evidence. We learn to understand the difference between causal association and mere co-occurrence. In matters in which we have no expertise, we learn to identify people we can rightly call experts and depend on their opinions. In matters where experts are divided in their opinions, we learn to suspend judgement and await further confirmation of one view or another. Following these rules does not guarantee we will always be right—sometimes the vast body of experts get things quite wrong—but it does reduce the likelihood of being wrong. Given the rapidity in which rumor and false information spreads through the Internet, this is a set of skills that needs to be emphasized as part of the curriculum at every grade level in public education.

Another general intellectual skill relevant to phronesis is the ability to consider multiple factors simultaneously. We know that all things arise out of the interaction of multiple causes and conditions. Some are salient, or immediately obvious, and others are less immediately obvious. Young children tend to focus on just one salient aspect of a situation and can't take everything relevant into account when making a judgement. As we grow older, we develop the capacity to decenter off what is most salient and consider other less immediately salient factors that are also relevant to the matter we are considering. As psychologists Jean Piaget and Barbel Inhelder (1974) have shown, when water is poured from a narrow beaker into a wider beaker, young children will state that the total amount of water has become less, because the water level in the wider beaker is lower than it was in the narrower beaker. They are taking the height of the water column into consideration because it is the most salient characteristic of the visual array but ignoring the increased width of the water column. They are not yet able to coordinate changes in three dimensions to order to derive a concept of unvarying volume. In adults, we see this same tendency when it comes to solving more abstract kinds of problems, including social problems. This is the kind of thinking that leads some to conclude that the best way to solve the problem of crime is to build more prisons rather than to also consider addressing issues like poverty, inequality, poor schooling, and inadequate substance abuse treatment that contribute to the rate of criminality.

Another intellectual skill we acquire over time is to be able to see things from someone else's perspective. Young children cannot do this. They can only see things from their own perspective. When asked to draw a picture of a doll the way someone behind the doll might see it, they draw the same frontal view they themselves see. They can only draw an imagined rear view when they grow older. As we grow older we can begin to imagine how other people see things from different perspectives. We also begin to understand that there isn't only one right perspective, and that we can get a larger understanding of situations by coordinating the perspectives of many people simultaneously. Many of the problems that come from living in a multicultural society come from just these kinds of failures to understand that others can have a different perspective that contains a partial aspect of some larger, more complex truth.

So far we have identified three general intellectual skills that are precursors of phronesis: epistemological skills, the ability to engage in combinatorial thought, and the ability to consider multiple perspectives. We can certainly add more skills to the mix. We can add the ability to understand abstract relations and operations in addition to concrete relations and operations, which only develops in late childhood, adolescence, and adulthood. This allows us to mentally solve verbal problems involving seriation (e.g., "If Charlotte is taller than Suzanne, and Suzanne is taller than Anne, is Charlotte taller than Ann?") as well as to understand the abstract meaning of concrete expressions, like "shallow brooks are noisy."

We can also include the rules that allow us to infer whether a situation is a specific case of a more general situation and whether the rules of the more general situation apply. When I was first hired as a hospital psychologist, a wise supervisor told me I was allowed to make every mistake twice: the first time because I didn't realize it was a mistake, and the second time because I didn't realize it was the same mistake again. Being able to see what disparate situations have in common is itself a real skill.

Wisdom of the Body

All of these epistemological, inferential, logical, combinatorial, perspectival, and abstract skills belong to ways of knowing that are linear, verbal, and hypothetico-deductive. As crucial as these skills are, there are other ways of knowing that might be called "intuitive," "paralogical," "organic," "embodied," and "holistic" that also have an important role to play in wisdom. They constitute our whole organism's implicit felt sense of the totality of its ongoing process and circumstances.[2]

If you do not already have an immediate sense of what this embodied knowing is, it may be hard to explain. We tend to associate cognition only with our heads and ignore the fact that our bodies know things as well. I am not just pointing to simplistic cases, as when our minds and bodies are disconnected—for example, when a friend tells us we're angry, and we strenuously deny it—but then we "check in" with our bodies and feel our jaw and fists clenched, and the adrenaline pumping through us. A better example is when we feel an inchoate sense that something is troubling us but aren't quite sure what it is. We can "check in" with that inchoate feeling at the place where we can bodily locate it, usually somewhere mid-chest. As we do so, a word or image might emerge that captures some aspect of that feeling. We can then inquire whether that word is exactly right. If it is, the body relaxes a bit. If it isn't, the body feels it's wrongness. It's like when we are trying to find an elusive word that's at the tip of our tongue, and a friend offers us a wrong suggestion. While we still can't remember the word, we can know with great certainty that our friend's suggestion isn't quite right. It's as if the missing word possesses a kind of definiteness of its own.

But let's go back to our inchoate feeling of unease. If we persist in waiting for a word to emerge that will serve as the key to unlocking the feeling, we will eventually get better approximations that describe aspects of the feeling more adequately: "It's a kind of jumpiness ... no, disquiet is a better word ... it has something to do with what I said to my boss yesterday about wanting a raise ... no, that's not quite right ... it's about my fear that I may lose my job because I'm not quite good enough ... yes, that's it." And so the process goes. When we finally have the right words for it, the feeling shifts, and then as we work with that changed feeling, new aspects of our sense of the situation we find ourselves in begin to emerge. One way to describe this is a kind of ongoing conversation with our bodies.

We get these embodied senses of knowing something all the time. We meet someone new, and we don't know why, but we feel queasy in their presence. There is something about them that disturbs us but we can't quite put our finger on it. Or just the opposite. We meet someone new and feel an immedi-

---

[2]. For a detailed account of what this means, see Gendlin, 2018. Much of what follows in this section is drawn from my reading of Gendlin.

ate connection to them as if we had known them in a previous life. Or we are about to make a major life decision that our friends and family have talked us into, but we feel some residual resistance to it in our bodies, but we don't know just what that resistance is really all about.

Now all of these felt senses may be valid or invalid. We may be queasy about our new acquaintance because we are prejudiced and they are of a different skin color. We may be attracted to the appealing new person because they remind us of someone from our past but are really nothing like that person in ways that count. Or our resistance to that new life decision may be simply fear of the unknown, and we would do best to push ahead with the decision regardless. On the other hand, these felt senses may also convey vital information that is in the body but "out of mind" and that we ought to heed. Maybe the person we feel queasy about really is a psychopath. Maybe there are cogent reasons why that new life decision is wrong for us. The key here is not that these gut intuitions are always right but that they always deserve our attention and our best understanding of what they may potentially be telling us. We ignore them at our peril. And the only way to understand them is to engage in a process of discovery with them—a process that is not a straightforward logico-deductive process. Indeed, sometimes the keys to understanding these felt senses come to us in our dreams, or from keeping a diary about them, or by engaging with them through art and music.

What I am suggesting here is that these embodied ways of knowing complement our logical-analytic ways of knowing, and that the people we call truly wise are people who do both well—who can think logically *and* listen to their bodies *and* recognize when and where each of these is called for. Being able to take all of the available information from head, heart, and body into account is an important aspect of phronesis. This is not a matter of "trusting one's gut," but of taking one's gut to into account when making decisions.

I spent nearly three decades mentoring novice psychotherapists at a major university clinical psychology internship program. These were extremely bright, well-motivated students from top universities who had already completed their coursework for their doctorate degrees. I would spend hours each week listening to their taped conversations with clients and providing feedback on how they might improve. Most of them became good therapists, but there were some who could never quite manage to say the right thing, in the right way, at the right time despite their considerable intelligence. The ones who had the most trouble were the ones who had the greatest difficulty tapping into their own embodied experiencing. A lot of good therapy consists of simply helping clients to get in touch with what their bodies already know but their minds do not. A question like, "why did you say that?" prompts clients to speculate profitlessly in their heads, while a question like, "what's your body's whole sense of this problem?" often directs clients to the heart of the matter. You can't help someone do this, however, if you can't do it yourself.

I could often identify the best novice therapists from the way they casually spoke in our mentoring sessions. Some were always in their heads and spoke in an emotionally detached, intellectualized way. It's as though their words went straight from their brains to their mouths. Other's spoke more from the heart. You could see them physically feeling their way through an answer—pausing now and then to check in with their bodies— making sure what they were saying accurately reflected what was most important to their whole selves at that moment.

I once had a meditation teacher who epitomized this process. She spoke mostly with her eyes closed, all the better to bodily focus, and her speech was riddled with pauses as she listened to her body reacting to what she had just said and then reflected on whether her words exactly matched what she intended to convey. When the right words came, they seemed to flow from her whole being, her body subtly dancing with her words. Her conversations went right to the heart of whatever matter we were discussing. In many ways, she epitomized for me what a wise person is like.

Mindfulness and Metacognition

Speaking of meditation teachers, the Buddhist tradition introduces another aspect of practical wisdom. It encourages a set of practices that modern psychologists sometimes refer to as meta-cognition—"thinking about thinking"—but that really amounts to the cultivation of awareness of one's own mental processes. Thoughts and emotions often enter our stream of consciousness without our stopping to notice or reflect on them. It's not that these thoughts or emotions are "unconscious" but that they occur without our specifically making a mental note that they occurred and without any effort to evaluate their value for us in terms of our well-being. The Buddhist tradition recommends that we cultivate *mindfulness,* the ability to take a step back and observe our own mental processes so we can decide how to respond to them. We can make a judgement about each thought—is it beneficial to me if I go on thinking this way, or is it harmful to my well-being? If it is beneficial, we can endorse the train of thought and allow it to continue. If it is harmful, we can either stop thinking it, or can change the thought to make it more beneficial.

For example, after making a mistake, someone can have the thought, "I must be a complete idiot!" If one fails to note and evaluate the thought, the thought can have emotional consequences that can ruin the rest of one's day. One can plunge into a negative spiral of reminding oneself of all the mistakes one has made in the past, ruminating about them, and thinking about how stupid one is. Is any of this helpful to well-being? Absolutely not. On the other hand, if one notices the thought as it occurs, one can simply either drop it or dispute it. Acknowledging mistakes and exerting care not to repeat them is beneficial but exaggerating and overgeneralizing from them ("I am a complete idiot!") is not.

It's the same with unwanted emotions. States of anxiety, anger, or sadness can be self-perpetuating, often supported by the exaggerated, overgeneralized, or erroneous thoughts that help maintain them. Cognitive-behavioral psychologists have done a good job of cataloging the kinds of thoughts that are the prime culprits for negative emotional states. Thoughts like, "I must always be perfect," or "Everyone must always love me and approve of everything I do." The trick to dealing with unwanted emotions is to first accept them and not deny them, push them aside, or castigate oneself for having them—and second, to examine the thoughts that accompany them and evaluate their usefulness and validity.

The process of being mindful of thoughts, sustaining beneficial thoughts, and dropping harmful ones can be compared to the process of cultivating a garden—one nurtures the desirable plants and starves out the weeds. As we get better at this, it increases our equanimity. If we are mindful of our thoughts, we can prevent ourselves from indulging in the kinds of exaggerated, overgeneralized thoughts that can disturb our mental calm. Increased equanimity, in turn, can strengthen the moral virtues of temperance and conscientiousness, which depend on even-temperedness for their exercise.

An Attitude of Open Inquiry

Our ability to think both logically and intuitively, take all the relevant information into account, and arrive at an informed opinion also requires a crucial attitudinal component—an attitude of open inquiry. There are amazingly smart people—perhaps you've met some—who only use rational argumentation to buttress their pre-existing beliefs and poke holes in their opponents' arguments. It is a lot harder to remain committed to a process of open-ended inquiry in which one isn't emotionally invested in having one's beliefs confirmed, but instead in arriving at the closest possible approximation of truth.

It's hard to recognize self-defensive reasoning when we're the ones engaging in it. It requires self-reflection, the ability to temporarily place one's ego-related concerns in brackets, and to adopt a more impartial stance—something that does not come naturally to us. While it's impossible to maintain this attitude all the time, it is possible to cultivate it so that it becomes easier to recognize when we're failing at it in situations that call for it. Sometimes it takes someone else to point it out to us. When that happens, it's best we consider the possibility they might be right rather than leap to our own defense. This is one reason why interpersonal dialogue is a crucial aspect of the search for truth.

This need for open inquiry is even more important in matters of values than matters of facts. Our values are what we hold most dear, and thus what we are most motivated to defend. Issues concerning values, however, are never permanently settled. Whenever we think we have arrived at final clarity, we soon encounter a new exception to the rule, a voice not yet heard from, or a change in social relations which require opening a renewed round of inquiry. We see this in the ever-evolving re-definition of who holds specific rights protected by law in Western societies—first only property-owning adult white males, then all adult white males, then all adult males, then all adult males and females, and finally all adult persons. There are continuing debates, yet to be resolved, over the rights of children, embryos, and non-humans.

These conflicts regarding values tend to get resolved, when they do, through a lengthy historical process. When there is no initial consensus, a consensus is often arrived at after decades of contention that can allow society to settle on a new rule. Sometimes these issues of value seem permanently settled—no one seems to want to argue on behalf of slavery anymore—sometimes they just recede in importance in the face of more urgent dilemmas, and sometimes they are settled for only now, ready to be reopened at a later date. We see this process at work in debates over the right to privacy in an age of surveillance; over the value of reparations to injured social groups; over the nature of consent in sexual relations, medical research, and internet data; over the balance between individual rights and social responsibilities; and over what is permissible in genetic research. All these issues involve conflicting values and conceptions of the good that are difficult to weigh and balance, and there is never such thing as getting that balance right forever and for everyone. Any consensus arrived at is always open to critique from some new perspective or the emergence of some novel social factor, and thus always requiring a continuing process of inquiry.

When I say these issues are often resolved through an evolving historical process, this should not be understood as meaning that society is always evolving "for the best." It is just a way of noting that consensuses often eventually appear where there was none at the start, and that consensuses often take a long time to emerge. Sometimes the emerging change is generational as older people who hold a particular viewpoint die off. Sometimes the emerging change is the result of exhaustion—the way Protestant and Catholic states learned to co-exist in Europe after centuries of war. Sometimes the emergent change is due to new social realties—military assault rifles, nuclear weapons, birth control, motor cars, climate change, pandemics. That new emergent consensus may not be for the best, however, which is why whatever new consensus emerges must remain open to further inquiry and critique.

Philosophical Wisdom

So far, we have discussed two conceptions of wisdom: wisdom as a cultural fund of practical advice on how to best live, and wisdom as *phronesis*, or the faculty of practical judgement. The Aristotelian and Buddhist traditions both mention a third kind of wisdom that Aristotle called *sophia* and the Buddhists call *prajña*. We can call this kind of wisdom "philosophical" wisdom as opposed to practical wisdom.

For Aristotle, *sophia* entails the knowing of "extraordinary, amazing, difficult, and divine things"—the direct apprehension of highest fundamental principles and the starting points of all things. For Mahayana Buddhists, *prajña* means understanding the interrelatedness of all things and how their ultimate nature is beyond conceptual dualities. For Theravada Buddhists, it is an understanding of karma, how craving for things to be different causes suffering, the insubstantial nature of the self, and how all is impermanent. For Daoists, it is understanding the way of nature.

Let us note that Buddhists, Daoists, and Aristotelians disagree on what philosophical wisdom entails, and that every philosopher since has had his or her own take on the matter. It's above my pay grade to resolve these differences of opinion, so I will not dive deeply into the exact nature of philosophical wisdom. What I would say, however, is that studying the great philosophers on these matters and pondering these questions directly contributes to personal flourishing. It deepens one's sense of awe and mystery about our world, and sense of humility about what one knows. It enlarges one's capacity to view life from multiple perspectives, transcending the limitations of one's own specific life history, time, and place.

We are also more likely to approach life with a "philosophical attitude," which entails the capacity to take a step back from immediate experience and investigate it with curiosity and not take everything that happens to us as a personally directed affront. It allows us to bear untoward events—especially those that are not genuinely catastrophic—with grace, dignity, and equanimity—and perhaps a dose of humility and humor. This is an important part of what most of us mean by "wisdom."

— 4 —

On Flourishing

Introduction

Living a flourishing life means being the person we aspire to be and having our lives embody the ideals and values most meaningful to us. In the previous chapter I suggested we can judge values by the degree to which they promote flourishing, and that virtue and wisdom are the prerequisites for flourishing. So far, however, we have left flourishing only loosely defined. Flourishing means living lives that are decent, meaningful, fulfilling, and admirable—but what kinds of lives meet these four criteria? When we think about creating a society that promotes individual and collective flourishing, what kinds of lives are we aiming for, and how might we best foster them?

This chapter is an attempt to clarify the nature of flourishing by investigating its various domains. I will explore eight domains of flourishing in depth: *relationship, accomplishment, aesthetics, meaning, whole-heartedness, integration, and acceptance.* This list is intended to be illustrative rather than exhaustive—others may imagine domains I failed to include. While I will identify a plurality of ways in which people can flourish, I will also identify the features all flourishing lives share in common.

Let's begin by noting that there is no such thing as perfect flourishing. We all flourish to a greater or lesser extent; we may also flourish in some domains while languishing in others. However good our lives are, they can always be better. Any life includes moments of dissatisfaction, boredom, loss, anger, grief, pain, failure, and disappointment. In addition, one lifetime is never long enough to develop all one's potentials. We also have conflicting goals and desires that are impossible to simultaneously fulfill; we can't be junior law partners and beach bums at the same time.

Even if our lives were eternal and our desires harmonious, we would still be incapable of perfect flourishing. That's because none of us is perfectly wise or has access to all the information one might need to make perfectly good decisions. We can't know in advance how a specific choice will turn out for us, but only judge it after we have lived through its consequences. Even then, we can never really know whether things might have turned out better or worse had we made an alternative choice. When we choose one college over another, one career path over another, one life partner over another, the road not taken remains unknown. As a result, we all make mistakes in judging what relationships, achievements, skills, activities, and possessions might make us happy, what strategies are most likely to secure them, and how to best implement those strategies. Given these limitations, it isn't surprising that many people fail to flourish.

Flourishing, however, isn't simply the product of good judgement, strong effort, and virtuous character. Our lives are subject to a wide variety of adventitious factors—obstacles, challenges, temptations, opportunities, accidents, misfortunes, random bits of luck, external pressures, and other propitious and adverse circumstances. No matter how good we may be at certain things, we need some degree of good fortune if we are to put our abilities to good account. The best we can say about the relationships between judgement, effort, character, and flourishing is that these relationships are probabilistic rather than certain. All things being equal, judgement, effort, and character pay off more often than ignorance, sloth, and vice. But all things are never quite equal. We all know of people we disapprove of who end up with wealth, fame, and happiness we do not think they deserve.

Nevertheless, despite the not infrequent worldly success of con artists, pirates, drug lords, petty tyrants, and assorted other low-lives, being a jerk is still not usually a recipe for flourishing. As hard as they may try, many of the above fail to flourish or attain more than transient worldly success. Many end up in prison, dead, or shunned by society-at-large. They must expend an inordinate amount of effort watching their backs, keeping their lies straight, and eyeing their escape routes. We can question the degree of serenity and inner peace they can attain, and the depth of lasting love, affection, and friendship that characterizes their relationships. A drug lord's life may have its moments of success and glory, but it is probably not a flourishing one.

Conversely, we know of people born with excellent natural endowments who live lives subject to abuse, violence, deprivation, and discrimination and fail to flourish through no fault of their own. If a seed is to flourish, it must first fall on fertile ground. A person of good judgement, effort, and character may, given enough adverse circumstances, find himself or herself perishing, floundering, or withering rather than flourishing.

Flourishing people sometimes mistakenly claim all the credit for their well-being. They lack perspective on just how fortunate their lives have been. As coach Barry Switzer famously quipped, "they are born on third base and think they hit a triple." While we have reason to take pride in those character traits we have worked hard to develop, we should also appreciate how much of our flourishing depends on the unmerited fortunate circumstances life has bestowed on us. Life is not fair in this regard. There is no reason that good fortune should be ours rather than someone else's. We should cultivate gratitude for our good fortune, humility for our successes, and nurture a moral obligation to see that those goods society has control over are fairly distributed so that all have a chance at flourishing. This is why Aristotle thought flourishing people involved themselves in the civic lives of their communities.

Happiness and Flourishing

We say we want to be "happy," but it's not entirely clear what we mean by it. Imagine you are always happy no matter what happens. Imagine that you feel this same unvarying degree of cheerfulness even if your child is kidnapped or your pet run over by a car. If someone were to ask how you felt during these moments, you would reply "never better" and mean it.

Or imagine an intravenously administered drug that could make you radiantly happy for months on end. During those months, you would lie happily in a comfortable hospital bed while nurses administered parenteral nutrition and tended to your catheter and ostomy bags.

These are two ways of being happy you probably wouldn't choose for yourself. Oh, you might choose the happiness drug if your current situation were absolutely, unrelentingly, and hopelessly bleak: if you were suffering, for example, from an intractable painful fatal illness. But other than that, almost certainly not.

Thought experiments like these demonstrate that what we really want isn't just a *feeling* of happiness. What we really want is to feel those positive emotions that are the result of appropriate causes: doing good things and having good things happen to us. We want to do and experience the appropriate causes of well-being.

What are the appropriate causes of well-being? While the list of appropriate causes might vary from person to person, for most it would include things like:

1. Mastering a new skill;
2. Accomplishing something worthwhile;
3. Being completely absorbed in an activity;
4. Beginning, maintaining, and enhancing loving relationships;
5. Caring for and nurturing others;
6. Creating and appreciating beauty;
7. Experiencing pleasant sights, sounds, smells, tastes, and touches;
8. Experiencing the pleasures and thrills of surprise, novelty, and adventure;
9. Being valued, appreciated, and esteemed by others;
10. Living in accordance with one's values;
11. Experiencing safety, ease, and repose, and;
12. Being meaningfully connected to something larger than oneself (family, faith, community, nature, or a noble cause).

To a large extent, flourishing depends on having as many of these things in one's life as possible. It also means having as few of the causes of ill-being as possible. These would include experiencing, anticipating, or ruminating about:

1. Sickness, injury, pain, and disability;
2. Lack or loss of resources and opportunities;
3. Physical danger;
4. Lack or loss of relationship;
5. Loss of values, meaning, and identity;
6. Being shunned, shamed, criticized, and dis-esteemed by others;
7. Failure

But in addition to having and doing good things and avoiding bad things, we also need the capacity to experience the emotions that are appropriate to good occasions and circumstances. Not everyone can do that. Some people are clinically depressed and unable to appreciate good things when they happen. When people are seriously depressed, they have an incapacity to experience pleasure called *anhedonia*. They minimize the emotions associated with positive events by interpreting those events through a biased set of generalized beliefs, including the beliefs that they are inadequate or bad, that the world has nothing worthwhile to offer, and that nothing will ever improve.

But you don't have to be depressed to curtail positive emotions consequent to good events. Some people are pessimists who regularly discount their accomplishments or good fortune. Rather than savoring their accomplishments, they undercut them by reminding themselves that they failed to do something completely perfectly, or as well as someone else might have done. Rather than savoring pleasant experiences, they may remind themselves that the pleasure won't last, or wasn't quite as good as what they had anticipated. They hold themselves and life experiences up to standards they cannot possibly meet.

So, what do we mean when we say we want our lives to be happy? We probably mean several things. First, we want our life to contain as many as possible of the appropriate causes of well-being and as few as possible of the appropriate causes of ill-being. Second, we want to be free of clinical depression and blessed with nervous systems that allow us to fully experience the pleasant feelings associated with things that are the appropriate causes of happiness. Third, we want to possess a set of mental attitudes that enable us to appreciate and savor pleasant experiences without undercutting them and endure unpleasant experiences with equanimity, and without ruminating on them or blowing them out of proportion. Fourth, we want to cultivate the requisite knowledge, virtues, habits, and skills that enable us to successfully pursue the appropriate causes of happiness and successfully maintain them. Fifth, we want a bit of good luck, since so much of our success in pursuing the appropriate causes of happiness is not just due to our attitudes, knowledge, virtues, habits, and skills, but also a matter of being at the right place at the right time.

Happiness and living an objectively good life often coincide, but not always. Misalignments may sometimes occur. People in the throes of mania feel deliriously happy while destroying their lives and the lives of those around them. Moral saints like Mother Theresa can lead lives worthy of emulation yet experience despair. In a letter to her confessor Mother Teresa wrote:

> In the darkness ... Lord, my God, who am I that you should forsake me? The child of your love—and now become as the most hated one. The one—you have thrown away as unwanted—unloved. I call, I cling, I want, and there is no one to answer ... Where I try to raise my thoughts to heaven, there is such convicting emptiness that those very thoughts return like sharp knives and hurt my very soul. Love—the word—it brings nothing. I am told God lives in me—and yet the reality of darkness and coldness and emptiness is so great that nothing touches my soul. (Scott 2013, 107–113)

And then there are, as mentioned earlier, those jerks who experience undeserved success. So, we need to be clear that happiness and leading a worthwhile life are not necessarily the same thing. On the other hand, most of us aspire to lives that meet the dual criteria of being both happy and good—and genuine flourishing, as we are defining it here, requires some degree of both.

Domains of Flourishing

Earlier in this chapter I enumerated the appropriate causes of well- and ill-being. It is now time to explore these causes in greater depth. I have grouped them together under more general headings that we can think of as domains of flourishing.[1] Every flourishing life is flourishing because of some degree of attainment in several or all these domains. These are the domains of 1) Relationship, 2) Accomplishment, 3) Aesthetics, 4) Meaning, 5) Whole-heartedness, 6) Integration, and 7) Acceptance. The multiplicity of these domains reflects the irreducible pluralism of human aims and purposes—that all our higher goals—freedom, equality, justice, wealth, power, respect, beauty, intimacy, security, excellence, serenity, sanctity, and ecstasy—do not form one harmonious whole, but often conflict. Some people flourish in a life primarily focused on accomplishment, some in a life primarily about relationships, and others in a life devoted to aesthetics. Most who flourish manage to do so in multiple domains, seeking accomplishment in some endeavor while tending to relationships and leaving space for aesthetic expression and appreciation. This often means engaging in difficult trade-offs—think of all the discussion today about work-life balance—but one does so in the belief that making these trade-offs leads to a life that is richer and fuller than a single-purpose life.

In claiming these domains define flourishing for us—that is, for those of us who live in modern industrialized societies—I am not claiming they also define flourishing everywhere throughout human history. The kinds of flourishing that are possible depend, to a large extent, on the opportunities available within given social structures and cultural milieus. Hunter-gather societies, feudal societies, and industrialized democracies offer different sets of opportunities for and obstacles to modes of flourishing and vary in how different virtues may be emphasized and expressed. With that said, let us now turn to the domains that define flourishing for us in our modern way of life.

---

1. I developed these domains borrowing from psychologist Martin Seligman's (2011) PERMA approach to defining flourishing. PERMA is his acronym for Positive Emotion, Engagement, Relationship, Meaning, and Accomplishment. I have kept Seligman's Relationship, Accomplishment, and Meaning domains, incorporated his Engagement into my Whole-heartedness domain, and added the domains of Aesthetics, Integration, and Acceptance.

On Flourishing

Relationship

When my uncle was 92 years old and still in relatively good physical and mental health, he told me he was ready to die. "Everyone I know is gone," he said. That wasn't strictly true—his adult children were still living, as were his grandchildren. But his wife, siblings, and lifelong friends had all passed from the scene—he had outlived all his peers. While his children adored him, they lived at some distance and were primarily occupied, as is often the case, with pursuing their careers and raising their own children.

When my father was 91 years old, he expressed a similar sentiment. He was the last of seven siblings still alive. His wife had passed, as had all his in-laws. I was still around of course, but not really "around"—I lived 1,200 miles away and was focused on my career, marriage, and children. My sister, who lived nearby, visited him daily, checking in, preparing meals, and making sure he took his medications. He had many adoring nieces and nephews—they still recall "Uncle Eddie" fondly—who traveled from afar to visit on occasion, but they were not his peers.

After my mother passed, my father found a girlfriend whom he enjoyed traveling the world with. The girlfriend, I regret to say, was possessive, spiteful, and a pathological liar, and during their two decades together she succeeded in alienating all my father's lifelong friends and prevented him from making new ones. She eventually developed Alzheimer's Disease and was moved to a nursing home nearer to her own children. Once she was gone, he had no friends left to call on the phone, play cards, golf, bowl, or share coffee with.

Towards the end of his life, my father lost interest in showering or getting dressed, preferring to stay in bed and watch television. It was painful to see this decline in a man who, in his prime, was the beloved member of a large extended family, a war hero, a successful businessman, a devoted husband and father, a man who could make or repair almost anything with his hands, a pillar of his synagogue, an avid fisherman and golfer, and the life of any party.

These episodes from the lives of my uncle and father illustrate the importance of staying embedded in a network of relationships for our flourishing. Contemporary research shows that a lack of close personal relationships profoundly affects emotional well-being and physical health: lonely people are not only unhappy, but are at greater risk for depression, cardiovascular disease, cognitive decline, and premature death.

The House We Live In: Virtue, Wisdom, and Pluralism

Aristotle wrote that a human being is a *zoon politikon*—a "political animal," by which he meant that sociality is an inherent part of our nature. Philosopher Martin Heidegger pointed to the same dimension when he wrote that human being was a "being-with-others." The predominant modern Western ideal of "individualism"—the idea that we are each, somehow autonomous individuals—is a fundamental misstatement of our genuine nature. We are intrinsically social animals. While we each have our own distinctness and individuality, we are all embedded within social systems and function as parts of larger wholes.

Nature has made sure of this. We are born helpless—unable to support our heads, feed or defend ourselves, or change location on our own. We need to be taken care of for the first years of our lives. This means nature had to endow the people we depend on with an interest in taking care of us. Parenting is a hard job, as any parent can attest. No one would persist at it, given all the other opportunities the world offers to occupy and fulfill us, if they didn't care a great deal about their offspring and be willing to do almost anything—even sacrifice their own lives if need be—to help them survive and thrive.

Wherever there are people, there are communities to which they belong. The premodern indigenous societies of Europe, the Americas, the Artic, Africa, Polynesia, and Asia did not consist of single-family groupings. Nomadic societies usually contain 20–30 members, while hunter-gatherer societies usually contain about 30–40 (Bowles and Gintis 2011). These small societies periodically gather with neighboring and more distant societies to engage in community celebrations and rituals that can include thousands of participants. These small societies trade with each other and members typically marry outside their own group.

When human societies develop agriculture, the average size of communities swell as more people can be supported within a single locale. When they industrialize, community size increases further. As of 2018, there were 467 cities with over 1,000,000 inhabitants, and an additional 598 cities with over 500,000 inhabitants. People flock to cities for a multitude of reasons. That's where the work is, but it's also where the amenities are—the restaurants, coffee houses, concert halls, parks, theaters, museums, hospitals, administrative centers, public transportation, and the other accoutrements of civilization.

We affiliate together for many reasons—sharing skills; trading and bartering; cooperating in finding and growing food, child rearing, clearing land, and engaging in labor intensive terraforming, water management, and building projects; the production of tools, household utensils, clothing, and decorative goods; and participation in a common defense—but also for the sheer joy of company itself—finding love, companionship, friendship, and dancing, making art, and singing together.

We are also language users, and language is a social activity par excellence. Language is something we pick up from hearing others speak it. It enables us all to live in a shared, socially constructed world. Our ability to engage in complex conceptual and abstract undertakings depends, to a large part, on language—our ability to do history, philosophy, natural or social science, mathematics, criticism, and literature. Our ability to accumulate knowledge, share it, and pass it down to the next generation is language dependent. Language also allows us to step outside of the immediate present and think in the past, future, and conditional tenses. It allows us to learn of happenings out of immediate sight and earshot and imagine counterfactuals.

Nature has equipped us to live in socially constructed worlds. Many of our reactive emotions are explicitly social: envy, resentment, jealousy, adoration, love, empathy, compassion, pity, pride, and shame. These emotions have no content without a social context: they are emotions about relationships.

As I look about my office, I can appreciate how much I owe to others: everything in my office—desk, chair, pens, pencils, paper, and computer—were invented and made by others. The language I am writing this book in is the language of Angles and Saxons, Chaucer, Shakespeare, the King James Bible, Noah Webster, and Yogi Berra. In addition, I can appreciate how much of my individuality is, in part, the result of modeling and internalizing other people. I find bits and pieces of my parents in the way I walk, speak, and act, as well as bits and pieces of friends I admired, idols I aspired to be like in adolescence, and teachers who mentored me.

All this is preface for stating the obvious—that there are good reasons why our relationships play a central role in our well-being. All the philosophers we have mentioned in our discussion of the virtues saw a central role for friendship in their understanding of human flourishing. For example, Aristotle wrote:

> Without friends no one would choose to live, though he had all other goods; even rich men and those in possession of office and of dominating power are thought to need friends most of all; for what is the use of such prosperity without the opportunity of beneficence, which is exercised chiefly and in its most laudable form towards friends? Or how can prosperity be guarded and preserved without friends? The greater it is, the more exposed is it to risk.

And in poverty and in other misfortunes men think friends are the only refuge. It helps the young, too, to keep from error; it aids older people by ministering to their needs and supplementing the activities that are failing from weakness; those in the prime of life it stimulates to noble actions—'two going together'—for with friends men are more able both to think and to act.
(Aristotle 1973, 509)

Similarly, the Buddhist tradition cites the following conversation between the Buddha and his attendant Ananda. Ananda said,

"This is half of the holy life, that is, good friendship, good companionship, good comradeship." The Buddha replied, "Not so, Ananda! Not so, Ananda! This is the entire holy life, Ananda, that is, good friendship, good companionship, good comradeship. When a bhikkhu [monk] has a good friend, a good companion, a good comrade, it is to be expected that he will develop and cultivate the Noble Eightfold Path." (Half the Holy Life 2020, 1524)

Our relationships with others can be characterized along multiple dimensions including: 1) their centrality to our identity and well-being, 2) their degree of mutual attachment, intimacy, and respect, 3) the degree to which they are instrumental or ends-in-themselves, 4) the degree to which they are characterized by differentiations in roles, power and status, 5) the degree to which they are governed by gender norms and/or legal and contractual obligations, and 6) whether they are sexual or non-sexual.

A relationship of a husband to a wife is surely different from the relationship of a parent to a child, a boss to an employee, a mutual friendship, or a liege-lord to his serf. A good deal of Confucian philosophy is dedicated to codifying appropriate roles in different kinds of relationships.

But of course, marriages, to take just one kind of relationship, also differ along all these dimensions. People may marry for love or to get ahead. The power in a marriage may be equally or unequally shared. Members may or may not respect each other. They may be emotionally intimate or distant. Marital partners may think they need to agree on everything and do everything together or each may be mostly doing his or her own thing. Attachment can take many forms that represent a variety of mixtures of love, friendship, tenderness, generosity, ownership, dependency, and need for control.

It is too much to expect that any two people would be exactly equally matched on all these variables. In addition, any two people in a relationship may have different views of role expectations, how decisions get made, how money gets spent, how children should be raised, and what virtues and spiritual qualities they ought to actualize. Resolving these differences within modern marriages takes a certain degree of flexibility, an open flow of communication, and a willingness to compromise and yield when possible. It also requires a degree of emotional maturity so that every disagreement or spat doesn't send one into a downward emotional spiral. All the moral and intellectual virtues discussed in Chapter 2 come in handy here: practical wisdom, equanimity, benevolence, truthfulness, courage, temperance, and conscientiousness.

Making an intimate relationship work means needing to think intelligently about what we want from the relationship and what sort of person we want to be in relationship with. This can be difficult to do while in the throes of infatuation. The things that initially attract us to others—their physical appearance, whether they are "our type," their popularity and social status, their "coolness," the presence of common backgrounds and experiences (or exotic ones), their talents, the qualities they have that might complement or complete us, the unconscious fantasies they fulfill based on early childhood dynamics—are in many ways irrelevant to whether they will be compatible with us in the long run—whether they are capable of intimacy, are trustworthy, will be fair in jointly making decisions, or will agree with our ideas about childrearing. Physically attractive, popular, outwardly successful people can be just as emotionally immature, selfish, controlling, or close-minded as anyone else. That's one reason why people ought to get to know each other over a long period of time before deciding whether to settle down in a more permanent way.

Of course, people "settle" for all kinds of bad reasons. Perhaps they have a low opinion of themselves and think the flawed person in front of them is the best they can hope for—they would rather settle than be lonely. Or perhaps they are dependent types who feel a sense of desperation unless there is someone nearby they can cling onto to take care of them. Or perhaps they are despondent people looking for a magical being who will transform their lives and make them happy. Or perhaps they consider their somewhat advanced age and think life is passing them by, and that this other person is available. Of course, not all settling is bad. No one is perfect—it's not as if there is some perfectly matched person out there who will meet all our present and future needs and desires.

The key point here is that we need relationships to thrive, and that successfully maintaining relationships requires both a degree of practical wisdom, and virtues such as courage, benevolence, fairness, equanimity, truthfulness, and conscientiousness. While they are not the only things that matter—

physical attractiveness, sexual prowess, charm, and a sense of humor also help—in the long run, they probably matter more. That's because relationships fundamentally depend on mutual trust—the trust that one's partner has one's best interest at heart, and will be reliably there to support, protect, and defend one's well-being.

Another key point is that we shouldn't put all our eggs in one basket. Some people invest all their energy in a single relationship, and if that person should happen to change, leave, or die, they are left alone and bereft. It is better—if one can—to also cultivate relationships within one's extended kinship network, along with a variety of friendships, acquaintanceships, and vocational and avocational connections.

This is harder to do today than in the past due to people's increased mobility. It also gets harder to do with advanced age. People in childhood, adolescence, young adulthood, and middle age seem better at establishing new relationships than people in their senior years. This is, in part, because younger people are more likely to meet new friends in school, at the office, at parties, while traveling, or through their children's after-school activities. Meeting new people is built into their life structure. Older people must make more of an effort to leave the house and find venues where they may discover people with mutual interests.

We should also note that the fraternal and sororal organizations that used to promote connections among adult peers—church groups, the Elks, the Moose, the Rotarians, the Chamber of Commerce, the Knights of Columbus, the Masons, the Shriners, the Order of the Eastern Star, Hadassah, B'nai B'rith, the Veterans of Foreign Wars—are steadily declining in membership and not drawing many younger members. People still connect with others through a variety of volunteer activities, but to a large extent these types of fraternal and sororal relationships are being replaced by on-line relationships, as people meet based on similar interests in on-line communities of various types. We should note that people who spend more time on-line are less happy than those who are involved in real-world activities and relationships. One can imagine many possible reasons for this: perhaps they are unhappier to begin with, and find greater difficulty dealing with real-world relationships, and on-line relationships are the best they can manage. Perhaps the easy accessibility of on-line communication seduces them away from the harder work of initiating and maintaining real-life relationships. There can be an addictive quality to on-line relationships that draw one away from real-world relationships requiring more time, effort, and skill—ones that might prove to be, in the long run, more rewarding. One troubling recent phenomenon is the way people can get caught up in on-line extremist communities, gradually cutting their ties with family and real-world friends.

Most people highly value their families and friendships and consider them crucial to their well-being, but are they *essential* for flourishing? Are there ways of life that are poor in social relationships but still happy, meaningful, and fulfilling? What about hermits, or monastics who take a vow of silence, or high-functioning persons with autism who find relationships perplexing and somewhat aversive?

First, just because one is living the life of a hermit is no indication one has left the social world and all it implies behind. One's thoughts (thought quietly to oneself in a language learned from others) and feelings may still be preoccupied with remembrances of past social relations, and the feelings of anger, hurt, and disappointment that led to one's withdrawal from active social life. One continues to carry the social world within, in much the same way that one continues to maintain a sense of ongoing relatedness with loved ones who are gone.

One particularly egregious example can be found in the diary of the hermit and Unabomber, Ted Kaczynski, in which he explained his motivation for his crimes for the presumed benefit of some imagined future interlocutor:

> I certainly don't claim to be an altruist or to be acting for the 'good' (whatever that is) of the human race. I act merely from a desire for revenge. Of course, I would like to get revenge on the whole scientific and bureaucratic establishment, not to mention communists and others who threaten freedom, but, that being impossible, I have to content myself with just a little revenge.
>
> Kaczynski, 1998

Clearly, the social world, albeit a malign one, is still foremost in his thoughts.

My own experience as a psychotherapist working with higher functioning people on the autistic spectrum is that they, too, retain a sense of relatedness, even when their relationships with other people are extremely attenuated. One of my adult autistic clients showed me the photograph album she had maintained over the years. The album did not have a single human image in it, but was filled, page after page, with photos of her cats. Clearly, people can find ways to maintain a sense of connection to a kind of social world through their relationships with pets, or even through their relationships with houseplants, whom they may talk to, care for, and nurture.

I do not want to make the claim that having close personal relationships is a necessary part of well-being for everyone. There are people who, for a variety of reasons, find themselves alone in life. These people can still find meaning, purpose, and pleasure through their vocations, hobbies, travels, enjoyment of literature and the arts, the causes they choose to champion, the skills they nurture and develop, and their religious pursuits. Even if these people regret the absence of fulfilling personal relationships, they would be making an error if they allowed that regret to spoil whatever other sources of fulfillment were available to them. No one gets to lead a life that is complete in every imaginable way, and for people with the right sort of personality, a friendless life can still be a good enough kind of life. It's just that, for most of us, a life with close personal relationships is a superior kind of flourishing than a life without them.

What if one is unhappy with the relationship one is in? People are always looking for advice as to how to improve or "fix" bad or otherwise unsatisfying relationships, and marriage counseling is and always will be a thriving profession. As Tolstoy noted, every unhappy family is unhappy in its own way, and there is no such thing as "one size fits all" advice.

It's hard to know when things are irretrievably broken and its best to count one's losses and move on, or when there are enough good aspects remaining in a relationship that it makes sense to persist in trying to repair and restore it. That is a question one must sit quietly with until inner clarity emerges, and once it does, one has to have the courage to accept it and be truthful with oneself.

Obviously, if one finds oneself repulsed by one's spouse, or one feels a rock certainty that their spouse cannot be trusted with things that are of central importance to oneself, then things are almost certainly not going to get any better. In terms of general rules on how to fix things, people must decide what sorts of flaws in their loved ones—and everyone has their flaws—are tolerable or acceptable, and what sorts of flaws are deal breakers.

Unless we are judges or policemen, we cannot force grown adults to do things they do not themselves see the sense in. Attempts to control one's spouse in order to improve them are more likely to breed resentment than improvement. Shaming loved ones is also rarely the royal road to marital bliss. On the other hand, we can try to explain to significant others how their behavior makes us feel and suggest why changing their behavior might benefit both them and us. We should also understand that we too have our flaws, and some of our loved one's complaints about us may also be, at least partly justified. Open communication, willingness to listen, flexibility, refraining as much as possible from shaming and blaming, and mutual respect, are always in order. As psychologist John Gottman (1994) points out, the most destructive things one can do to the communication process are to 1) respond defensively, 2) stonewall, 3) criticize, or 4) show contempt for one's partner. While we all must criticize our partners sometimes, it should be rare compared to how often we express our appreciation to them. While we all respond defensively or close ourselves off occasionally, it's how often we do so that matters. It shouldn't be our default mode. Contempt, on the other hand—eye rolling, acting superior, calling one's partner names—is never called for, and once it becomes a more than a rare occurrence, it's a sure sign that things are seriously wrong. One can never err by showing too much mutual respect. Note that the ability to maintain open communication and repair breaches of empathy are aspects of emotional and social intelligence that we described as aspects of Aristotelian *phronesis,* or practical wisdom in Chapter Three.

Accomplishment

One of the most essential components of being a flourishing self is our sense of ourselves as effective agents in the world. One could almost say, as the philosopher Spinoza (2005) did, that the central fact of human existence is our striving to maintain and further our existence and acquiring and expanding those powers that allow us to maintain and develop our lives.

When we see infants and toddlers learning to grasp things, roll over, sit, stand, walk, and speak, we are watching human beings expanding their powers so they can maintain their existences. Psychologists call this *funktionslust*, or the sheer exuberant pleasure toddlers and young children take in exercising new physical powers such as crawling, running, or throwing things. Later, they experience the same joy in learning how to skip, jump, hop, and tumble. Each of these new skills vivifies our sense of ourselves as effective agents—our sense of capability.

Eventually, skill development becomes associated with worthwhileness and value—our skills and abilities bring praise and recognition from others, and we are deemed useful members of society. Or conversely, our failure to master certain skills—learning to read or play ball—fills us with feelings of shame and inferiority. No child wants to be left behind a grade in school or be the last chosen for a pick-up softball game.

When most people look back over their lives to assess whether they have been satisfactory, they often look to their accomplishments. Some of these are familial—having a satisfying marriage or successfully raising children. Some are academic—having completed high school, college, or graduate school. Some are economic—being an adequate breadwinner or attaining a certain annual income or household worth. Others are more individual and specific—being good, for example, at a professional, athletic, or creative pursuit. Some are associated with notable acts of courage, endurance, generosity, or civic virtue.

But one does not have to look back on a life well-lived to understand the value of accomplishment to our sense of well-being. We can experience this in the small gains and triumphs that mark the passage of our daily lives: successfully completing a new level in a video game, solving a crossword or jigsaw puzzle, mastering a new skateboard trick or guitar lick, passing an exam, completing a homework assignment, salvaging a sickly plant, knitting a sweater, or successfully preparing a new recipe. Our days are filled with goals we establish, new tasks we set ourselves, and small victories and defeats along the way. With each new skill learned and mastered, with each new task completed, we experience not only the immediate satisfaction of attaining a goal but reinforce our sense of ourselves as competent agents and worthwhile beings.

There is an art to building a sense of mastery and competence that involves setting achievable goals matched to one's level of competence. Often this means breaking larger goals into subgoals and learning skills by the progressive mastery of successive small steps. One learns to read starting with the alphabet, play piano starting with the C major scale, and ride a bicycle starting with training wheels. The art of learning a new skill begins with finding the appropriate starting point and then determining the right-sized increments in difficulty. One must practice a new skill many times before one "has it under one's belt" and is ready to advance to the next level of incremental difficulty.

Often, the hardest part of skill learning is tolerating the frustration associated with practice attempts. One has a sense of trying to do something but not quite getting it, and then repeating the same attempt over and over with slight variations until one finally succeeds. People often require encouragement during the process to keep going until there is the intrinsic reward that comes from success.

As one practices, the body is also learning how to accomplish the task at hand. Maybe one must develop one's muscle strength, or perceptual discrimination, or eye-hand coordination, or new neural circuits. Skill learning is "bodily" learning and accommodation every bit as much as it is "mental" development.

Sometimes we "plateau" in learning a new skill, staying at the same skill level despite what can seem like an inordinate amount practice, until we finally break through what once seemed like an unsurmountable barrier. Repeated practice during these plateaus can be discouraging and demoralizing, and again, people often benefit from encouragement and extrinsic rewards for continued practice if they are to persist to the point of breakthrough.

Temperamental virtues like conscientiousness, persistence, and patience can help one through these fallow periods if one has previously cultivated and inculcated them. The process through which parents and teachers help children cultivate these temperamental virtues is itself a study in skill development. Most of us can remember the childhood process of learning our penmanship, multiplication tables, and spelling, and how much encouragement, contingent rewarding, urging, and cajoling was needed, and how much endurance, persistence, and frustration were required on our part. The successful inculcation of these temperamental virtues probably play as much or even more of a role in adult success than intelligence itself. As Thomas Edison said, "genius is one percent inspiration, and ninety-nine percent perspiration." Similarly, Malcolm Gladwell (2008) proposed the 10,000-hour rule—that beyond raw talent, becoming truly expert at something—whether becoming a concert-level pianist, a chess grandmaster, or a gifted neurosurgeon—requires 10,000 hours of devoted practice.

As we grow older and have fewer remaining years to our lives, the question of our legacy begins to loom large. What have we done with our lives that mattered and/or will live on? This question is tied to the question of meaning which we will address later in this chapter. There is a way in which our lives are like works of art—they are our most important creations—and when we look at their overall arcs—we want to think we have accomplished something good with them.

Sometimes we have done something extraordinary—resuscitated a drowned child or saved one's platoon from enemy fire—singular deeds that seem, in and of themselves, to justify our lives. Sometimes we have attained notable achievements—created a life-saving vaccine, discovered a new principle in physics, painted a masterpiece, written a beneficial new law, negotiated a peaceful settlement, captured a notorious criminal, or published a well-received novel. Most of us, however, live lives without such extraordinary accomplishments. To say our lives are worthwhile only if we have done so is to hold ourselves to an untenable standard. For most of us, it is enough if we can say that we have loved and taken care of our families, raised our children to become decent, competent adults, been fair and generous with our friends and neighbors, and behaved as good citizens. Given the vicissitudes of life, to have accomplished this is accomplishment enough.

Aesthetics

There are certain "facts" about the world that do not exist at the level of description reserved for describing the behavior of atoms and molecules but only emerge from the interactions of human beings with their world. Morality is one of these "facts." Atoms do not obey moral laws, but human beings have a general understanding that human actions can be morally right or wrong, even when they disagree on the particulars. The virtues—benevolence, fairness, truthfulness—are meaningful categories for human beings.

"Aesthetics" is another one of these emergent "facts." While beauty cannot exist in a universe without observers, all human beings have the capacity to experience beauty. We may disagree as to what we find beautiful, but we can all agree that beauty means something for us, and that "we know it when we see it." We do not usually have to decide whether something is beautiful or not—the beauty of a sunset or a melody strikes us with a certain immediacy.

It also seems clear that experiencing beautiful things contributes significantly to our flourishing. Wherever and whenever there have been humans, there has been art, music, and dance. As soon as we're capable as a species of rubbing two sticks together to create fire, we're busy painting caves, dancing, singing, dying cloth, making jewelry, and decorating pottery.

The appearance of the home my wife and I live in attests to the centrality of aesthetics to everyday life—the pleasing way the colors of its painted surfaces complement each other, the decorative paintings hanging on its walls, the well-wrought artifacts adorning its shelves, the pleasing contours of its sofas and chairs—the way all of these cooperate to "pull things together"—it's evident my wife and I exercised a great deal of thought, care, trouble and expense into making our house a "home"—a dwelling place that enriches our lives beyond the shelter and safety it provides.

We can say something similar about the time, effort, and expense we put into grooming, dressing, and decorating ourselves, or into hearing music, attending concerts, films, and theater, visiting museums and botanical gardens, reading poetry and fiction, gardening, and a-thousand-and-one similar pursuits that have an aesthetic aim. Is there anyone who doesn't take delight in pursuing an art or craft that allows one to create something of aesthetic value—playing an instrument, designing clothing, gourmet cooking, writing poetry, drawing, painting, knitting, making ceramics, planting a garden, singing, or developing one's physical grace as an athlete or dancer? How much poorer our lives would be without any of these things.

Why does creating and experiencing beauty play such a central role in our lives? For one thing, beauty is aligned with sensory pleasure. We all want to experience pleasant sights, sounds, smells, tastes, and touches. But when we say that something is beautiful, we mean something more than merely saying it is "pleasant." Beautiful things also touch our emotions. They transport, move, and overwhelm us. They lift our lives up beyond the mundane and ordinary. They add a new dimension to our lives beyond that which is merely necessary and sufficient. We don't need beauty to live, but a life with beauty is vastly preferable to one without it.

The sight of a sunset, the call of a wood thrush, the scent of the sea, or a taste of chocolate can instantly transform our moods, taking us outside of the world of our immediate concerns and connecting us to something larger. This something "larger" may be our connection to nature, our imagination, or our highest human ideals. There is a way, for example, that the music of Bach or Beethoven not only transports us, but reminds us of what is best and most noble about the human spirit.

The power art, music, and literature have to connect us with the higher aspects of our selves should not be surprising. Art arose, often enough, within spiritual and religious contexts, whether we are talking about the first cave paintings, the origin of Greek theater, Native American dance, or the sacred music of the Gregorian chant and Catholic Mass. The artistic impulse and the religious impulse have never been far apart.

But of course, music can connect us with more than our nobility. It can also connect us with what is most passionate, primal, or erotic about our lives. When we dance and sing with others, it can also be a way of letting go and letting loose, as well as a way of merging with a group identity. Beethoven sonatas, 12-bar blues songs, and gospel hymns all transport us to different human realms and possibilities.

While some things (rainbows, sunsets) are immediately beautiful to all—we don't have to learn anything to appreciate them—there are other kinds of aesthetic appreciation which require some degree of knowledge—being able to appreciate all the notes in the bouquet of a fine wine, or fully appreciating a Shakespearian sonnet. Some music is immediately accessible to almost everyone—pop tunes, folk music, rock anthems, Pachelbel's Canon—whereas other music takes sophisticated musical knowledge to appreciate, such as the Bartok or Carter string quartets. There is also music one can appreciate on first hearing, but that acquires greater depth and meaning as one hears it repeatedly over the course of a lifetime, such as Bach's *Goldberg Variations*.

When we are cultivating our musical taste, we are developing a better understanding of the historical context of the work of music—what is unique or innovative about it, or how it relates to other cultural developments—as well as appreciating the complex elements that contribute to its structure—being able to hear and follow different voices of counterpoint or understanding key changes and chord progressions. Similarly, when cultivating our taste in visual art, we are learning to appreciate the history of perspective, changing representational and non-representational styles, ideas about color and symmetry, changing standards of beauty, changing ideas about the sorts of people and things that are appropriate to paint, new techniques of applying paint, and how painting reflects and comments on changing aspects of our culture. Anyone who has watched a toddler rock back and forth to music can sense how immediate aesthetic pleasure and gratification can be, but the educated eye, ear, and palette opens new worlds of appreciation that widen our horizons.

Music, art, and literature not only serve as aesthetic and spiritual resources, but moral resources as well. A good deal of moral advancement consists in extending our empathy beyond those who share our own culture to those who belong to different cultures. Listening to the art, music, and literature of other cultures is one way in which we learn to appreciate not only our common humanity, but also the ways in which other people's cultural experiences differ from ours and the unique contributions they make to world culture. It also means extending our empathy to people living under different sets of circumstances. When we read Philip Roth we understand more of what it means to be Jewish in America; when we read James Baldwin, we learn more of what it means to be Black in America. We learn about war from Leo Tolstoy, courtship from Jane Austin, ennui from Honoré de Balzac, and poverty from Charles Dickens. We get to imaginatively inhabit different worlds and different lives.

Artistic appreciation and creation are, as philosopher John Dewey (2005) noted, ways of intensifying our experiencing. Moments of intensity—whether experienced in aesthetic contexts, or during the thrills of an adventure, or in heightened religious experience, or in the exertions of athletic competition, lift us out of the routine humdrum of our lives, adding vitality and depth of meaning.

Aesthetic creation intensifies experience even more than aesthetic appreciation. Many artists, musicians, and writers discuss the experience of "inspiration," of how images, melodies, feelings, characters, dialogue, and ideas seem to come to them from somewhere outside of themselves, as if their conscious egos were being invaded or assisted by forces from celestial or chthonic realms. In addition, there is the joy of mastery as one learns to wield a paintbrush, play a musical instrument, learn a new dance step, or express one's thoughts within the confines of a rhyming scheme. There is the emotional satisfaction that comes from singing a song that deeply expresses one's mood or allows one to briefly inhabit a different one. There is the vivification and enlivening of the self when some private aspect of the self is expressed in some new and powerful way. There are the joys of collaboration, when one performs in a play, plays in a band, or sings in a choir. Finally, there is the aesthetic satisfaction of having created something new, beautiful, and meaningful—whether a poem, melody, quilt, ceramic, drawing, film, sculpture, article of clothing or jewelry, piece of furniture, or culinary dish.

Given the central place aesthetic experience plays in our lives, it is ironic that public schools often must struggle to justify keeping art and music classes in their curricula. Education isn't just preparation for earning a living, but preparation for life itself. It is an essential component of teaching children to live lives that are flourishing and not simply subsisting or economically productive. Teaching the arts teaches children to be both the recipients of and participants in a vast, rich, and dynamic cultural heritage, and that they can be creators as well as consumers. The expansion of sensibilities one acquires through art, music, and literature is also an essential part of preparing children for citizenship in pluralistic and multicultural democracies.

Whole-Heartedness

The usual lists of virtues, attainments, and relationships that contribute to and constitute flourishing rarely mention the quality of mind, activity, and relatedness I call "whole-heartedness" and that psychologist Marsha Linehan (1993) calls "doing things one-mindfully." I prefer the term "whole-heartedness" because it reminds us that consciousness is not merely ideational and "in the head," but also consciousness of the body and the qualities of feeling we usually associate with the "heart." It entails a more integrated mode of awareness that includes thought, emotion, and sensation.

To be whole-hearted means to be fully committed to what one is doing—in for a penny, in for a pound. If something is worth doing, it is worth doing whole-heartedly and unreservedly—whatever it might be. Whole-heartedness means giving our undivided attention to what we are doing and throwing our whole being into its pursuit. We don't just go through the motions or do things absent-mindedly. It means being forward facing: when problems and conflicts arise, we directly engage them, rather than avoiding them, procrastinating, or acting passive-aggressively. We are fully present to our lives in each moment. When we do things whole-heartedly, we experience the full richness of the texture of our lives. Even the most mundane, repetitive tasks—washing the dishes, doing the laundry, brushing one's teeth—can be invested with renewed vitality, interest, meaning, and satisfaction. When we are whole-hearted in our relationships with others, we are *present* for them. We give them our full attention. We make authentic contact with them and they experience us as being there, with, and for them.

Zen Buddhist monastic training focuses on developing and embodying this single-minded whole-heartedness in everything one does. The Japanese Soto Zen tradition speaks about "*menmitsu no-kafu.*" Taking the morphemes in this phrase one-by-one, *men* means "close, intimate, or densely woven," *mitsu* means "cotton fabric," *ka* means "family," and *fu* means "wind" or "manner." Together, the phrase names the "Zen family style" of exquisite, careful, considerate, intimate, warm-hearted, continuous attention to detail that characterizes Zen practice. This is evident in the way monks are trained to focus single-mindedly on the sensations of breathing during *zazen* (sitting meditation) and the sensations in their feet during *kinhin* (walking meditation). A good deal of Zen monastic training is learning how to embody *menmitsu* as monks go about their daily activities—donning their robes, sweeping the walkways, refolding their bowing cloths, assembling and disassembling their eating bowls, lighting incense, and so on. You and I, dear reader, are not necessarily called to the same degree of exacting, meticulous attentiveness as the monk in our personal, professional, and public lives. But we could do well to take a page from their training.

Why don't we show this kind of whole-heartedness and presence in everything we do? Why do we disconnect, or partially disconnect, from many activities and encounters? Why do some people seem to shrink from genuine contact with the world? There are a multiplicity of reasons for it.

Sometimes we are engaged in an activity that is not of our choosing; someone else is demanding it of us and we don't really see the point of it. In that case, we often stay primarily engaged with our own private thoughts while physically going through the motions. Sometimes we have performed a rote task so many times we can "do it in our sleep." In that case, we are tempted to turn at least some of our attention to other more intrinsically pleasurable activities, like chatting, listening to music, or daydreaming.

Some people are so traumatized by events that they hide inside themselves, avoiding genuine contact with an outside world they perceive as inherently dangerous. Some people think that when conflicts arise, it's best to side-step and avoid them and delay any day of reckoning whenever possible.

Sometimes, people avoid genuinely "being there" with others because they are angry, frustrated, or disappointed with them. They would rather avoid real contact than risk expressing their feelings and stirring up conflict. Sometimes, people are absorbed in "doing their own thing" to the exclusion of paying attention to someone else. Sometimes, other people are boring and hard to attend to. Sometimes, situations require us to multitask—to walk and chew gum at the same time. Sometimes, what we are doing is simply not as intrinsically rewarding as something else occurring at the same time and that more rewarding activity draws our attention. The invention of the smartphone has provided us with the potentiality of finding rewarding, enjoyable, and entertaining things to do with minimal effort any time of the day—one's that can pull us away from less stimulating tasks in the non-virtual world.

Probably the most common reason for divided attention, however, is our becoming preoccupied with some past event or future possibility. We may be anticipating upcoming events, or ruminating about past events, or working at resolving a problem that is gnawing at us. In these cases, the pull to dwell on whatever is preoccupying us takes away from attending to whatever behavior we are presently engaging in. Sometimes we are half here and half there, and sometimes almost all there and hardly here.

It can be useful to "check in" at random points throughout the day and take mental note of whether you are being whole-hearted or only partially attentive to your ongoing activity. Most people are surprised to learn how absent they are from their lives, and how much time they spend "in their heads," or half-attending while fiddling with their smartphones. It's as if we are ghost-walking through our lives.

One problem with being only "half there" is we are missing a good deal of our lives in the process. If we are reading the newspaper while eating breakfast, we are missing the taste of our food. If we are ruminating about a past argument in the shower, we are missing the feel of the water against our skin. If we are mulling over a work-related problem while playing with our children, we are missing out on engaging with our children—and they are missing out on us. It is the little things we miss out on that are often the most meaningful pleasures available to us on any given day—the laugh of a child, the colors of a sunset, the song of a bird, the scent of the sea or newly mown grass, the taste and warmth of a cup of tea. We can enjoy our lives more if we can "get out of our heads" and savor these myriad small pleasures as much as possible.

How can one increase one's capacity to be whole-heartedly present? One way to do it is to follow the lead of those Zen monks and take up a daily practice of formal mindfulness meditation. This is a type of meditation that emphasizes being in one's body rather than being in one's head: one becomes intimately acquainted with the myriad bodily sensations—warmths and coolnesses, itches and tingles, tics and twitches, the feeling of air moving in and out of the body, the sensation of one's pulse, areas of tension and restriction—that are issuing from every square inch of our bodies all the time and that we only rarely attend to. Mindfulness meditation also emphasizes being with whatever presents itself right now, rather than time-traveling in our minds to the past and future. What's present can be a bodily sensation, sight, sound, emotion, mood, quality of mind, or thought. Moment-by-moment one learns to stay present and be aware of everything the present moment encompasses. This is good training for learning how to be undividedly present to our lives.

But formal mediation is not the only way to cultivate this quality of whole-heartedness. If one develops the habit of checking in at various random points throughout the day to see whether one is fully present, one can quickly learn to discriminate when this quality is at hand and when it is not. Simply noticing when one is not really "fully here" can be a signal to "take a breath" and bring oneself back—at least momentarily—into full presence. The more one trains oneself to become aware of when one is not aware, the more one can habitually bring whole-heartedness into one's life. This is a quality of the heart/mind that can be truly cultivated.

As an experiment, try washing the dishes the way you usually do—as an annoying but necessary chore to be gotten out of the way as quickly as possible so that you can get on to something more enjoyable—and then try being fully present to washing the dishes as if it was the best possible way to spend your time. If you like, imagine washing the dishes with the same care and attention you would were you bathing a newborn baby. Pay attention to the feel of washing them—the temperature of the water against your skin, the fine muscle movements in your hands, the smell of the dish detergent, the squeak of the clean dish. Then you can try the same experiment while eating your breakfast, walking your dog, brushing your teeth, or doing the laundry. When you succeed in doing this, every moment in your life becomes something to find meaning and satisfaction in. Your day is no longer a disconnected set of satisfying moments separated by an endless stream of dull necessities.

Several years ago when I was still practicing clinical psychology, I had a client who, because of a history of past horrific abuse, was numb to emotions and bodily sensations. At some point in therapy, after a degree of trust had been established, she performed a meditation called the "body scan" in which she attended over the course of 45 minutes to every portion of her body in sequence, noticing whatever sensations arose. The initial results of the body scan were upsetting to her. Her new awareness that her arms, legs, and torso had weight made her feel uncomfortably fat and briefly re-triggered an old eating disorder. Being able to feel her body made her feel vulnerable—someone could physically hurt her again. But after two weeks, while sitting on her front porch, she experienced a warm spring breeze brushing against her face. As she wrote in her diary, it felt as if she had been "kissed by God." Feeling her body not only opened her up to the possibility of being hurt, but also the possibility of experiencing pleasure, aliveness, and vitality. Her willingness to allow herself to be present with her body eventually extended to a willingness to feel emotions, including grief and laughter.

I don't want to give the false impression that a little bit of practice will make you whole-hearted all or most of the time. I have been practicing formal mindfulness meditation for 25 years, and my wife can tell you how absent-minded I still am. I am still probably more absent-minded than the average person. But I know I am much better at being present than I was before I began practicing, and that the quality of my life has significantly improved as a result. Whenever I catch myself not being whole-heartedly present, it is relatively easy to restore a sense of full presence.

I volunteered for several years as an associate chaplain at my local hospital. I would make rounds on a medical-surgical floor, meeting with each of the patients in turn, and discussing whatever was on their minds. My main goal was to be as fully present as I could with each of them—to give them my full attention and be emotionally available. Hospital patients often experience the need to be seen and heard as full persons with all their hopes, dreams, fears, regrets, and accomplishments. All too often, the experience of illness and hospitalization makes them feel as if they are just a collection of medical symptoms or something broken to be mended.

It was both taxing and rewarding work. Thankfully, my medical-surgical floor had a meditation room, and whenever I felt attentionally or emotionally depleted I could sit quietly and meditate until I felt ready to return to my rounds. This meant learning to discriminate when I was capable of being fully present, and when I wasn't and needed to restore myself.

However meaningful these meetings may or may not have been to my patients, they were rewarding and meaningful for me. There is something inherently enriching in meeting people where they are, getting to know them deeply, and listening to and responding to what is most urgent for them. In many ways, it restored my faith in humanity—something one might easily lose as one reads the daily newspaper—my sense that most people when you get to know them, despite their many imperfections and flaws, are trying as best they can—albeit with lapses—to live meaningful, decent, and admirable lives.

Chaplains can't do their jobs well if they are not fully present. Full presence, you might say, is their stock and trade. Patients can tell right away if you are authentically there for them, or just perfunctorily going through the motions. Full presence is not only the stock and trade of chaplains, counselor, and therapists, however, but of also air traffic controllers, surgeons, basketball players, soldiers, and firemen. Their complete attention is not on the personhood of others, but nevertheless, the situations they find themselves require an absolute attentiveness. No one wants a surgeon who is only half attentive, or not whole-heartedly committed to doing his absolute best in every single moment.

The literature on flourishing often mentions the state of mind psychologists call "flow" (Csikszentmihalyi 1990). Flow is the peak experience of being fully engaged in a skillful activity in which the demands of the activity and one's abilities are evenly matched, and in which awareness of oneself and time seem to disappear as one is completely absorbed in the activity. We often see this occur while playing professional sports, or during a musical or dance performance, or during periods of artistic creation or scientific problem solving. Psychologists say that the more moments of flow in our lives, the more enriched and meaningful they feel. I am in total agreement with this observation. These moments often seem sublime. The literature on flow, however, suggests these moments can only occur amidst complex high-level performances. My dimension of whole-heartedness suggests that we can bring at least some of the qualities associated with flow to mundane aspects of our everyday lives, investing even ordinary activities with the qualities of depth, meaningfulness, and satisfaction.

Meaning

The difference between being alive and being some bit of inorganic matter—a rock, a crystal, a cloud—is that things "matter" to living beings—they "mean" something. When we say that some thing or event "means" something to a living being, we mean that this thing or event has significance in terms of furthering or impeding the living being's aims and goals, and consequently, its flourishing.

All living beings have "aims" or "goals," although these aims and goals may or may not be reflected in conscious intentions. We might begin by stating that all living beings engage in activities that have the effect of maintaining and enhancing their existence. Even amoebas must find and take in nutriment, metabolize it, and avoid contact with potentially toxic aspects of their environments if they are to persist. Biologists are uncomfortable saying that amoebas have survival, growth, or reproductive "goals." They will do almost anything to avoid saying it. These terms seem to imply something like conscious intent, and biologists never like to ascribe human-like processes to so-called "lower" organisms. And yet, we so-called "higher" organisms do have goals and intentions, and our ability to do so had to have had its origins somewhere along the line in evolution. At what point in evolution does something like intentionality first emerge? There probably isn't a single point in time when going from nothing like intention to something like intention occurs. In any case, I am more comfortable than biologists in saying that all living beings behave in order to stay alive—that living beings have purposes, period.

But let's put this argument aside. I don't need to be right about it to say that humans have intentions, goals, and aims. And whenever we ask, "what's the meaning of 'X?,'" we are really asking, "what is the significance of 'X' for maintaining and enhancing our lives." To take a simple example, we can ask what is the meaning of a "chair." You cannot define a chair by its parts: it can have one leg, three legs, or four, you name it. It may or may not have a back. It may or may not have an arm rest. It may be wood, metal or plastic. It may be large, medium, or small. The only thing that counts for a thing's being a chair is that it is something designed for humans to sit on, or that humans think of it as something to sit on. It has a use or value in terms of our comfort or convenience. Of course, a chair can be used for multiple purposes. We may not only sit on it; we may also hang a coat on its back, or if we are small children, hide under it in a game of hide-and-seek. If it is a wooden chair and the power goes out during winter, we could chop it up for firewood to keep us warm. A chair may have all these potential meanings—we could say it is embedded in a mesh of possibilities for use, past, present, and future. But the point is, the meaning of the object for me is its potential utility in furthering my process of living.

It's the same when we inquire into the meaning of abstract terms such as the meaning of love or the mathematical symbol "π." The meaning of "love" is all the things your experience (and society) tells you about the relevance of love for enhancing or impeding your life, "it's the thing that makes life worth living," or "it's the thing that distracts you from your career," and so on. The meaning of "π" is also all the things it means for your life and our common social understanding of things—"the thing I need to remember when figuring out the area of a circle from its radius," or "the thing I need to understand if I'm going to pass math."

But it's one thing to say that things and events have a meaning for us as living beings, and another to ask existential questions like, "what is the meaning of life?" or "Is my life meaningful?" When we ask, "what is the meaning of life?" the only proper response is, "for whom?" Things do not have meanings in themselves but are only meaningful in terms of their relevance to living beings. Since, so far as we know, there is nothing outside of life for life to be relevant to, the question is largely meaningless. If one believes in God, one can ask God what life means for Him but until one gets to ask Him directly one would only be guessing.

On the other hand, "Is my life meaningful?" *is* a meaningful question. Again, we must ask, "for whom?" We could ask, "is it meaningful to me?" or we could ask, "is it meaningful to others?" George Washington's life is much more meaningful to most Americans than my father's life, but my father's life is more meaningful to me.

Usually, what we are really asking is, "Is my life significant in some way?" and by significant, we mean, "has my life made, or is it making, a difference of some kind?" Does it matter to others that I've been here, lived how I've lived, and done what I've done? We hope we've made, on balance, a positive difference—that the people we know or whose lives we affect live lives that are appreciably better and happier because of us. We hope, like George Bailey in *It's a Wonderful Life*, that the world is a better place because of how we've lived our lives. We hope that our spouses, children, and grandchildren can say that; we hope that our friends, neighbors, acquaintances, and co-workers can say that; and we hope the people whose lives are touched by our work, whatever work we do, can say that.

While our families are often our greatest arenas of influence, the vocational, creative, and civic arenas are a close second, third, and fourth for most of us. The most satisfying life tasks outside of family life are those that have some potential to be of value to others. First and foremost, people want jobs and careers that can help sustain their own and their family's lives but, if they have the opportunity, they also want jobs and careers that are of value to others. Teachers, ministers, chaplains, health care professionals, counselors, childcare workers, and social workers may do this in a very direct way. So may plumbers, electricians, and carpenters. So may fireman, policemen, and other first responders. So may writers, actors, singers, dancers, sculptors, painters, clothes designers, and other artistic creators. So may civil servants, legislators, and administrators. So may assembly line workers or craftsman who help make and produce products that are useful or beautiful. So may farmers and dairymen who grow our food, truckers who bring produce to market, and grocery clerks who stock the shelves.

There are many ways we can be of value to others in our work and careers, but the word "may" in all these sentences informs us that all these careers and vocations can also be causes of harm. We are all aware of bad teachers, ministers, doctors, policemen, civil servants, legislators, administrators, factory farm owners, and the like, whose actions detract from social well-being. In all these roles, it is possible to lose (or never have had) the intention to be an agent of good, and to become corrupt, careless, lazy, overly focused on ease and self-gain, or to succumb to compassion fatigue and bureaucratic inertia.

And then there are jobs whose only rewards are extrinsic but which are unsatisfying in and of themselves and which offer little if anything—or may even be destructive to—wider social well-being. There are dull, repetitive, mind-numbing, or physically taxing jobs where one's labor goes into producing a final product that is essentially unlovely, toxic, dangerous, useless, or wasteful. These are soul-destroying jobs that make people question the meaning of their lives, especially if they lack other arenas (familial, athletic, creative, social, religious, or political) for generating meaning.

And then there are jobs that are exploitative and antisocial at their core—loan sharking, pimping, thieving, conning, being a mob "soldier," child trafficking, dealing in narcotics, and so on. And let us not leave out whole industries and professions which, although they may be legal and have limited value, on the balance cause more harm than good. Here we can include lawyers, politicians, and public relations personnel who promote the sale of or deny the toxicity of harmful products, or who promote climate change denialism, or work to limit people's access to the ballot. We can also include corporations that manufacture military grade weapons for civilian use, overproduce and aggressively market opioids, or mistreat domestic animals. You can add your own malefactors to the list.

The point of this list of mind-numbing, antisocial, or harmful occupations is that working in these jobs detracts from our ability to feel our lives are meaningful. Some people may live under sets of circumstances in which these are the only kinds of work available to them. They can then justify working in them because they must earn a living and support a family, and surviving and helping their families survive is the thing most central to their well-being. But people are better off in terms of their overall well-being and the meaningfulness of their lives when they can aspire to something more intrinsically rewarding and worthwhile.

This is a good place to note the role of cognitive dissonance, the way people lie to themselves to make it more acceptable to do bad things in order to survive. They often engage in self-deception, trying to convince themselves what they are doing is not harmful but is in fact socially beneficial in some way. Factory farm owners probably tell themselves that they are doing a social good by producing food efficiently and cheaply. Assault rifle manufacturers probably tell themselves they are helping to defend constitutional rights and provide citizens with the means to defend themselves. Pimps probably tell themselves they are meeting a social need by providing sexual outlets to lonely or frustrated men. Loan sharks probably tell themselves they are lending money to needy people who can't obtain loans through the normal banking system. One can always come up with some argument to justify one's behavior, however flimsy or unconvincing it might be to others.

The point I am emphasizing is that a meaningful life cannot be built on lies and self-deception. We have a moral obligation to hold a mirror to ourselves and honestly reflect on whether the way we are living is mostly harmful or beneficial to others. If honest reflection leads us to conclude we are acting in harmful ways, then our self-respect and dignity demand we seek more beneficial ways of furthering our interests in the world. Many people, as they seek second careers in mid-life, do just that.

I realize there are certain morally deformed individuals who are so callous, indifferent, incurious, and/or self-absorbed that no amount of reasoning and appeal to their ostensible higher natures could possibly convince them they ought to care more about their moral integrity and the harm they cause others. Fortunately, they are few, and I did not write this book for their benefit.

Since you, dear reader, have read this far, I assume you are not among them.

So far, we have looked at meaning in terms of making a beneficial difference in the world, but there are other sources of meaning as well. One is the feeling of connection to something larger than oneself. Understanding that our lives have contributed to the well-being of others is one way of connecting to something larger than ourselves. Our lives, then, have not been just about ourselves. But there are other ways of connecting as well. People also derive meaning in their lives from connections to a religion, a people, creativity, nature, or a cherished cause or ideal.

Let us begin by exploring the relationship between meaning and religion. The very word religion comes from the Latin word *religare*, meaning to bind together. Religion binds a community together in worship, but also binds individual lives to a creed and faith. Being a Christian, for example, means being an active co-participant in God's plan, a co-participation that imbues one's entire life with meaning and purpose. One is here to assure that God's kingdom is established on earth as it is in heaven. One is part of the sweep of history, from the day of creation until the final judgement. Religious people may feel the presence of God in their hearts—that he is there to watch over, protect, and guide them in every moment of their lives. If they lead the right sort of lives, they can expect an eternal afterlife in God's loving embrace, rejoining their loved ones who have passed on. This is a meaningful life, to be sure.

But there are other religious ways to live one's life besides a Christian one. Other religions offer some of the same benefits in terms of meaning and purpose. Buddhists don't believe in a creator God, for example, but believe they are living their lives as they ought—in accord with the *Dharma* and realizing their Buddha-nature. They think of themselves as on a path that leads not only to their own personal liberation, well-being, and happiness, but also the liberation of all beings. Their lives, like the lives of Christians, are part of a larger meaningful story about human happiness and purpose.

Religious mystical experiences can also be a source of meaning. These experiences may be spontaneous, come after extended periods of prayer, meditation, and/or fasting, or may be induced by psychedelics. People who have these experiences often report a sense of unity with the universe or of a divine presence along with an experience of partial or full ego dissolution and profound feelings of serenity and love. These experiences are often accompanied by intuitions into what seems to be a "deeper," "higher," or "truer" reality than that which ordinary experience allows. As philosopher Walter Terrence Stace noted, a mystical experience "of only a few moments' duration" can transform a person's life: A life previously felt to be "meaningless and worthless" can come to acquire "meaning, value, and direction" (Stace 1961, 60–61).

Today's world religions were once yesterday's cults. Cults can provide the same sorts of meaning that many derive from mainstream religions. In fact, cults may confer even more meaning because they allow one to feel as if one is a member of a vanguard elite. QAnon is an example of one such emerging quasi-religious cult that allows its members to feel as if they are in on a shared secret understanding of the true nature of unfolding socio-political events—an understanding that depicts an imminent war between ultimate good and evil and assures its believers they are on the winning side.

Religious belief is only one way of finding meaning beyond oneself in the world. Many religious and non-religious people find meaning in the causes they devote themselves to. The Marxist revolutionary believes he is living his life in accord with the larger sweep of history, and the dialectical forces that determine it. He is furthering the next step in the establishment of justice in the world. The same feeling of being part of history's arc of justice can be found in advocating for or devoting one's life to fighting for the rights of women, people of color, the LGBTQ+ community, or a nationalist or anti-colonialist cause. The same kind of meaning can also be found in fighting for ethnonationalist and fascist causes. What matters isn't the objective goodness or badness of the cause, but feeling one derives that one is fighting for some imagined better future.

Other people may gain meaning from their professional or creative work. They may feel their work is creating something of lasting value to those they professionally engage with, or to the world at large. The scientist who makes an important discovery has discovered something that affects the development of science going forward and joins Galileo, Newton, Darwin, Einstein, and the community of other greats who have advanced human knowledge and culture. The artist who creates a new metaphor, a beautiful artifact, or something that changes the *zeitgeist* in a new kind of way also joins a pantheon of creators who have advanced human culture. They have an importance not only now but in a legacy that gives them a kind of immortality.

People also derive a larger sense of meaning through their connection with nature. Looking up at the Milky Way or out at a vast expanse of sea, perceiving the grandeur of a mountain range, listening to the sound of a stream, standing amidst a field of wildflowers, sitting mesmerized by a waterfall, or just walking quietly in the woods—these are all moments of contact with nature that enrich and potentially add meaning to our lives.

The kinds of meaning we derive from nature can vary. The starry vault may make us feel inconsequential, fill us with wonder and awe, or make us question the reason for our existence. This can start us on a search to discover new sources of meaning in our lives. On the other hand, that same stary vault may connect us with something vast—the feeling we are an intimate part of the infinite and all that exists. In either case, nature opens us up to the possibility of "more"—a "more" that goes beyond the boundary of our skin or the briefness of our lives. Nature tells us that there is more to life than the cramped apartments where we live, or the offices and cubicles where we spend our workdays.

There is the vast tree of life, of which we are a small offshoot. There is the vast history of evolution on our planet, to which we are a recent arrival. Our planet is one small part of the vast web of creation, in an incomprehensively large universe which may just be one of many. There is wonder in imagining our intimate connection to all of this. One can end up feeling like an alien presence in an indifferent universe, or one can end up feeling at home in a complex mesh of interdependence with all that lives and co-evolves with us.

There was a time not too long ago when biologists thought of humankind as in a war against microorganisms and viruses. Now we are learning how much our lives depend on our gut microbiome and the viral bacteriophages that cull and cultivate it. Biologists used to think our immune systems were systems for sorting out what was "me" from what was "not me." Now they are coming to understand our immune systems are selective, counting many bacteria and viruses as beneficial friends, and sometimes mistaking cells with our own DNA as an enemy. As we learn more, we come to see how we are nature and nature is us.

Integration

If certain values are of great importance to us, then flourishing includes the idea of manifesting these values in every aspect of our lives. This is not always the case, and people may compartmentalize their lives or have only loosely organized or fragmented selves. When our central values permeate every domain of our lives, we experience a sense of integrity and wholeness that becomes an important component of our flourishing.

Examples of people who manifest their central values in only some parts of their lives are legion: The congenial member of the community who is an abusive husband or father at home; the politician known for his signature support of women's issues who creates a toxic workplace for the women in his office; the pastor who embezzles church funds; the pedophilic priest, coach, or scout leader; the policeman who takes bribes; the professor of moral philosophy who is cruel to colleagues and students.

To this list we should also add those people for whom compartmentalization is an essential aspect of their being. This would include double agents, undercover policemen, moles, and serial killers. It would also include persons with dissociative disorders whose alternative personalities serve to wall off trauma or manage situations their dominant personalities are too depleted to handle.

People with these compartmentalized selves do not always understand the benefits of greater integration or what their inner dividedness costs them. Let's just say that living in these ways involves a level of self-deception and deceitfulness towards others and this alone prevents one from obtaining certain goods that most people value. Included in these goods are the genuine intimacy that comes with being truly known and accepted, the deserved approval of those we interact with on a most frequent basis, and our feeling of common membership in the human community. One must also live with a perpetual fear of disclosure and getting caught in the act. For those people, like undercover policeman, who have basically decent personalities but must pretend at being repugnant human beings, there is the risk of this rubbing off on one's inner self, of coarsening or soiling oneself, and the possibility of moral self-injury may be inherent in the role.

Of course, if a person thrives on the heightened intensity that comes with danger or the sense of narcissistic superiority that comes with successfully outwitting others, these may offset some of the losses to well-being described above. One can also justify some of these roles when undertaken in the pursuit of a larger common good, like protecting one's country or taking down the mob. But when undertaken on one's own behalf in pursuit of one's personal interest, the goods deriving from facing danger and being clever lose much of their attractiveness, and one must find ways to be comfortable with the truth that most people would shun you or be appalled by you if they knew what you were truly about. Being all right with this is not as easy as it might sound, because most of us retain some wish to be on good terms with the rest of the world. Of course, if you are quite all right with being thought of as a monster, something is already seriously wrong with you. There is no way anyone could convince you of why it might be in your best interest to reform yourself. That is why banishment and imprisonment will always exist as a last resort even for the most enlightened of societies.

Most of us fall short of the goal of having our values manifest in every domain of our lives. Even if we tend to be very good at this, we frequently find ourselves in stressful, seemingly trivial, or novel situations in which we react without adequately consulting our central values. Someone who is generally careful about what they eat may binge on junk food under stress. Someone who is generally considerate of other's feelings may snap at colleagues under the pressure of a deadline. Someone who generally believes in playing by the rules may run a red light when no one is watching and he or she is in a hurry. Someone who generally finds stealing abhorrent may take pencils or paper clips home from the office for personal use. Someone who generally values telling the truth may shade the truth to protect him or herself from minor embarrassment.

These kinds of inconsistencies and imperfections of character are all too human, and no one is completely exempt from them. The temptations to stray are strong enough, the odds of getting caught low enough, and the costs of always doing the right thing high enough that this will probably always be the case. Many of these imperfections are, by themselves, of small consequence. I can always restart my diet or apologize to the person I snapped at tomorrow, and no big harm done. However, we lose something if we become overly comfortable with our foibles and imperfections. I'm not suggesting we should become harsh self-critics or unrelentingly self-scolds. But we would be better off if we all had the aspiration to improve our self-consistency and tried somewhat harder to live consistently with our values.

The people who manage to do so—who manage to a considerable extent to express their values in almost everything they do and achieve an admirable kind of self-coherence—are the kinds of persons we come to value as religious and/or civic saints. Think of people like Albert Schweitzer, the Dalai Lama, Mohandas Gandhi, Nelson Mandela, Jane Goodall, Pope Francis, Mother Teresa, John Lewis, Martin Luther King, Jr., and Jimmy Carter. None of them are beyond reproach, but they are people so identified with their values that their very names become symbols of human aspiration. It is too much to hope that we ourselves will become exemplars of values coherence to the same extent that they are, but they become the heroes and heroines we can use as touchstones to measure our own values coherence by.

There are other kinds of wholeness beyond moral wholeness that also play a role in flourishing. The psychiatrist Carl Jung (1960) devised a psychotherapeutic system based on the idea of life as a process of growing into wholeness. Without getting into the specifics of his theories, he saw our initial personalities as formed against the backdrop of a larger sea of undeveloped potentials that could become activated over the course of a lifetime and needed to be integrated with our conscious personalities. For example, a man might define his identity in accord with certain cultural stereotypes of manliness, and then discover he also has qualities society defines as feminine that he needs to accept, realize, and integrate into his personality. Similarly, a hard-core, no-nonsense, logical, skeptical, scientifically-oriented person might suddenly discover previously unrecognized spiritual needs and resources that have to be integrated into who she is. A person whose life has been dominated by feeling and intuition may find that they need to become more logical, and vice versa. The important idea is that we can always discover parts of ourselves that need acceptance or further development, and that need to be reconciled with our old ideas of who we thought we were. Consider the situation of a man who discovers his feminine side and acts tough during the day but dons women's clothing at night in the privacy of his home. It may be a step up from acting tough all the time and never accepting his feminine side, but only a partial step up. It may well be that the vocational and social niches he occupies provide few affordances for greater integration. If he were to become truly whole, however, he would be able express toughness or tenderness in any situation where these qualities were called for. It's not that cross-dressing is "wrong," but that it reflects a lower degree of personal integration.

What are the benefits of wholeness for our well-being? We have a broader range of energies, potentials, and emotional and intellectual resources available for us as needed. We have an undivided sense of purpose, so that we are not warring with ourselves, undercutting ourselves, or at a loss for direction. We behave with a consistency others can appreciate and depend on. Most importantly, we have an inner sense of our own integrity. We act more and more as the persons we aspire to be. Perhaps most importantly, that inner feeling of wholeness, integration, and living in accordance with one's values allows us to unreservedly approve of ourselves and our lives and is the ultimate source of self-respect.

Finally, we must speak about another kind of integration. We live our lives in multiple domains in our diverse roles as family members, friends, coworkers, citizens, worshippers, and creative artists. If these roles are not rigidly separated, there are ways our experiences in these diverse domains can mutually enrich each other. Work, for example, can be not just part of one's professional life but a means of providing for one's family. The skills learned in negotiating conflicts at home are transferable to dealings with co-workers and in the civic arena. The satisfactions we derive outside the home can lend vitality to conversations at the family dinner table. The creative spirit we bring to our artistic endeavors can enliven our workplaces and homes. Ethical development in our spiritual life rightfully informs all these domains, and vice versa. An integrated life means allowing these diverse aspects of our life their own space to live and breathe but also allowing them to freely communicate and mutually enrich each other.

This kind of mutual integration can be contrasted with arrangements in which one domain encroaches on, envelops, or dominates the others. An overly demanding work life can steal energy, time, and attention from one's family life; totalitarian states encroach on and dominate family, artistic, and spiritual life; all-demanding religious regimens can encroach on individual, familial, and social freedom and development; overly strong family ties can lead to a nepotism that impairs business and civic life.

Acceptance

The previous domains of flourishing involve maximizing factors that are at least partially under our control. Not everything is under our control, however. Trouble and hardship come to everyone and skillfulness in dealing with unavoidable adversity is another important aspect of flourishing.

There are people who never recover from a loss. Someone close to them dies, or their business fails, or a medical procedure goes awry, or they are the victims of a violent crime. Often, they feel they cannot get on with their lives if the loss is not somehow redressed. When one psychotherapy client of mine had a son who was declared brain-dead by doctors, my client made the decision, after some hesitation, to terminate his life-support. She later profoundly regretted that decision—she would rather have tended to her son at home for the rest of her life, even if he were permanently comatose, than to have made the decision she did. Although she had made the decision with her doctor's and family's support, she was perpetually haunted by it and couldn't move on with her life. She even considered going to the cemetery to dig up her son's remains and bring them home.

Another psychotherapy client of mine underwent a surgical procedure that left a small keloid scar on her abdomen. She felt as if her body had been vandalized and sued the surgeon for malpractice. As far as she was concerned, he had ruined her life. The court case dragged on for years. She felt there could be no happiness for her until and unless the case was successfully resolved.

This kind of inability to recover from loss, this lack of resilience, is a fatal impediment to flourishing. Why are some people able to recover from terrible loss and move on while others remain stuck in grief, regret, and recrimination? How does one in fact "move on" from loss to acceptance?

Let's begin by noting that "moving on" is a process with no definable beginning or discernable end. Except in trivial cases, it is not something one simply chooses to do. While there are sets of attitudes and beliefs that are conducive to moving on, there are also sets of circumstances we either help create or passively undergo that also partially determine the outcome of the process of acceptance. If one loses a spouse or a job, for example, it matters whether there are other potential spouses or jobs down the road or whether that loss *is* the end of the road. Let us also note that there is no return to the *status quo ante* after one has moved on. The life experiences we undergo change us for better and for worse, and the idea of a return to the old normal is a fantasy.

The losses that are the most devastating are the ones that are most central to our identity and well-being. Our well-being is the result of many inter-affecting sources—familial, vocational, avocational, recreational, social, aesthetic, and religious—and a loss in one area can be compensated for to some degree by a gain in another. People who have more sources of well-being at their disposal at the time of the loss—a rich support system, a satisfying career, many interests and creative outlets—are going to be more resilient. People can also discover new sources of well-being after a loss—a new friend, a religious conversion, a different life mission, or a new creative outlet. What becomes available to us is a matter of openness to new possibilities, but also the result of unpredictable chance encounters—a new neighbor moves in, a friend invites us to join a bible study or meditation group, an adult education program offers an interesting new course, we hear a podcast that initiates a new chain of thought, and so on. Often moving on is the end result of many similar changes that offer new opportunities for connection and growth.

What are the attitudes that promote acceptance and moving on? Some are temperamental and probably reflect innate factors and early childhood experiences. Chief among these are a sense of basic trust and hope. Some people have a faith that if one just waits and keeps on keeping on, that good things will again come into one's life. Some of this may be religious ("the Lord will provide," "God doesn't give us more than we can handle") but much of it depends on having had good-enough parents in a childhood unmarked by trauma and adversity. The psychoanalyst Erik Erikson (1950) thought this attitude of "basic trust" develops (or fails to develop) during the first year of life when infants are helpless and must depend on benevolent parenting for their well-being. After that, we find ourselves to be either dispositional optimists or pessimists—we expect the world will provide, or we expect disappointment.

Another important aspect is our cognitive schemas—the ways we tend to think about adverse circumstances. There are ways in which our thought processes can magnify adverse circumstances making them feel worse than they are, make them right-sized, or minimize them making them seem less severe than they are. For example, we can catastrophize about events, making events that are merely unfortunate seem like the end of the world. An ambitious student who doesn't get into his number one ranked college may feel his or her life is tragically doomed, or a person who is rejected by a potential love match may feel condemned to a life of loneliness. Thinking more reasonably about such events—that many people who don't go to Harvard lead perfectly good lives or that there are more fish in the sea—helps keeps these loses from becoming fatal blows.

People can also have a tendency not only to think overly negatively about life events, but to ruminate about them—that is to think persistently about them—as well. We keep returning to the place that hurts the way our tongue keeps exploring a tooth that has chipped. Perhaps this is supported by the idea that if one has a problem, one ought to keep thinking about it until one reaches a solution. Sometimes, however, when we have an unresolvable problem it is best to put it aside for a while—to sleep on it or distract ourselves—until possibilities for new solutions make their appearance.

We should also acknowledge the role of refusal to accept reality as an impediment to the restoration of flourishing. Sometimes our initial reaction to events is, "I can't believe this is happening" or "I can never accept this." There are patients who disbelieve their doctor's diagnosis of cancer, parents who can never accept their children's disclosure that they are "gay," and politicians who can never accept they lost an election fair and square. This obstinate refusal to accept reality becomes an insurmountable barrier to moving on.

Let's take the example of a parent refusing to accept his or her child is gay. What does this refusal accomplish for the parent? It does nothing but rupture the bond between parent and child, cutting the parent off from the future benefits of their potentially ongoing relationship. It leaves an unfillable hole in the life of the parent—it is as if the child had died. It leads to endless self-recriminations ("how did I fail as a parent?") or unresolvable resentments (blaming evil cultural influences or the child's bad friends). Even if one thought being gay is against the word of God, one could still accept one's wayward child in one's heart and accept one's helplessness to control one's child's thoughts and feelings. Of course, that kind of helplessness is an unpleasant feeling. The parent who "refuses to accept" his or her child's sexual orientation can perhaps cling on to an illusion of control, that if the parent never accepts it they may eventually influence the child to be different. But that is an illusion that does no one any good except to temporarily allay the feelings of helplessness.

Clearly, the parent would be better off admitting his or her helplessness and inability to control the situation. The parent is no different than other parents in this sense of helplessness as they watch their growing children create their own lives according to their own lights. At best, the parent may come around to seeing the child's gayness as acceptable, or may come to think, "although I worry this is not good for my child, I can do nothing about it. Who knows? Maybe my child will eventually come around on his or her own." Even if the parent never approves of being gay, and even if (as is almost always the case) the child does not "come around," the parent can still come to imagine ways in which the child's life may be a good-enough, if second-best, kind of flourishing life.

What about the person who denies he has cancer? What does this accomplish and what does it cost? What it accomplishes is a diminishment of immediate anxiety around possible future death, pain, or disability. In the short run, this can be temporarily helpful to flourishing. What does it cost? It prevents one from receiving treatment that might potentially improve one's life in the long run. It means one will not have an opportunity to go through the process of grieving that might end in an acceptance of the end of one's life. It also prevents one's family and loved one's from coming to terms with one's eventual death, should that be the outcome. It's possible to see death, not as an enemy, but as an inevitable part of every life. There is also a way in which patients and families can come together to accept an oncoming death with dignity and grace in a manner that enriches and ennobles the lives of survivors going forward.

So far we have been discussing acceptance in moving on from disruptive life events, but acceptance also plays an important role in the moment-to-moment process of daily living. Every moment involves encountering life experiences that vary in pleasantness. We have a natural tendency to want to savor and prolong pleasant experiences and avoid, shorten, or terminate unpleasant ones. This only becomes a problem when we refuse to accept that pleasant experiences are transient or when tolerating unpleasant experiences becomes a necessity.

As an example, let's imagine you are sitting down to meditate in order to relieve your stress. You hope for a relaxing and pleasant experience. As soon as you sit, however, you become aware of all sorts of conditions that are unconducive to that pleasant state you hope to attain. The room you are in may seem too cool or warm. Garbage trucks, ambulances, and cars with boom boxes pass outside your window making unwanted noise. Your stomach may be upset or your back might ache. You may notice your mind is too unsettled or sleepy to focus on your breathing. At this point, you might decide this is the wrong time or set of circumstances in which to try to meditate—maybe you should try later or tomorrow when everything is just right.

Of course, one quickly discovers that everything is never "just right." One would be better off if one just accepted the warmth, the noise, the ache, the unsettledness—making a mental note that they exist and accepting they are, at least in this moment, a necessary part of the process. This process of letting things be as they are even if we don't prefer them is a powerful and transformative process. If we say, "Even though the room is warmer than I would like, I can accept it," we can then investigate what this particular "too warm" is like— notice how we feel it in our bodies and investigate its qualities. We can do the same with the noise, the ache, and the unsettledness. As we investigate these qualities without resistance, they often transform. They become interesting in their own right. Even a feeling like boredom can become interesting once we decide to investigate it with freshness, openness, and curiosity. Rather than be annoyed with the things we don't prefer, they can become opportunities for "making friends" with them. Life with them becomes tolerable, and maybe even something more positive than "tolerable." Some of them—old thought patterns we think we shouldn't have, for example—we can even welcome in as old friends, smiling and laughing at their persistence rather than brow-beating ourselves for not having transcended them.

The willingness to practice acceptance during meditation can become a metaphor for treating all of life this way. There are all kinds of unalterable life circumstances we can turn into enemies by resisting rather than accepting them. People in our lives whom we, for the most part, love who also have annoying behaviors we can never change. What a relief when we no longer need to control their behavior and can accept them as they are despite their imperfections. The chronic pain we have that prevents us from enjoying our lives—what a relief it is to accept the pain as part of one's life without obsessing over how horrible it is and letting it dominate our moods and control our lives.

The House We Live In: Virtue, Wisdom, and Pluralism

I once had a forty-year-old chronic pain patient who introduced himself by saying "my doctor says I have the back of a hundred-year-old man." He stopped working, was on long-term disability, and ceased sexual relations with his wife due to pain. His wife was none too happy with this and was on the verge of divorcing him. Several months into therapy (and antidepressant medication) he was working two jobs and had resumed sexual relations with his wife. I foolishly asked if his pain had lessened. "No," he said. "My pain's just the same but it used to be at the center of my life and now its somewhere off to the side." He wasn't happy with the pain, but he had come to accept it and was able to get on with living despite it.

Earlier, in the Wisdom chapter, I mentioned the Chinese fable of the man at the frontier who lost his horse. The moral of the fable was that we can never know whether something is for the good or for the ill until we reach the end of the story. Another patient of mine who suffered from depression came to a therapy session and reported that he had lost his job and his mother had died that week. My first thought was, "this will make his depression even worse." As it turned out, he hated his job and detested his mother, and both these "losses" came as a relief to him. His depression cleared almost instantaneously and he moved on with his life. I mention this, because we never know whether something that might be initially viewed as a misfortune can turn out, in surprising ways, to be a blessing in disguise. An unwanted divorce can initially be the cause of despair but being freed from a bad marriage may be the inflection point that allows one to seek and find a more satisfying love relationship in the future. Being fired from a job one is bad at is discouraging but it also liberates one to find some job one might be better suited for.

One doesn't necessarily have to believe that "everything happens for the best" or "whenever one door closes, another opens" to understand that crises can also sometimes be opportunities, or that tragic and traumatic experiences can also be the impetus for significant growth. Sometimes tragedy and suffering deepens people's characters and gives their life greater depth and meaning. In Sophocles' *Oedipus in Colonus*, the unfortunate Oedipus, having already met his tragic fate, is now a blind, wandering exile nearing death. Yet, Oedipus has grown in stature and wisdom through the vicissitudes of life and Sophocles presents him as a person characterized by a hard-earned dignity and inner peace.

Many of my psychotherapy clients whose childhood histories reflect an almost unendurable series of traumas and tragedies—and who lived through extended periods of adulthood suicidality, alcoholism, and repeated psychiatric hospitalizations—emerged through this fire to become wise, empathic, and admirable people. The characters they eventually forged as adults were, in some ways, superior to those of people who had lived easier lives and took their comfort for granted. Despite struggling with residual problems, they developed extraordinary levels of wisdom and empathy and became genuine assets to their communities. None of them would have chosen this path—their lives never became "easy"—but there was an inspiring nobility about them.

Part of the process of forging these deeper new selves involved accepting their pasts—that those pasts genuinely happened, that they were just as bad as they felt at the time, that they were dependent on and helpless before the adults who tormented them, and that their extended families and society did nothing to rescue them and sometimes made things worse. Acceptance means allowing the grief, fear, and anger associated with the past to be what it is—to do one's mourning and at the same time, begin to construct a tolerable life. Moving on, in this case, means learning that the future need not be a repetition of the past; that one now has adult capabilities and is no longer helpless; that one can cultivate new skills that allow one to grieve without becoming overwhelmed; that some people can be trusted and that vulnerability and intimacy are possibilities; that asking for help will not always be punished. The people who can never move on from the consequences of childhood trauma are those who can never accept their past and who dissociate, repress, drink, drug, engage in reckless thrill seeking, injure themselves, and do everything they can to avoid dealing with it.

Of course, the idea that acceptance is a necessary precursor to beneficial change is not a new one. It lies at the heart of every 12-step program. The first step in Alcoholics Anonymous, for example, is to accept one is an alcoholic. Alcoholics Anonymous members learn to recite the *Serenity Prayer* that asks God to grant them the serenity to accept the things they cannot change, the courage to change the things they can, and the wisdom to know the difference.

Acceptance strategies also lie at the core of newer cognitive-behavioral therapies like Linehan's (1993) Dialectical Behavioral Therapy (DBT), and Hayes, Strosahl, and Wilson's (2016) Acceptance and Commitment Therapy (ACT). They are premised on the idea that resistance to pain causes surplus suffering. Becoming stuck in ruminative thoughts like, "I can't believe this happened!" or "I can never accept this!" or "why me?" is never helpful. The best response is always, "OK. I don't like it, but it did happen. What's the best thing to do, now that it has happened?"

Finally, let us note that acceptance in terms of self-acceptance and self-affirmation of one's identity, even if it is an historically socially disapproved or marginalized identity, is at the heart of modern liberatory movements. This includes the 1960s-1970s Black Power Movement ("I'm Black and I'm proud!") and the current LGBTQ+ movement ("We're here, We're queer, Get over it!") which foster not only self-acceptance, but also positive affirmation of one's gender identity and sexual orientation.

Are There One or Multiple Paths to Flourishing?

Tolstoy wrote that all happy families are alike, but all unhappy families are unhappy in their own way. I have already alluded to this aphorism in my discussion of relationships. I used it to introduce the multiplicity of ways in which relationships can go badly, but I think Tolstoy had it wrong when it came to happy families and flourishing people. There appears to be a multiplicity of ways in which people's lives can go right, and a multiplicity of ways to flourish. We each have our unique natural endowments, our unique patterns of strengths and weaknesses, and our unique histories of unhappy or fortuitous upbringings and educations. We bring different sets of interests, preferences, and abilities to the table and the same kind of life will not be a flourishing life for all.

Some will have lives that emphasize the satisfactions of family life, and others lives that emphasize the satisfactions of professional or creative life. Some will find meaning in religion, some in politics, some in advancing science, and others in communing with nature. Some will prefer the life of the mind, while others will prefer a life of adventure and exploration. Some will have lives that emphasize continuity with tradition, others will have lives that emphasize novelty and innovation. Some will find their greatest joys in reading great works of literature, some will be gourmands whose happiest moments involve savoring the tastes of well-prepared meals, and others will get their greatest satisfactions on the athletic field or dance floor. There are a wide variety of ways in which we can experience accomplishment, meaning, and connection.

That said, are there commonalities shared by all flourishing lives? Is there something uniting these lives under a common understanding of flourishing? The philosopher Valerie Tiberius (2018) offers one intriguing approach to this question. First, she defines values as patterns of "relatively robust desires and emotions that we can endorse as giving us reasons relevant to planning and evaluating our lives." In other words, our values are what we think ought to guide and govern our actions, and what we ought to use to evaluate the overall goodness of our lives.

Tiberius then observes that everyone has a unique set of values that are the most important ones for oneself, whether they be values concerning relationships, vocations, avocations, ideals, skills, achievements, personal traits, moral or spiritual endeavors, aesthetic interests, or amusements and pastimes. What flourishing lives have in common are not specific sets of values but the realization and satisfaction of a person's *own set of values* over the course of a lifetime.

Tiberius then qualifies her definition: for a life to be flourishing, the values one strives to realize must be appropriate for oneself. "Appropriate" values are ones which are well-suited to our individual natures, compatible with our other values, and that we can reflectively endorse. If we highly value something that we are unable to accomplish—if we value becoming a singer but are tone deaf, or a basketball star but are only five feet tall—our values are not appropriate for us. If we are extraverts and value pursuing careers requiring an introverted way of life—becoming a computer programmer or joining a monastery where one undertakes a vow of silence—we again have a value incompatible with our natures. Similarly, if our values conflict so that realizing one means undercutting another, we are limiting the amount of value fulfillment we can attain.

Tiberius also requires that appropriate values be ones we can reflectively endorse. By this, she means that when we think about our values we can affirm they are the sort of values that will rationally contribute to our overall well-being. Someone might think about how pleasant the life of a beach bum might be, for example, but when they examine the idea more closely, they decide it conflicts too much with their other values (being rich or socially useful) to be able to endorse it as an appropriate value for themselves.

Flourishing, for Tiberius, means not only that we have values appropriate for ourselves, but that we, to a large extent, succeed in realizing them. People can judge their degree of flourishing by how well they are succeeding in realizing and satisfying their personal values.

Tiberius's model of flourishing, as helpful as it is, raises some difficult questions. Do we really want to say, as Tiberius seems to be saying, that a mobster, if he successfully realizes his values, has attained the same level of flourishing as a humanitarian? Even if we agree they have the same degree of subjective happiness—and I am not sure that is true— it seems that—for most of us— being a humanitarian is superior in some way to being a mobster. We would prefer that our children grow up to be humanitarians rather than mobsters.

While Tiberius makes important points in demonstrating that our values must be appropriate for us as individuals and that there is a great diversity of ways in which we may flourish, she is wrong in suggesting that all appropriate values are equally good or that there are no reasonable grounds for judging the goodness of values.

At this point, I refer the reader back to the chapter on the virtues and what makes a habit/value constellation a virtue. We stated that virtues must be both self-regarding and other-regarding—that they not only have the probability of making our lives better, but also have a probability of contributing to the general social welfare. Given that we are all social beings, a life with values that are only centered on one's personal satisfaction and to hell with everyone else is a symptom of stunted humanity and not a sign of human excellence. It is never enough that we live just for ourselves. We ought to live in such a way that the world in general ends up a better place because we are here.

A logician might argue that one can never logically prove that living a life that is only self-regarding is an objectively lesser kind of life. They are, in a very narrow sense, correct. But this is a point that the great sages of the past—Aristotle, Confucius, the Buddha, Jesus, Hillel, the Hebrew prophets, Mohammed, Spinoza, Kant, and Mill—all agree on. It is something every non-psychopath and non-narcissist will also agree on. It is the Golden Rule that lies at the heart of every moral philosophy. When there is so much universal agreement on what being a decent human being entails, one would need very strong evidence to convince one otherwise. The burden of proof is not on those of us who insist that we ought to adopt values that take the well-being of others into consideration but on those who might wish to reject it.

To summarize so far, we now have many individualized paths to flourishing—the realization and satisfaction of our appropriate values—but also the caveat that these values be other-regarding and well as self-regarding. I now want to add one more consideration to the idea of flourishing I am developing here, and that is the idea of open-ended inquiry.

Our lives are never complete until they are over. During one's lifetime, one hopefully continues to develop one's skills, cultivate one's virtues, and expand one's wisdom and understanding. Our lives are, in a real sense, the products of our imagination and creativity. We are always learning from experience, imagining new ways in which our lives can go better, creatively solving new dilemmas as they arise, and integrating new facets of our personalities as they develop or are uncovered. A good life is not a static life—one in which we achieve a final kind of perfection and rest on our laurels. A good life is one that stays in motion, and as the philosopher John Dewey (2013) insisted, a life of open-ended inquiry into its possible meaning. In this dynamic vision, a life that is closed to inquiry and creativity is a lesser kind of life even if one lives in accordance with a set of prescribed virtues. A life lived strictly according to a closed set of rules—be they old ones handed down from antiquity, or new ones issuing from charismatic authority—may be a good-enough kind of life, but not the best possible kind of life.

Why is a life of open-ended inquiry better than a life committed to a prescribed set of beliefs? There are three reasons why. First, the life of inquiry takes the value of truthfulness more seriously. Just as our lives should be as courageous and benevolent as possible, they should also be as truthful as possible. In the wake of the European Enlightenment, a commitment to truth means a commitment to reason, inquiry, and empiricism. If we are asked to believe something without sufficient supporting evidence, it is our ethical responsibility to investigate the belief responsibly and honestly and to come, whenever possible, to our own conclusions. If we decide we must defer to experts because we lack the time or the expertise, then we have the responsibility to understand what makes a particular person an expert on the this or that belief. Does this person have the where-with-all to test this belief him or herself or is this person just repeating what someone else said? When experts disagree among themselves, we have the responsibility to defer judgement and await further evidence.

Second, a life of open-ended inquiry is superior to a life committed to a prescribed set of beliefs because our flourishing depends, to a very large extent, on our ability to use practical reason to determine which goals and strategies are most likely to lead to flourishing. If practical reason is shackled by dogma, it is trying to accomplish this with one hand tied behind its back. Earlier we discussed how, as we move out of childhood, our lives are made better by reflecting on our internalized values and determining whether they are a good fit with all the other things we hold dear. Adolescents and adults normatively go through this process of refinement, elaboration, or revision of their previously internalized values as part of their development and growth. Adherence to a ready-made dogma forecloses that process and limits the extent we can reasonably chose and effectively pursue those goals that would genuinely enhance our well-being. A prescribed set of beliefs may allow us to flourish to some degree if they are a good-enough set of beliefs, but they can rarely be as suited to our individual natures as those we arrive at through dialogue and open-ended inquiry.

Third, a life of open-ended inquiry is superior to a life committed to a prescribed set of beliefs because our concept of flourishing entails a commitment to the welfare of the community. This means discerning, as best one can, what norms, customs, goals, habits, laws, and beliefs lead to enhanced welfare for a community and which serve as obstacles to collective flourishing. Is society better off if women submit to their husband's authority or better off if they determine their own futures? Is society better off when society polices traditional gender roles or better off when people are free to express their gender as they feel called to? Is society better off if abortions are illegal or if they are decided on by women and their doctors? Is society better off when we lock up criminal offenders and throw away the key or when we treat them with dignity and rehabilitate them?

These issues can be decided according to an *a priori* set of rules or they can be addressed empirically, letting the evidence speak for itself. Sometimes the old rules are best, sometimes the old rules have become—or perhaps always were—obstacles to flourishing. Sometimes the old rules made sense given past social conditions, but no longer do so.

Once one has decided an empirically-based solution makes better sense than the old way of doing things, a new problem emerges: what is the best way of implementing change? Is there a possible way forward? Sometimes there is too much resistance to change and a way forward is not yet possible. Or maybe it is possible, but the conflict that might ensue between the *avant-garde* and the old guard wouldn't be worth the effort. Or maybe it is possible to implement the change in a piecemeal, evolutionary way—two steps forward, one step backward, then repeat. Or maybe the amount of suffering that would occur if the change were delayed or too piecemeal is enough to outweigh the cost of ensuing conflict. These are difficult decisions to make, but the best way to approach them is empirically, weighing the best information available, testing the waters, and using practical wisdom to determine the best course moment by moment.

I have one more comment to make about lesser kinds of flourishing lives. Not only can a good-enough kind of life be too cramped, rigid, and stultified—as when one adheres to a prescribed set of rules—but it can also be too shallow. Our lives are better off when they are deeper—when we learn to cultivate our tastes in order to appreciate new and more complex satisfactions. When we learn not to take everything at face value but develop a curiosity about why things are as they are. When we develop and use our imaginations and creative capacities to enrich our experiencing. One doesn't need to be an intellectual or creative genius to cultivate these qualities. Everyone is capable of some level of inquiry, imagination, and creativity in the conduct of their daily lives. This process of continued growth and development of our potentials and possibilities is a necessary aspect of a flourishing human existence.

Conclusions

A flourishing life is one that, as much as possible, successfully maximizes the appropriate causes of well-being and minimizes the appropriate causes of ill-being. The intellectual and moral virtues (practical wisdom, courage, benevolence, conscientiousness, temperance, equanimity, truthfulness, and justice) are indispensable for accomplishing these ends, and there is considerable cross-cultural agreement about which habit/value constellations can be properly identified as virtues.

Relationships, accomplishments, aesthetics, meaning, whole-heartedness, and acceptance are key domains of human flourishing. These are the appropriate causes of well-being, and benefit from the cultivation of skills, tastes, and imagination. Higher levels of flourishing are associated with higher degrees of personal integration and wholeness as well as a commitment to an open-ended process of growth and inquiry.

We have also noted that one's happiness, skills, tastes, and virtues are all contingent on a certain amount of good fortune. That good fortune includes a good-enough genetic endowment, good-enough parenting, a minimum of traumatic events, and an environment that offers sufficient opportunities for realizing one's potentials. Some of these are currently outside of anyone's control but some could be more equitably distributed by novel social arrangements that recognize the value of fostering everyone's flourishing as much as possible. The odds of leading a flourishing life can also be increased through an education that focuses not only on developing employable skills but on cultivating the moral virtues and relationship skills, developing wisdom and the capacity for inquiry, developing the capacity for aesthetic appreciation and creativity, and preparing one for citizenship in a pluralistic and ever-changing world.

While there may be many paths to flourishing based on individual personalities and abilities, all paths to flourishing share something in common. While the values we organize our lives around must be values that are appropriate to our unique individuality, they must be other-regarding as well as self-regarding. We are social animals through and through and must find ways to harmonize our own desires with the general good of the communities in which we live and the natural environments that sustain them. Anything less is not genuine flourishing.

—5—

Only Connect

"Only connect! That was the whole of her sermon ... Live in fragments no longer." E.M. Forster

Ethical Renewal and the Crisis of Democracy

The last decade has come as a shock—an occasion for disillusionment—for anyone paying close attention. Liberal narratives of the inevitable march of progress and the eventual success of democracy, globalization, cosmopolitanism, scientific reason, and multiculturalism lie in tatters. There is a renewed appreciation for the difficulties involved in transcending tribalism, identity politics, and historical grievances and resentments, and of curbing unlimited human desires for power and wealth. There is also a new skepticism about the possibility of arriving at a consensus based on reasoned inquiry.

This shouldn't have come as such a surprise. Philosopher Richard Rorty (1989) uncannily foreshadowed our current impasse over thirty years ago:

> I do not think that we liberals can now imagine a future of "human dignity, freedom and peace." That is, we cannot tell ourselves a story about how to get from the actual present to such a future. We can picture various socioeconomic setups which would be preferable to the present one. But we have no clear sense of how to get from the actual world to these theoretically possible worlds ... This bad news remains the great intransigent fact of contemporary political speculation... (Rorty 1989, 181–182)

Rorty believed that social scientists could propose all the ideal remedies they like—it's always possible to imagine better ways of doing things—but remedies—at least remedies that are more than cosmetic—couldn't be implemented given how history has determined our current sociopolitical climate. Rorty thought this problem was intrinsic to modernity itself and not something we could remedy through "better philosophical accounts of man, truth, or history."

I am somewhat more optimistic than Rorty. I agree there is no arc of history that makes moral progress inevitable—the current spate of dystopian futures in literature and cinema allows us to vividly imagine possible scenarios of social regression and collapse. Nevertheless, the history of the past two centuries also gives us cause for hope. Slavery persisted from the dawn of civilization until the end of the civil war. It took a change of consciousness to end it—a change that began with a small group of Quakers in the late 1700s before eventually becoming the common sentiment of humankind. The women's rights movement began with a small assemblage of women and their male allies in Seneca Falls in 1848. It took a full seven decades until suffrage was attained in 1920. While there is still nowhere on earth where women's rights are fully realized, in the 173 years since Seneca Falls modern people around the world have come to change many of their basic assumptions about the role of women in society—a change that continues to ripple across the globe. Similarly, almost a half-century intervened between the social awakening symbolized by New York City's 1968 Stonewall Riots and the Supreme Court's 2015 *Obergefell v. Hodges* decision making marriage equality the law of the land.

These changes did not "just happen." A whole set of alterations in social conditions had to occur before they became possible. For example, the ending of the British slave trade could not have happened a century earlier when much of Britain's mercantilist economy was still dependent on it. By the early 1800s however, the industrial and capitalist revolutions had shrunk the slave trade to just 5% of the British economy rendering it easier to contemplate its demise. Restricting the slave trade also dovetailed with British military interests during the Napoleonic Wars, since it throttled back the supply of slaves available to French colonies. While these changes made the British ruling class more amenable to ending slavery, that end was also dependent on newly emerging ideas about dignity and the rights of human beings, ideas fueled—however unintentionally—by the rhetoric of the American and French revolutions. As Victor Hugo noted, "nothing is more powerful as an idea whose time has come."

In this analysis, moral advances partly depend on new ways of thinking about values as well as small groups of zealous people fighting for their propagation over extended horizons of time. The British parliament voted down bills to end the slave trade multiple times in the sixteen years between 1791 and 1807. The 1791 abolition bill was defeated by 75 votes, while the 1807 abolition bill passed by 267 votes. This represents a huge swing of elite opinion in only 16 years. The current impasse of American democracy can also be overcome by a new moral vision, and people willing to advocate for it over time despite initial setbacks. We can accomplish almost nothing, however, without first arriving at a new operating consensus on values and a new vision for how we might flourish together.

Unlike the Great Awakenings of the American past, this new moral vision can't be based on the revitalization of a single faith tradition. We are now a nation of Christians, Jews, Muslims, Hindus, Sikhs, Buddhists, humanists, atheists, agnostics, and the "spiritual but not religious." Any new vision must be transcultural and aspire to universality—it must build on the commonalities and overlapping consensuses between traditions and address the concerns and aspirations of people in all walks of life.

The previous chapters laid the framework for a moral vision based on human flourishing. It cataloged a set of virtues common to ancient Aristotelian, Confucian, and Buddhist philosophies as well as contemporary world religions and humanisms—values that are independent of commitments to specific theological or metaphysical beliefs. It deems values to be good when they promote individual and collective flourishing, and not because they are aligned with a specific vision of God or nature.

The previous chapters also outlined how values evolve as part of a process of collective social inquiry so as to remain appropriate to changing social conditions. Many things that made sense for frontiersmen a century-and-a-half ago may not make sense for urbanites today. Innovations in medicine, technology, communication, transportation, manufacturing, trade, and finance have transformed every aspect of modern life and call for a renewed understanding of values. Our ancestors never had to imagine responses to nuclear weapons, global warming, mass extinctions, the Internet, school shootings, ICU life-support, genetic engineering, or artifical intelligence.

It is now time to discuss how a moral vision based on human flourishing can help address the problems afflicting pluralistic, multicultural democracies. It is a moral vision that has important implications for how corporations conduct business, how nation states conduct domestic and foreign policies, and how we educate children, regulate social media, and navigate the cultural divide.

The Centrality of Relatedness in Moral Traditions

Chapter 2 defined virtues as self-regarding and other-regarding. Like Janus, the two-headed Roman God, they look inward and outward reflecting the central fact that we are not just individuals but belong to families, communities, nations, an international order, an ecosystem, and a planet. While we aspire to flourish as individuals—to develop our interests and talents, preserve our freedom of choice, express our uniqueness, and honor the traditions in which we were raised—all of this must be counterbalanced with respect for the well-being of our neighbors and their traditions, and honoring our responsibilities to the larger communities we belong to by birth and fate. This is a moral vision that balances individualism and relatedness.

The first century BCE Jewish sage Rabbi Hillel got this balance exactly right when he asked, "If I am not for myself, who will be? If I am only for myself, what am I?" (Pirkei Avot, 1:14). His adage gives priority to our personal needs and desires but then immediately recognizes if we are only for ourselves we aren't even human. This adage is more relational than the libertarian credo that "my right to swing my arm ends at your nose." Libertarianism posits we may do whatever we please so long as we do not harm others but includes no positive obligation to help others. It doesn't require us, for example, to care about Mencius's child falling into that well—but caring about that child is part of our essential natures and if we numb ourselves to it we are dispensing with a core part of our humanity. Remember that *humaneness* is Confucius' master virtue, just as *lovingkindness* and *compassion* are key Buddhist ones.

Relatedness and caring are major themes in all the world's religions. The New Testament admonishes us to love our neighbors as ourselves (Mark, 12:21), while the Old Testament exhorts us to love the stranger (Leviticus, 19:33–34). St. Paul tells us in *Corinthians* 13:13 that love—*agapē*—is the greatest of virtues. In his *Canticle to the Sun*, St. Francis sings of his love for all God's creation:

> Be praised, my Lord, through all your creatures,
> especially through my lord Brother Sun,
> who brings the day; and you give light through him.
> And he is beautiful and radiant in all his splendor!
> Of you, Most High, he bears the likeness.
>
> Praised be You, my Lord, through Sister Moon and the stars,
> in heaven you formed them clear and precious and beautiful.
> Praised be You, my Lord, through Brother Wind,
> and through the air, cloudy and serene,
> and every kind of weather through which
> You give sustenance to Your creatures.

> Praised be You, my Lord, through Sister Water,
> which is very useful and humble and precious and chaste.
> Praised be You, my Lord, through Brother Fire,
> through whom you light the night and he is beautiful
> and playful and robust and strong.
> Praised be You, my Lord, through Sister Mother Earth,
> who sustains us and governs us and who produces varied fruits with
> colored flowers and herbs. (Saint Francis of Assisi, n.d)

St. Francis's participation in God's love for His creation parallels the relationship to nature found in Indigenous American traditions. Ogalala Lakota medicine man Black Elk expressed this reverence, love, and connection in his vision of the sacred hoop:

> I was standing on the highest mountain of them all, and round about beneath me was the whole hoop of the world. And while I stood there I saw more than I can tell and I understood more than I saw; for I was seeing in a sacred manner the shapes of all things in the spirit, and the shape of all shapes as they must live together like one being. And I saw that the sacred hoop of my people was one of many hoops that made one circle, wide as daylight and as starlight, and in the center grew one mighty flowering tree to shelter all children of one mother and one father. And I saw that it was holy ... but anywhere is the center of the world. (Neihardt 2014, 26)

On another occasion Black Elk says:

> The Six Grandfathers have placed in this world many things, all of which should be happy. Every little thing is sent for something, and in that thing there should be happiness and the power to make happy. Like the grasses showing tender faces to each other, thus we should do, for this was the wish of the Grandfathers of the World. (Neihardt 2014, 120)

We see similar expressions of caring and connection in the Buddhist tradition. According to the *Karaniya Metta Sutta*:

> As a mother would risk her life
> to protect her child, her only child,
> even so should one cultivate a limitless heart
> with regard to all beings.
> With good will for the entire cosmos,
> cultivate a limitless heart:
> Above, below, & all around,

unobstructed, without enmity or hate.
Whether standing, walking,
sitting, or lying down,
as long as one is alert,
one should be resolved on this mindfulness.
This is called a sublime abiding here & now.

(Thanissaro Bhikkhu 2004)

There is a meditation practice associated with this text called *metta* (lovingkindness) meditation that helps practitioners cultivate benevolent intentions towards self and others. The meditator first expresses benevolent wishes for his or her own health, happiness, and well-being, and then directs the same wishes to a friend, a neutral person, a disliked person, and all living beings in turn. This practice reflects the belief that benevolence is not just part of our intrinsic nature but also a skill we can cultivate to promote flourishing. The Buddhist tradition makes clear that kindness and compassion are not just transitory feelings but intentions that can inform benevolent actions.

The African *Ubuntu* tradition stresses individuals do not exist apart from their communities. The Nguni Bantu word *ubuntu* (often translated as "humanity") is associated with the phrase "I am because you are." Cognate terms are found in many African languages. Scholar Michael Onyebuchi Eze explains Ubuntu as follows:

> ... my humanity is co-substantively bestowed upon the other and me. Humanity is a quality we owe to each other. We create each other and need to sustain this *otherness* creation. And if we belong to each other, we participate in our creations: *we are because you are, and since you are, definitely I am*. The "I am" is not a rigid subject, but a dynamic self-constitution dependent on this *otherness* creation of relation and distance (Eze 2010, 191–192).

Ubuntu stresses the need for humane relations and the need to work harmoniously with others for the welfare of the entire community.

Humanitarian and theologian Albert Schweitzer called this intimate sense of caring and connection to all beings "reverence for life." This reverence lies at the heart of not just the world religions, but the non-theistic humanistic traditions as well. Benevolence towards others (*rén*) was Confucius' paramount virtue. When a student asked Confucius if there was a single principle he should practice all his life, Confucius gave a single word answer, "*shù*," a word that connotes reciprocity, consideration, and empathic understanding.

He then explained, "that which you do not desire, do not do to others" (*The Analects of Confucius*, 2015, 25:14).

In a more contemporary context, philosopher John Dewey (2013) tried to imagine a secular American faith that could bind atheists and religious believers together in shared common purpose. Dewey used the term *natural piety* to define our palpable connection to "the community of causes and consequences in which we, together with those not born, are enmeshed in the widest and deepest symbol of the mysterious totality of being the imagination calls the universe" (p. 78). This is a natural piety that connects us not only with the totality of existence, but with the future as well.

In his book *A Secular Age* (2007), philosopher Charles Taylor wonders whether there are sufficient moral resources to draw upon to motivate most people to transition from loyalty to family, clan, tribe, or nation state to the more universal benevolence that is the cornerstone of the modern moral order. People do not make this transition easily because they have conflicting intuitions about loyalty to the proximal social institutions to which they belong and their more benevolent sentiments for humankind in general. That is why the conflict between loyalty to family and an impartial sense of justice was the primary conflict addressed by much of classical Chinese philosophy, and why all the axial religions stress a more universal love, benevolence, and interrelatedness.

This necessarily brief survey of Judeo-Christian, Buddhist, Ogalala Lakota, Ubuntu, and contemporary humanist traditions illustrates how all (or almost all) axial and post-axial religions and humanisms—be they Western, Asian, African, or Native American—provide us with moral resources to help make the transition from an unadulterated individualism or loyalty to a small in-group to a wider identification as an integral member of a broader human community and perhaps even to all life. This does not mean the transition is necessarily easy or that everyone can make it. It does mean that if we wish to make it, we can draw on a wide set of adages, legends, teachings, practices, and parables to help us on our way.

The One-sidedness of Western Individualism

This theme of belongingness, relationship, empathy, care, and connection seems to have gotten submerged as Western culture has elaborated new and important ideas about individualism, inalienable rights, and authenticity. This new emphasis on individuality is a salutary historical development that played a crucial role in breaking from feudalism and the emergence of

Protestantism, secularism, humanism, liberalism, romanticism, and modern psychology. It also played a crucial role in establishing the importance of individual conscience. As a result of these developments, modern Westerners have a sense of themselves as more fully individuated from their families than people in many East Asian and African cultures. Charles Taylor (2007) calls this new Western emphasis on individuality over relatedness "the Great Disembedding."

This radical Western individualism has had undeniable benefits. In the early twentieth century it served as a bulwark against statism and totalitarianism. It remains the animating force behind modern personal liberation movements, helping to free many from stifling and antiquated social and gender roles. It becomes problematic, however, when it is emphasized at the expense of relatedness, connection, and caring.

I find it helpful to view our present overemphasis on individualism through the lens of modern psychological theories of personal and cultural development. The twentieth century Austrian psychologist Heinz Werner (1957) thought that individual and cultural development reflected a balance between the reciprocal processes of differentiation and integration. Differentiation is the process by which we separate phenomena from their backgrounds and wholes into their myriad parts. Integration is the reciprocal process of coordinating individual parts into articulated wholes and reintegrating them with their backgrounds. Werner saw this process unfolding in the embryonic, perceptual, motor, and cognitive development of children and in the way cultures mature. He thought development progressed from initial stages of relatively undifferentiated globality to later stages of increasing differentiation and integration.

For example, when very young children draw a picture of a person, they often draw a crude circle without clearly differentiated legs, arms, head, or torso. At a later stage they add differentiated details but aren't quite sure how they fit together. At this stage a child might draw a person's arms extending from the neck rather than the shoulders. The face might have eyes but the eyes lack pupils, lashes, and brows. Children can only draw all the differentiated parts and how they fit together into an organized whole at a later developmental stage.

We might view the cultural and historical development of biological science through the same lens. Biology is adept at differentiating living beings into parts: tissues into cells, cells into organelles, organelles into their constituent molecules. This has led to great advances in knowledge, but biology has not been quite as adept (at least not yet) in understanding how these component parts self-organize into living wholes.

When we try to imagine how the differentiated systems of the body work together as an integrated whole we begin devising hybrid fields of study like *psychoneuroimmunology*. Similarly, when we started to wonder how organisms interact with their environments we devised the new field of *ecology*. These newer fields point to a kind of holistic integration but take us only part way there. In living organisms, every "part" has an impact, trivial or large, on every other "part." Of course, from the organism's own perspective there are no parts, only a whole.

Science has no tools for handling this astonishing degree of complexity. How do trillions of cells coordinate their activities to produce integrated beings with a unitary consciousness, intentionality, purpose, and sociality? Of course, these cells were never separate entities to begin with—they were part of a self-organizing whole from the start. Organisms are, as biologist Francisco Varela put it, *autopoietic* or self-producing (Maturana and Varela 1980). Unlike machines, they make their own parts, transforming energy and matter from outside their bodies into animate internal structure. Nicholson (2019) emphasizes how internal cellular structures are never fixed but constantly regenerating and reconstituting themselves, so that it might be better to think of them as fluid dynamic processes.

Heinz Werner's dual reciprocal process theory is not the only psychological theory of its kind. The Swiss Psychologist Jean Piaget called his dual reciprocal processes *assimilation* and *accommodation*. Assimilation means taking something external into oneself and making it one's own, while accommodation means adapting oneself to the exigencies of the external world. Piaget viewed child development as an ever-shifting balance between these dual reciprocal processes. When children pretend the nozzle of a garden hose is a gun they are assimilating the nozzle to their imagination. When they learn their multiplication tables, they are accommodating their minds to external demands. Piaget's theory emphasizes the balance between changing the world to suit oneself and changing oneself to adapt to the world. We could say that individualism is primarily assimilationist in that it is all about adopting the world to suit oneself. Relatedness, on the other hand, requires greater degrees of accommodation—understanding how one's needs and desires differ from those of others—and taking their needs and desires into consideration.

The American psychoanalyst Sidney Blatt saw child and adolescent development proceeding along two similar dual reciprocal tracks: the establishment of an individual identity and the establishment of healthy relationships. Having healthy relationships means seeing others as separate from oneself and as having equal existential worth. It means treating others as ends rather than using them as means. People with a variety of personality disorders—dependent, antisocial, or narcissistic—see others as "things" to be manipulated. How using them makes them feel is not their concern.

Blatt developed a scoring system for the Rorschach inkblot test based on Werner's and Piaget's theories as well as psychoanalytic theories of interpersonal relations. He used his scoring system to assess peoples' ability to establish healthy relationships. In the Rorschach test, psychologists ask people to describe what comes to mind when they look at non-representational inkblots. Blatt scored client's responses in the following way: He gave the lowest possible scores to seeing whole human figures in areas of the blot which don't resemble humans in any reasonable way. Answers like these meant perceivers were assimilating the blots to their imaginations rather than accommodating their perception to adequately conform to blot contours. Blatt gave a somewhat higher score for seeing human body part details—eyes, hands, ears—in places that reasonably fit the blot contours. He gave even higher scores for seeing whole humans in appropriate areas of the blots. He gave higher scores still for seeing humans in interaction in appropriate areas, and the very highest scores for seeing humans actively cooperating. Blatt and Ford (1994) used these Rorschach scores to predict improvement in emotionally disturbed adolescents who were being treated in a long-term residential therapeutic setting. His scores predicted adolescent improvement with uncanny accuracy.

In his later work, Blatt looked at Western cultural development from the perspective of the dual tasks of developing an individual identity and developing healthy relationships. Blatt concluded that the contemporary West overemphasizes individuality at the expense of relatedness. He believed this overemphasis resulted in a higher social valuation of "masculine" domination and control over "feminine" caring and relatedness and contributed to a psychological epidemic of "alienation and narcissistic self-absorption" (Guisinger and Blatt 1994).

It's possible to think about our culture's individualist emphasis as a stage in a dialectical historical process which needs to be corrected by a compensating emphasis on relationship, connectedness, and caring. Modern market capitalism developed hand-in-hand with this overemphasis on individualism. Western economists often portray the human being as a *homo economicus,* a creature devoted solely to rationally calculating its own advantage.

Ayn Rand's (1957/1992) philosophy of Objectivism also reflects this kind of radical individualism. She viewed human beings' personal happiness as their sole moral purpose.

These are overly thin conceptions of human beings. Human beings care about their own happiness, but they care for others as well. They understand their well-being depends on more than just desire satisfaction, but on the well-being of those they care about and their community. This means not only pursuing one's own narrow aims but living in a well-ordered society governed by mutual care and respect and on a sustainable planet capable of supporting life for oneself and one's descendants. We ought to care not just for the world as it is, but also for the future—as the Iroquois say, "until the 7th generation."

Individualism and its Discontents

A good deal of the West's recent moral shortcomings are the result of men (they have usually been men) and nations ruthlessly pursing their narrow short-term self-interests—masters of the universe, captains of industry, and conquerors of nations and nature. Once one conceives of oneself as an individual apart from nature and the community of humankind, one becomes an island fortress struggling to dominate and control what lies outside the self. This is the mindset of individual self-interest, mastery, domination, and control that promoted the colonial subjugation of much of Africa and Asia. It is the mindset that allows corporations to heat up the atmosphere; pollute soil, water, and air; kill off pollinating insects, birds, and fish; and raise domestic animals in inhumane factory farms. It enabled European-descent Americans to retain their sense of moral superiority while owning slaves and exterminating indigenous peoples.

It is also the mindset that allows the CEO of Amazon to earn 300,000 times the starting salary of an employee in one of his distribution facilities (Sarokin, 2020), or the CEO of Disney to earn 2,338 times the wages of a theme-park princess (Mosteller 2021). In 2021, American CEOs earned 339 times their median employees' wage (Eavis 2022), the highest CEO-Employee differential in the world (Sarokin 2020).

One doesn't have to believe in equality to believe there is something wrong with these vast differentials. Hard work, risk, skill, and innovation deserve to be handsomely rewarded, but reward differentials of this magnitude aren't necessary to attract talent. Neurosurgeons are willing to work for 5% of the average CEO's salary, yet there is no shortage of bright and capable people willing to become neurosurgeons. We could reduce CEO compensation by more than half and businesses would still find talented people willing to take the helm.

The Gini coefficient is a measure of the distribution of wealth in a society. A Gini coefficient of 0 indicates perfect equality, while a Gini coefficient of 1.0 indicates that 100% of a country's wealth is owned by a single person. The current U.S. Gini coefficient (.48) is higher than comparable European, Asian, and North American industrialized democracies. It has risen precipitously over the past half-century–especially since the Reagan presidency—as wealth has become increasingly concentrated in fewer and fewer hands (United States Census Bureau 2015). The top 1% of Americans now own a third of the country's wealth, while the bottom 50% own less than 2% (United States Federal Reserve 2020).

Some of this growing inequality is due to increases in CEO compensation, some to taxation policies that favor the rich, some to the decline of labor unions, and some to the outsourcing of manufacturing jobs. It is also the result of laws that treat corporations as people, allowing them to pour huge sums of money into the political process and tilt the playing field to their advantage. When you combine this with the fact that many candidates for legislative office are themselves multi-millionaires, the result is a political system disinclined to meaningfully address inequality.

It's impossible to overestimate the impact of extreme inequality on almost every aspect of the current crisis of American democracy. It has locked-in the lower socio-economic status of Blacks, Hispanics, and Indigenous Americans while raising the status anxiety of Whites struggling to remain in the middle class, pitting the narrowly conceived interests of these groups against each other. It has led to a corrosive distrust and resentment of the political, economic, and social elites due to the (not unjustified) belief they are rigging the system for their own benefit. This corrosive distrust now extends to every institution—Congress, the courts, the executive, the media, and corporations, as well as the legal, medical, scientific, and academic professions. This distrust and resentment fuels American populism, erodes the legitimacy of the electoral process, and was responsible for hundreds of thousands of U.S. deaths during the COVID pandemic.

These failing aspects of our socioeconomic system are supported by a triad of pernicious beliefs that: 1) a corporation's sole responsibility is to its shareholders, 2) a government's prime economic interest is its country's gross domestic product (GDP), and 3) the best measure of a person's flourishing is his or her financial success. These beliefs treat wealth as the be-all-and-end-all of existence.

It's not my intention to denigrate money—we would all like enough of it to live comfortably and pursue what matters most to us—but money ought to be a means for building a flourishing life rather than an end-in-itself. The point of money is what it can offer in terms of basic food, shelter, education, medical care, leisure, and the ability to pursue one's interests. It matters little if the national GDP increases annually, but 50% of the country worries over basic levels of food, shelter, healthcare, and education. If Jeff Bezos walks into a bar, the average wealth of the people in the bar goes up by several billion but that doesn't make them any better off.

If corporations are people (as current law would have it), then many corporations meet the psychiatric diagnostic criteria for antisocial personality disorder—the steadfast pursuit of narrow self-interest regardless of harm to others. The idea that a corporation's prime obligation is to its shareholders but not equally its workers, community, end-service users, or environment is literally killing us. Medical researchers tell us that when a cell stops cooperating with neighboring cells and focuses solely on its own metabolic and reproductive needs, that cell has become a cancer cell. Individuals and corporations that pursue their narrow self-interests at the expense of the community are analogous to these cancer cells.

Fixing the House We Live In

Domestic Policy

It doesn't have to be this way. Laws can be changed. Corporations can be held legally responsible for the harms they cause workers, communities, consumers, and the planet. Corporations and their officers could be held legally accountable for workplace safety, consumer injuries, and environmental harms. While workers, consumers, and environmentalists can sue for damages under some circumstances—legal proceedings that take forever due to the obstruction of well-paid corporate lawyers—why aren't these criminal matters as well? Why are gun manufacturers exempt from being sued? Why do we treat corporate officers who knowingly dump toxins in the environment, create products that injure consumers, or compel workers to labor under unsafe conditions any differently than we do street criminals? We treat white-collar crime much more leniently than street crime—the wealthy, if they see jail time at all, go to the best prisons while the poor go to the worst—but why? Why should a person caught with a few ounces of marijuana go to jail for years, while the owner of a company that dumps opiates on the market walks away with a fine that still leaves him a billionaire?

Before we can have a chance at changing these laws, however, we must first arrive at a new consensus on values—a consensus on our ethical responsibilities to each other and the planet. It is a consensus that the well-being of individuals and society, not wealth, is the proper end-goal for corporations and governments. Once we understand that—individually and collectively—we can begin to think about new legal arrangements more in line with that moral understanding.

I wrote earlier that allowing corporations to operate like persons with antisocial personality disorder is literally killing us. I want to take a moment to explore this more fully. Recent years have witnessed an increase in middle-aged deaths of despair in rural and rustbelt regions—deaths related to alcoholism, drug addiction, and suicide—deaths that reflect a collective social failure to promote individual flourishing. The large corporations that once provided good-paying jobs abandoned these regions for greater profit elsewhere, defaulting on their obligations to those who helped create their wealth. At the same time, government policies driven by lobbyists for wealthy interests siphoned tax monies away from the infrastructure, amenities, and services that supported flourishing in these communities and into the pockets of the already wealthy.

These increased deaths of despair and the failure to flourish they represent are then construed as personal moral failings rather than collective social ones. What, after all, can one expect from alcoholics and drug addicts, except alcoholism and addiction? While I do not want to minimize personal moral responsibility—the whole of Chapter 2 is devoted to it—the corporations and politicians who abandoned these communities have their responsibilities as well. As Confucius points out, individuals and the collectivity mutually affect each other—when the state is virtuous, the people flourish; when the people are virtuous, the state thrives.

These are not the only ways our allowing corporations to act like persons with antisocial personality disorder is killing us. We are also being killed by a gun industry that promotes the sale of millions of military grade weapons capable of inflicting mass casualties in schools, shopping malls, and houses of worship into private hands. In 2020, nearly 20,000 Americans died from gun-related violence and accidents (Thebault and Rindler 2021).

Corporate malfeasance contributing to global warming is the most alarming example of how our current values are killing us. Extractive industries like the gas, coal, and oil industries are continuing to pursue their profits and fight or stall governmental efforts to curtail global warming. All this is occurring even as climate change is already intensifying heat waves, wildfires, droughts, floods, and tropical storms. As bad as conditions are now, they will only get worse. This past year may have been the coolest year in the rest of our and our descendants' lives.

We are also already seeing mass migrations from drought-prone Middle Eastern and African regions roiling the domestic politics of Europe. This problem, too, is only going to get worse. As sea levels rise, the populations in low lying areas and small island nations will be forced to abandon their homelands, and as desertification proceeds regions that once sustained agriculture and nomadic herds are becoming uninhabitable.

And these changes are not just killing *us*. They are leading to what biologists are calling the Sixth Great Extinction. We are already witnessing significant declines in amphibian, bird, fish, and insect populations, and biologists tell us 1,000,000 species may be at risk for extinction by 2050. Our lives depend on resilient ecosystems, but we are failing to preserve them.

All this can change, but only if we adopt a moral vision that recognizes our mutual responsibilities to each other and the planet—a change that puts flourishing ahead of profit and unlimited personal and corporate freedom. A majority of us must come to agree that the current way of doing things is unconscionable and unsustainable. Once that happens, many solutions become possible.

It's not my intention to advocate specific solutions—I am not an expert in economics or ecology. Maybe we limit corporate contributions to politicians or publicly finance elections. Maybe we make the tax system more progressive. Maybe boards of directors and shareholders vote to eliminate unconscionable CEO salaries. Maybe we make corporate crimes against the planet criminal offenses. Maybe we tax carbon. Maybe we give workers and stakeholders seats on corporate boards. Maybe we socialize funding for health care and education. Maybe we reinvigorate labor unions. Maybe governments measure success by national well-being and not national wealth. There is no shortage of ideas about what could be done. What we lack is the moral consensus that would allow us to successfully implement them.

Foreign Policy

This same moral vision that can inform our domestic policies can also inform foreign affairs. While America suffered from decaying infrastructure and unequal access to decent housing, healthcare, and education, it spent trillions of dollars on military adventures in Southeast Asia and the Middle East that did nothing to improve general well-being here or abroad. Part of this reflects a lack of respect for the evolving international system and the way individual non-Western cultures chose their own unique paths to development. In this case it is not an individual or corporation acting out of narrow self-interest without regard to harms caused, but a nation state.

American foreign policy tends to veer erratically between a *realpolitik* that conceives of American national interest in narrow economic and geopolitical terms and an American exceptionalism that promotes democracy and free markets globally. Every nation state has an obligation to defend the well-being of its citizens, and a nation based on ideas rather than ethnicity must propagate its beliefs—to do anything less undermines its legitimacy. While sociobiologists tell us warfare is an unfortunate part of our human evolutionary inheritance (Bowles and Gintis 2011), the modern conditions of war have changed the stakes. Hunter-gatherer warriors could raid another tribe's horses and women and the world endured. Now even "small" wars cost millions of lives—the Vietnam War cost over 3,000,000 lives (Britannica 2020) and post 9/11 Middle Eastern interventions over 900,000 (Watson Institute 2021a)—and a nuclear war could end civilization.

Our foreign policy must be both inward and outward looking, promoting the well-being of our citizenry and concerned for the well-being of foreign nationals. We must be cooperative players in the international order, acting in concert with others. Strengthening and renewing international institutions is a vital part of our self-interest. Our policy must reflect a kind of national *phronesis:* an awareness of which ends are within our means and which are beyond them. It must also be cognizant of the true costs of adventures abroad for flourishing at home. Our post-9/11 Middle East interventions cost an estimated $8,000,000,000 (Watson Institute 2021b). Imagine what that money could have done to improve access to decent housing, education, and healthcare at home.

Our foreign policy shouldn't be steeped in a shared national narcissism—America *über alles in der Welt*—but in a realistic view of what enables our citizens to flourish in safety. The dominance of Euro-American cultures over the last half millennium is a historical anomaly. Before 1500 CE, the Chinese, Indian, Persian, Arabic, and Ottoman civilizations were more vibrant than the Euro-American ones (Darwin, 2008). Guns, germs, and steel enabled Europeans to colonize the Americas, and the resulting flush of new wealth helped finance European imperial ambitions in Africa and Asia. That historical anomaly has now reached an end, and America and Europe must adjust to new realities as the inheritors of the Chinese, Persian, Indian, Arabic, and Ottoman civilizations aspire to larger roles as regional and/or global powers.

The Sino-American relationship is fraught with particular difficulty. China, in its nationalist drive to overcome historic humiliations, is intent on reclaiming Taiwan, whereas America's interest in promoting democracy commits it to Taiwan's defense. It is not clear how this tension can be peacefully resolved. If China were to invade Taiwan and the United States did nothing, it would betray America's founding principles and undermine the credibility of its Asian and Pacific alliances. But if America went to war to defend Taiwan, it would be a war America would almost certainly lose. Assuming the United States and China could prevent it from escalating into a nuclear conflict, America would have to project its military power across the Pacific Ocean to a country only 100 miles from the mainland Chinese coast. The Chinese would be fighting for an issue central to their national identity, while America would be fighting for the abstract ideal of global democracy. While that idea is congruent with its founding revolutionary principles, it is of less central importance to its narrowly conceived vital national interests—and America has often abandoned its commitment to democracy abroad when it has proved expedient in terms of its economic or geopolitical interests.

If China succeeded in forcibly seizing Taiwan, life for the average American would continue mostly unchanged. The political debate over "who lost China" after the 1949 revolution contributed to the rise of McCarthyism in the United States, but other than that, the "loss" of China had little practical impact on the lives of average Americans. If American influence as a Pacific power were to wane, the short-term impact on the well-being of Americans would be marginal. Think how the British adjusted over the past century to the loss of Empire. Britannia no longer ruled the waves, but the average British citizen was not significantly worse off as a result. Any decline in the quality of life for the average British citizen had more to do with the self-inflicted wounds of Thatcherism and Brexit than the loss of empire.

This is not an argument for doing nothing to prevent a Chinese invasion of Taiwan. It is an argument for strengthening American Pacific naval and air power, helping the Taiwanese strengthen their own self-defense capabilities, strengthening alliances with other Asian Pacific democracies, and using the threat of diplomatic and financial sanctions to discourage an imminent Chinese invasion. There has also been a policy of "strategic ambiguity" as to whether the United States might respond militarily to such an invasion. President Biden recently removed some of that ambiguity when he expressed a willingness to employ military power to defend Taiwan. It is unclear whether this represents a change in U.S. policy that is likely to survive Biden's tenure in office. It is also unclear how much of a deterrent this actually is to Chinese ambitions given the relative weakness of American forces in the region. In any case, all these disincentives represent an attempt to kick the can down the road while hoping for the possibility of a peaceful resolution in the distant future.

Taiwan is not the only thorn in the Sino-American relationship. The growth of Chinese authoritarianism and the surveillance state under Xi Jinping and Chinese repression in Hong Kong, Xinjiang and Tibet run contrary to American ideals. America would no longer be America if it failed to criticize these developments and try to influence China to change. On the other hand, China views such criticisms as interference in its internal affairs. It touts its system as an indigenously-rooted alternative to American-style democracy, and views China and America as competitors for the imaginations of people around the world. They are failing at this right now—people around the globe aspiring for a better future want to immigrate to America and not China—but that can change as China grows in economic, cultural, and military might.

There are also difficulties related to trade and intellectual property but these are less intractable than ones more deeply intertwined with national identity and purpose. Managing the American-Chinese relationship is the great foreign policy challenge of the next fifty years, and successful management will require a kind of national *phronesis* that includes 1) understanding what genuinely contributes to individual and collective flourishing at home, 2) understanding the extent and limits of our powers, 3) tolerating national sociocultural differences as much as possible, and 4) learning how to navigate in a world where we are no longer the sole superpower. When we criticize Chinese human rights abuses, China responds by criticizing American racial and economic inequities, civil unrest, violence, and disorder. Pointing out another's flaws never excuses one's own, but the Chinese are right in a way. If we are going to successfully compete for the hearts and minds of people around the globe, we must put our own house in order and do better at promoting flourishing at home.

Finally, as I write this book, America and its allies are responding to the Russian invasion of Ukraine. As someone who fervently believes in democracy, it is hard not to sympathize with an emerging democratic nation struggling to maintain its freedom and identity in the face of a brutal invasion by a revanchist, expansionist, and kleptocratic autocracy. So far, America and its allies appear to be responding in a way that exhibits a degree of national and international *phronesis*—first, by establishing a broad-based international alliance and garnering United Nations General Assembly support; second, by providing Ukraine with military, economic and humanitarian aid; third, by sanctioning the Russian economy; and fourth, by keeping American and NATO soldiers out of direct combat. These actions reflect a carefully calibrated strategy that maximizes the chances for Ukrainian survival while minimizing the possibility of nuclear conflict. One can only hope the United States can maintain this steady-handed policy over time in the face of future changes in the composition of the House, Senate, and/or Presidency.

While it's good to see the United States standing up for a rules-based international order that punishes wars of conquest and regime change, let us not forget that the United States has historically been one of the biggest violators of this rules-based order—from its war with Mexico in the nineteenth century to its invasion of Iraq in the twenty-first. If America wants to help create, maintain, and strengthen this rules-based order, it must first set an example by refraining from violating it in the future. One reason many developing nations have declined joining the pro-Ukraine coalition is that they sense an element of hypocrisy in America's current muscular support for that order. They are, of course, justified in their suspicion. Only the future can tell whether America will continue to nurture this order or revert to past behavior that undermines it.

Education

A moral vision based on human flourishing also has implications for how we educate our children. Chapter 4 outlined eight domains of flourishing: *relationship, accomplishment, aesthetics, meaning, whole-heartedness, integration, and acceptance.* These are the domains that contribute to making lives satisfying, meaningful, honorable, and psychologically rich. If we want our children to flourish, we must teach them the skills that allow them to do so.

Current school curricula emphasize literacy and numeracy, as well they ought: these are the keys to employability, social mobility, and financial well-being in our knowledge economy. But psychologists tell us that young people are suffering from steadily increasing rates of anxiety and depression. Rates of adolescent anxiety disorders rose 20% from 2007–2012 (Data Resource

Center for Child and Adolescent Health 2021). and continue to rise, while hospital admissions for adolescent suicide more than doubled over the past decade (American Academy of Pediatrics 2017). Some of this is a consequence of the way social media amplifies adolescent anxieties over status, appearance, and popularity and provides a dangerous new venue for ostracism, ridicule, and bullying. Some of this may be a consequence of young people anticipating a post-education future marked by student debt and shrinking access to the middle class. This will be the first American generation since the Great Depression that will be less economically secure than the previous one. Some of this increase in anxiety may also be due to worries over the health of the planet they will inherit—an anxiety reflected in the dystopias so prevalent in young adult literature.

If young people are to thrive, schools must effectively address these issues. This means focusing more on ethics, values, and citizenship—the virtues and skills that are the prerequisites for leading satisfying, meaningful, honorable, and psychologically rich lives. It means devoting more of the curriculum to activities that promote civility, teamwork, and ethical problem solving. It means devoting more of the curriculum to cultivating aesthetic sensitivity, creativity, and self-expression. It means teaching how to negotiate social media and evaluate sources of information. It means developing the emotional and social intelligence skills that are the prerequisite for phronesis.

Making these curriculum changes will require a change in moral consciousness. It means understanding these "soft" skills are every bit as important to flourishing as literacy and numeracy. We cannot afford to focus exclusively on academic skills while leaving moral education to the home and street. Public schools are our primary institution for transmitting shared sets of values and cannot remain value neutral. Public schools in a democracy have the duty to promote values that allow pluralistic, multicultural democracies to function and flourish. This is one of the most important ways a national consensus on values, once established, can be sustained.

Social Media

In a previous section, I alluded to the corrosive effect social media has on adolescent mental health. Facebook's internal research shows Instagram (which is owned by Facebook—or Meta, as the parent company now calls itself) is harmful to the well-being of a third of its female adolescent users (Wells *et al.* 2021). But social media is harming more than adolescent mental health. It is also disrupting social harmony here and abroad. Social media business models are based on advertising dollars. The more time we spend engaged with them, the more profit they make. Facebook and other social media giants increase our engagement through algorithms that steer affectively "hot" information in our direction. It doesn't matter if the information is true; all that matters is that we "like" and share it. This includes "news" accounts—real or fake—about whatever horrible and stupid things those awful people on the other side of the cultural divide are doing. Using outrage to engage our eyeballs, they are amplifying our pre-existent affective political polarization and disrupting our social fabric. A recent Stanford University study showed Facebook users who deactivated their accounts became significantly less politically polarized over the course of a month (Allcott *et al.* 2020).

The social media giants play a major role in spreading political disinformation, conspiracy theories, health misinformation, and hate speech here and around the globe. Facebook, for example, has been used to stir-up hatred and violence against minorities in countries like Cameroon and Myanmar. Their pursuit of profit above all —like that of the tobacco, opiate, gun, oil, gas, and coal industries—is undermining the well-being of society. Social media companies must come to terms with the harm they cause in amplifying social discord, spreading disinformation, promoting addictive-like behavior, and increasing adolescent dysphoria. They must fundamentally change their business model, and if they are not willing to do so on their own, they must be compelled to through social pressure and government regulation. That means, first and foremost, preventing them from continuing to profit from hate speech, conspiracy theories, and disinformation.

Addressing the Cultural Divide

A flourishing-based ethics also has implications for how we talk to each other across the cultural divide. We need to find ways to tolerate and respect others we strongly disagree with. That doesn't mean that we allow a minority to control our lives, but it means we allow them, as much as possible, to live their lives in accordance with their own values so long as that does not cause undue harm to the public welfare. And it means that even when we think they are very wrong, we never forget our common humanity and our ethical requirement to treat them as we would like to be treated.

When I discussed the ethical questions raised by the abolitionist and the Bolshevik in Chapter 2—moralists who were willing to employ force to impose their views on others—I wrote that explaining to others why they are wrong almost never changes them. More often, it just causes them to dig in their heels. For example, I cannot imagine a conversation with a pro-Trump supporter that could change my mind about Donald Trump. Because I know that about myself, I suspect the opposite is also true: There is no argument I could make to a pro-Trump supporter that could convert them to my point of view. This intractable fact is the starting point for any exploration of communication across the cultural divide. Any conversation that begins with the intent of changing the other is doomed to fail. When social movements fade away they do so not because minds have been changed but because their adherents grow old and die and a new generation arises with different priorities and concerns.

Philosopher Richard Rorty noted when people change their minds it is not because someone else had changed it through a knock down argument, but because their life orientation has changed due to a multitude of other factors. He writes that sometimes:

> ... [P]eople change their central projects, change those parts of their self-image they previously found most precious. The question is, however, whether this ever happens as a result of *argument*. Perhaps sometimes it does, but this is surely the exception. Such conversions are typically as much of a surprise to the person herself as to her friends. The phrase "she became a new person—you would not recognize her" typically means "she no longer sees the point or relevance or interest of the arguments which she once deployed on the other side." (Rorty 2021, 92)

In other words, a cause a person once fervently endorsed can cease to be relevant to how one's central life purposes have evolved over time.

If we cannot change other people's minds through argument, what can we do? We can promote interactions that renew our bonds of common humanity. I may not be able to change your mind, but I can listen to your beliefs and explain why I believe mine. The goal of such an encounter is not a changing of minds, but mutual understanding. We can grow to respect that we each have convincing (for us) reasons why we believe as we do. In the process, we become human beings with differing opinions shaped by different life experiences and not enemies. We can advocate for our beliefs without treating each other like idiots or monsters.

For philosopher John Dewey, democracy was more than a set of formal institutions, but an ethos or personal commitment to a particular way of life. He viewed the airing of differences of opinion as an opportunity for both parties to inquire, learn, and grow. He expressed his idea most fully in an essay entitled *Creative Democracy—The Task Before Us*, written in 1939 in his eightieth year:

> Democracy as a way of life is controlled by personal faith in personal day-by-day working together with others. Democracy is the belief that even when needs and ends or consequences are different for each individual, the habit of amicable cooperation ... is itself a priceless addition to life. To take as far as possible every conflict which arises—and they are bound to arise—out of the atmosphere and medium of force, of violence as a means of settlement into that of discussion and of intelligence is to treat those who disagree—even profoundly—with us as those from whom we may learn, and in so far, as friends. A genuinely democratic faith in peace is faith in the possibility of conducting disputes, controversies and conflicts as cooperative undertakings in which both parties learn by giving the other a chance to express itself, instead of having one party conquer by forceful suppression of the other—a suppression which is none the less one of violence when it takes place by psychological means of ridicule, abuse, intimidation, instead of by overt imprisonment or in concentration camps. To cooperate by giving differences a chance to show themselves because of the belief that the expression of difference is not only a right of the other persons but is a means of enriching one's own life-experience, is inherent in the democratic personal way of life.
> (*Later Works* Vol. 14, 228)

Of course, there are genuine moral monsters—people who knowingly and deliberately lie in order to manipulate others and fulfill their will to power—with whom dialogue is not a genuine possibility. When these people venture into illegalities, they ought to be criminally prosecuted. In fact, failing to prosecute those suspected of plotting the illegal overturn of the 2020 election would make us complicit in hastening the demise of American democracy. Failure to prosecute would only embolden them and their emulators to engage in greater degrees of criminal activity in the next electoral cycle—and next time they might succeed.

But most people on the other side of the cultural divide (and here I am speaking of average citizens—not party functionaries and office holders) do not fall into that category. The fears and resentments that fuel their alienation and anger are existential responses to their life experiences. Even if they hold beliefs we find abhorrent, it does not mean they are abhorrent. Most are loving parents, decent neighbors, and contribute to their communities in meaningful ways. Treating them with contempt only deepens their resentment and the political divide.

The stance I have just outlined infuriates some progressives. "How," they might ask, "can you view people with racist views as decent human beings?" I understand their question. As a Jew, if I had lived in Nazi Germany, I wonder if I would have considered the average German who voted for Hitler a "decent human being." I understand the emotional difficulty one must overcome in order to see things that way.

But my answer is simple. We are all people of a time and place, and all of us—even the most enlightened among us—hold opinions history will one day judge as wrong and harmful. This is just the nature of human imperfection. We must take our neighbors as they are. We cannot, as the German playwright and poet Bertolt Brecht (2003) once quipped, "dissolve the people and elect another." If you think about the people you love, you can probably think of ways in which they could stand to improve. If you are waiting for perfect people to appear in your life, you will wait forever. Everyone you know or will ever meet is wrong about something. That doesn't make them your enemy.

I am not claiming that wrongful moral beliefs aren't harmful. They are, and we should do all we can to explain why we think so. But that does not make the people who hold them bad in a global kind of way. They can be more-or-less good people with very bad opinions. I am also not trying to make excuses for people who not only hold bad beliefs but also act on them. White people who hold private prejudices against Black people but treat them with overt signs of dignity and respect are not in the same camp with Ku Klux Klan members or politicians who suppress the Black vote. They share something in common with them, but they are not quite in the same category. The same could be said about straight people who privately feel gay sex is disgusting but support the rights of gay people to live as they choose. Are they prejudiced? Yes. But they are more-or-less decent people who are not engaging in active harm towards others.

Of course, one could argue that merely voting for Donald Trump is a harmful activity. True enough, but it is one thing to disapprove of people's actions, and another to disapprove of them as persons. If we held everyone to that standard of moral perfection none of us would pass the test. The Jewish tradition teaches that if God were to judge humans fairly, He would extinguish the sun. That is why the tradition extols His mercy. There are certainly things I did over the course of my lifetime that, in retrospect, I do not morally approve of. I would not want to be categorized by others for the worst mistakes I made in my life, nor do I want to do that to others. Few people are as bad as their worst mistake or as good as their greatest accomplishment.

In his autobiography, *And the Walls Came Tumbling Down*, the Reverend Ralph Abernathy (1989) recounts how the Reverend Doctor Martin Luther King, Jr., during the last days of his life, engaged in extramarital affairs and at one point shoved a woman across a bed during a heated argument. Abernathy's revelation of Dr. King's moral flaws doesn't undermine King's historic importance as a moral leader in the struggle for civil rights. The revelation of his violent temper doesn't transform his dedication to nonviolence into a hypocritical sham. One could even contend that his commitment to nonviolence grew, in part, out of his self-awareness of his own capacity for violence. Stories of people struggling to overcome their given natures are often more morally inspiring than stories of perfect saints, if only because perfect saints, if they existed, would have nothing in common with us.

I chose Dr. King for this example, but I could have easily chosen any of my personal heroes—Socrates, Aristotle, the Buddha, Confucius, John Dewey, Mother Teresa, Susan B. Anthony, Nelson Mandela, Abraham Lincoln, Frederick Douglass, Theodore Roosevelt, Ulysses S. Grant, Eleanor Roosevelt—and made the same point. The point is not that all idols have feet of clay. The point is that even the best of us are imperfect, and we would be better off accepting that fact.

Learning to tolerate others who are different from us lies at the heart of the modern liberal project. Everyone, whatever his or her beliefs, is entitled to respect, kindness, and compassion as a human being. That doesn't mean we allow everyone to do as he or she pleases, but it does mean everyone retains his or her dignity as a person. Even rightfully incarcerated criminals are entitled to the dignity and respect owed all people. That they are not afforded such is the great scandal of our criminal justice system.

We also learn to appreciate others' common humanity by interacting with them in ways other than having political conversations with them. We learn not to argue politics with Uncle Bob at the Thanksgiving table, but to appreciate that Uncle Bob, whatever his awful political views, remembers our birthdays and is kind to our children. We learn we can work together with people we disagree with over politics on common projects—serving food together at a soup kitchen, coaching together on a Little League team, fundraising together for the PTA, singing together in a chorus, belonging to the same photography or gardening club, or having one's children play together at playdates. The most important thing is not that we come to agree, but that we remain human in each other's eyes.

A flourishing-based ethics accepts that there are different paths to flourishing based on one's unique capabilities and interests. While it holds that non-dogmatic approaches to flourishing are superior to dogmatic ones based on tradition and authority, it doesn't demand everyone agree with such an approach. It asks that we respect each other's ways of life as much as possible. It hopes that given sufficient time to present its case, enough people will come to embrace it so that it will eventually become the majority opinion in modern pluralistic, multicultural democracies.

The sticking point comes when a committed minority believes it ought to try to force its will on the majority. The current divide in this country over abortion rights is one example of this kind of sticking point. The liberal position is to leave the decision about abortion up to women and their doctors. If someone thinks abortion is morally acceptable, they should be allowed to have one. If someone thinks abortion is morally objectionable, they are free to abstain. Polls consistently show a majority of Americans favor something like this position. While they might not necessarily approve of abortion under all circumstances, they think it ought to remain legal, at least before the age of fetal viability, under a variety of circumstances including pregnancy after a rape or incest, cases when the fetus is likely to be born profoundly disabled, and for the health of the mother.

This is an intolerable position for abortion opponents, however. From their vantage point, abortion is murder, full stop. We do not say to people, "if you think murder is morally acceptable you are free to engage in it, and if you think it is morally unacceptable, just abstain." We insist everyone abstain.

Now whether one thinks abortion is murder or not depends on one's belief about when human life begins—whether one believes it begins at conception, the age of viability, or birth. There is, of course, no empirical way to answer this question. It is a matter of how one defines human life based on feeling and/or religious tradition. People with different opinions could argue the point forever, and no new empirical evidence could resolve their dispute. Improvements in medical technology that allow premature infants to survive outside the womb at earlier gestational ages have affected attitudes toward late-term abortions for many people. But for most people, other issues also impact their opinions about whether abortion should be legal. Having a child is a life-altering event with enormous implications for a woman's (and her family's) future well-being. Having an unwanted child, or a child one isn't prepared to care for, or one at the wrong time in one's life, or dedicating one's life to caring for a child with profound mental and/

or physical disabilities can change lives in dramatic ways. For many, it can be the deciding factor between a flourishing life or a life of poverty and stifled aspiration. In addition, giving a newborn up to the vagaries of foster care and adoption is not a psychologically acceptable alternative for many pregnant women. It is harder, for example, to find adoptive parents for infants from racial minorities or with profound disabilities. Not every child gets adopted: there are presently 400,000 children in foster care in the United States. In addition, making abortions illegal does not stop them from occurring but only makes it more likely women seeking them would be at increased risk for injury or death from unsafe procedures. I suspect most readers are capable of sympathizing with the arguments on both sides. They can understand why some believe it is morally wrong, but also understand why it might be better to keep it a private decision.

Questions like these tend to get settled over time through the political process—or, like the Civil War, through violent conflict—or through the simple passage of time as adherents of various positions die off. There isn't any great push at present to revive many issues that once troubled the republic. There is, for example, no great outcry to restore slavery, debtor's prisons, Sunday blue laws, prohibition, or the right of Mormons to engage in plural marriage.

On the other hand, there are times when keeping a divisive issue on the front burner benefits the fortunes of a political party seeking its own advantage. Prior to the 1970s, Democrats and Republicans did not disagree over abortion. Barry Goldwater, Richard Nixon, Gerald Ford, and George H.W. Bush were all pro-choice. As California Governor, Ronald Regan signed one of the most liberal abortion laws in the country. A 1972 Gallop poll showed 68% of Republicans believed abortion ought to be a private matter (Halpern 2018). Evangelicals and Southern Baptists at that point were also not uniformly against abortion. There was a time, for example, when Evangelist Billy Graham and the influential Evangelical magazine *Christianity Today* both supported a woman's right to choose under some conditions. Initially, the Republican party decided to use abortion as an issue to court Roman Catholic voters and split the old New Deal coalition. Later, it used it to help motivate Evangelicals, who had previously been apolitical, to get out and vote for their candidates.

The Supreme Court's 1973 *Roe v. Wade* decision nationalized the abortion debate, providing Republicans with an opportunity to enlarge and energize their base. By making the right to abortion the law of the land, the Court bypassed the political process of individual states making the decisions. There are some who think that if conservative states had been allowed to ban abortions while liberal states had been allowed to legalize them the issue might never have risen to the level of national prominence it now has. Instead, each state government would have fought and refought this issue as the process played out over time.

There are strong reasons to believe this would not have been a satisfactory solution. Anti-abortion minorities in "liberal" states would have felt frustrated that their moral concerns were going unheeded. Women seeking abortions in states that banned them would have had to obtain them out of state or risk illegal ones at home. Pro-choice proponents would have 1) engaged in efforts to try to persuade voters in anti-abortion states to change their minds, 2) funded "underground railroads" to transport women to clinics where abortion was legal, and 3) pushed for federal legislation or a constitutional amendment to resolve the issue. At the same time, anti-abortion proponents would have fought for incremental federal restrictions and an eventual federal ban. A state-by-state solution wouldn't have been a genuine solution any more than past state-by-state solutions had been regarding slavery and Jim Crow.

Now that a conservative-majority Supreme Court has overturned *Roe v. Wade* with its *Dobbs v. Jackson Women's Health Organization* decision, it has temporarily returned the question of abortion back to the states and the unsatisfactory solution described above. For those who believe abortion is murder, "leaving it to the states" can only be a partial, stop-gap solution. Many states that ban abortions within their borders will try to criminalize out-of-state abortions and abortifacients-by-mail. If and when Republicans retake all three branches of the federal government, their base will push them to enact a nationwide ban. Anti-abortion proponents would view this as a final victory on behalf of the unborn, while pro-choice proponents would view it as minority-imposed religious tyranny. Presently, majorities in 30 states (and pluralities in 4 others) want to see some forms of abortion remain legal, while pro-choice minorities in 14 other states constitute over 40% of their populations (Cohn 2022). Any nationwide ban would be imposed against the will of the majority in most states, would be widely unpopular, and would generate the same contempt for the law that alcohol prohibition did in the 1920s.

How can this seemingly endless battle end? It can only end when and if, over the course of a long period of time, people who care fervently about this issue cease to care about it as intensely for various reasons or die off and are replaced by a generation with a different set of concerns. For example, there is some evidence that young people are not being drawn to Evangelicalism to the same extent their parents were—in part due to the increased politicization of the faith—and over time Evangelical political power may gradually ebb. In the past, Evangelicalism has waxed and waned throughout the various cycles of American history. Medical innovations that make abortions at home easier and safer or make premature infants viable at earlier ages can also shift the terms of the debate. In addition, there are a variety of long-term political and social factors that can also affect the outcome of the debate including continuing secularization and urbanization, changes over time to the composition of the Supreme Court, changes in the way elections are financed, changes in state demographics, and efforts to protect voting rights and eliminate the electoral college, the filibuster, and gerrymandering.

As an aside, the reasoning behind *Dobbs v. Jackson Women's Health Organization* causes many to wonder whether the Court will stop there, or whether it will seek to reconsider, as Justice Clarence Thomas suggests it should, other rights established by precedent but not explicitly guaranteed by the constitution—rights such as gay marriage (*Obergefell v. Hodges*), interracial marriage (*Loving v. Virginia*), access to birth control (*Griswold v. Connecticut*), and the decriminalization of homosexual activity (*Lawrence v. Texas*). Overturning these precedents would be consistent with the interpretive strategy of "constitutional originalism" which treats the Constitution as a sacred text to be read in much the same way as fundamentalists read the Bible and not as a living document whose ambiguities and judicial interpretive precedents allow us to creatively address the unique challenges of each era.

The boundary between the Republican political party and the Evangelical religious community is becoming increasingly blurred, with non-religious and non-Christian conservatives beginning to identify as "Evangelicals" (Burge 2021), and with the incorporation of Christian ritual and song into Republican public events (Dias and Graham 2022). As this boundary continues to erode, there is every reason to believe conservative Christians will push the Republican party to translate their anti-feminist and anti-LGBTQ+ agenda into law. If this happens, the culture wars will heat up further and factional affective polarization will intensify.

From the perspective of a pragmatic flourishing-based ethics, the prime questions regarding abortion are, at least theoretically, empirical. Does allowing abortion to remain legal promote individual and social flourishing or diminish it? If society allows abortion, does that cheapen human life or does it allow more people to lead flourishing lives? Does lowering the rate of unwanted births lower rates of poverty, illiteracy, crime, and incarceration? Does it allow more women to complete educations and find good paying jobs suited to their aspirations and talents? Does tolerating abortion pave the way to other practices that don't treat human life as sacrosanct such as assisted suicide and euthanasia? If that happens, is it good or bad for collective flourishing?

A pragmatic flourishing-based ethics bases its provisional conclusions on the best empirical evidence available, not on dogma and theology. There is some (limited) empirical evidence that legalizing abortion enhances individual and collective flourishing. For example, Ananat *et al.* found children born in states after abortion was legalized had lower rates of infant mortality, were more likely to graduate from college, and were less likely to go on welfare or become single parents. They conclude that "children who were 'born unwanted' prior to the legalization of abortion not only grew up in more disadvantaged households, but they also grew up to be more disadvantaged as adults" (Ananat *et al.* 2009, 36).

I have explored the abortion controversy at length because it points out a weak point in a multicultural ethics of flourishing. A multicultural flourishing-based ethics cannot provide clear-cut rules for deciding when a principled minority ought to try to force its will on a majority. All it can do is suggest we tolerate our differences and avoid civil strife as much as possible, but it can't specify when a difference becomes intolerable. That is a psychological rather than moral question. Usually something will be judged intolerable when it causes real, non-trivial harm to one's well-being or the well-being of those one deeply cares about. But sometimes, as in the case of the White pre-Civil War abolitionist or the contemporary anti-abortion crusader, it involves harm to the well-being of others one may never actually encounter face-to-face.

While a multiculturally-sensitive ethics of flourishing cannot settle every moral dispute, it can allow us to sidestep many. In this imperfect world, perhaps that is the best we can do. And it helps if most of us are working on the same page—searching for ways to enhance mutual well-being based, as much as possible, on empirical evidence and not dogma.

But I have digressed, and I want to return to the question about how to talk to each other across the political divide. How can we talk to each other about differences over abortion, immigration, racial equity, gender, voting rights, or any other controversial issue?

My answer is, "just connect." Just communicate in humane ways without trying to win arguments or score points. When the other person talks, try to provisionally see things from their perspective and understand why they feel as they do. Don't try to formulate a rebuttal while listening, but just try to understand. Don't present your own position until you have communicated back to the other person that you fully understand theirs and why they believe as they do—and they agree they have been correctly understood. When you finally present your position, don't present it as "here's why you're wrong," but as "here's how I see it differently." Don't expect the other person to change his or her mind during the discussion. If appropriate, appreciate the other person for their courtesy and frankness. It's all right to conclude, "I guess we disagree" with the implication that disagreement doesn't make the other disagreeable. This is the way we must learn to talk to each other. And sometimes, in the process of connecting in a humane way, people's positions evolve.

Former anti-Semite and White supremacist Derek Black—whose father was a Grand Master of the Ku Klux Klan—is a case in point. Derek's opinions changed gradually after going away to college. In college, he encountered Black and Jewish students who were willing to engage him in quiet, good faith conversations over dinner. In time, as he came to care about his interlocutors as friends, he realized his beliefs were hurtful to them and decided to change. Derek stated the best way to make change was to "start with one person you have a connection with. That's the most important and powerful thing you can do" (Hunter-Gault and Kane 2019). The vital word is "connection."

Atul Gawande (2013) describes the process of teaching best neonatal care practices to rural nurses in the Indian province of Uttar Pradesh who were resistant to changing their ways. The solution involved providing a cadre of nurse mentors who became personally acquainted with the village nurses over the course of many months. The rural nurses were willing to try new practices when the advice came from people they had established relationships with, and not from unknown experts. Gawande compared this to the way pharmaceutical company representatives persuade doctors to prescribe new medications. He quotes one representative as saying:

> Evidence is not remotely enough … however strong a case you may have. You must also apply "the rule of seven touches." Personally "touch" the doctors seven times, and they will come to know you; if they know you, they might trust you; and, if they trust you, they will change. That's why he stocked doctors' closets with free drug samples in person. Then he could poke his

head around the corner and ask, "So how did your daughter Debbie's soccer game go?" Eventually, this can become "Have you seen this study on our new drug? How about giving it a try?" As the rep had recognized, human interaction is the key force in overcoming resistance and speeding change.
(Gawande 2013, par. 41)

The message is: arguments do not change people, relationships do. I learned this as a psychotherapist. Patients change not just because the therapist makes a good argument, but because they come to feel understood and trust the therapist.

While this is a recipe for restoring civility and reducing affective polarization one relationship at a time, it is not, unfortunately, a recipe for preserving and extending democracy. Studies show that a decline in affective polarization does not, by itself, cause people to drop authoritarian beliefs and embrace democratic ones (Voelkel *et al.* 2021). We ought to be as civil to our opponents as we can—but make no mistake—we are in a vital struggle to preserve democracy. If we fail to make meaningful progress towards mitigating our current problems, a wave of populist resentment will soon put an end to the American experiment. A recent University of Virginia Center for Politics poll found 82% of Republicans endorsed the idea that America needs a "powerful leader in order to destroy the radical and immoral currents," and 52% favored secession from the union (University of Virginia Center for Politics 2021). These are not encouraging figures. If we are going to preserve democracy we will have to fight in its defense. We will have to preserve and extend the principle of "one person, one vote" and convince non-voters (through actions, not words) they have a stake in the system. How does that square with my earlier call for connection and civility? How can one vigorously fight for one's ideals and while staying in relationship with one's opponents?

One answer was provided years ago by Mahatma Gandhi and Dr. Martin Luther King, Jr. One can fight for what one believes in without hating others. One can fight while retaining and exercising the virtues of benevolence, honesty, courage, fairness, and equanimity. One can fight for something rather than against someone. Gandhi and King believed moral virtue inspires admiration and elicits shame in one's opponents. Gandhi called this *satyagraha*, or truth-power. It is not the naïve belief that good always prevails over evil, but the conviction that means must always be consistent with ends. One cannot create justice through injustice, or peace through war. As the Buddhist *Dhammapada* says: "Hostilities aren't stilled through hostility, regardless. Hostilities are stilled through non-hostility: this, an unending truth" (*Dhammapada* 2011, Verse 5).

This also means allowing others to live as they choose as much as possible as long as it does not significantly harm one's own well-being or the well-being of those one deeply cares about. While some things require a unified national strategy—foreign policy, climate change, national election rules—perhaps some can be left, as much as possible, to the laboratory of the states. We do not have to approve of everything going on in other people's bailiwicks. If we can allow some countries in the world to be Islamic republics, some to be monarchies, and some to be socialist states, perhaps we can allow some degree of diversity within our own national borders. But tolerance for that diversity cannot be unlimited, particularly when we see people we sympathize or identify with being grievously harmed. And the tolerance must be mutual, with conservative states accepting the right of liberal states to be as they are every bit as much as liberal states allow conservative states to be as they are.

In addition, a philosophical commitment to pluralism means no person or group has a monopoly on truth. It means people will always disagree on issues relevant to the good life. It means there is no such thing as ultimate perfection. There is no utopia in our future—a society of perfect justice where all flourish and live harmoniously. As Kant pointed out, "Out of the crooked timber of humanity, no straight thing was ever made." The best we can manage is small incremental steps in that direction. It means getting by with compromises that leave no one completely satisfied.

More importantly, it means understanding that what we believe to be the truth is always provisional and at least partly socially constructed. According to the American pragmatist philosopher Charles Peirce, the truth is that which intelligent, well-intentioned investigators will eventually agree on given inquiry over an infinite amount of time. When it comes to social truths, there can be no such final truths, however distant, because human nature and social organization evolve. We can only ask what seems true for us in our culture at this time.

Given there is no final truth, we are more likely to get things right when we listen to all the voices in a conversation. Everyone has a perspective that ought to be given consideration. Aristotle (1943) noted this in his *Politics*:

> The principle that the multitude ought to be supreme rather than the few best is one that is maintained, and, though not free from difficulty, yet seems to contain an element of truth. For the many, of whom each individual is but an ordinary person, when they meet together may very likely be

better than the few good, if regarded not individually but collectively, just as a feast to which many contribute is better than a dinner provided out of a single purse ... Hence the many are better judges than a single man of music and poetry; for some understand one part, and some another, and among them they understand the whole. (Aristotle 1943, Book 3:11)

Historically, Black, Latino, Asian, Indigenous, Female, Non-Christian, differently-abled, and gender non-conforming voices were excluded from the table, and including their voices is transforming our understanding of fairness and equity. Those who resent their inclusion because they fear it overshadows consideration of their own concerns also deserve a place at the table.

People are driven to embrace White or Christian nationalism out of a variety of authentic discontents. They feel increasingly marginalized in our changing culture. They feel their well-being slipping backwards. While most of that slippage is due to the siphoning of wealth from the middle class to the upper class, disinvestment in human capital, globalization, and the changing nature of the meritocracy in a knowledge economy—at least some of that slippage is related to loss of White and male privilege. Positions that used to automatically go to White males must now be competed for. Women currently make up 59.5% of all college students, with an ever-smaller percentage of White males applying for, accepted into, and graduating from college (Belkin 2021). The reasons for this are complex, but this will only guarantee further White male slippage going forward as college graduates make a million dollars more on the average than non-graduates over the course of their lifetimes, and as college educations continue to be a prerequisite for most good paying jobs.

The answer to this problem is not the restoration of male privilege. Part of the answer includes making two-year college more affordable and developing new shorter certification programs in specialty areas that don't require a broad educational background. It includes raising the minimum wage for everyone—especially for jobs that involve caring for children, the infirm, and the elderly. A society that values relatedness understands that jobs that involve caring for others are crucial for a humane, flourishing society. All of us were once children, and most of us will one day become elderly and/or infirm. Finally, four-year colleges should be gateways to cultural, moral, and intellectual flourishing for those so inclined and not the sole gateway to financial well-being and social respect.

We dismiss the concerns of the formerly privileged or those left out of the meritocracy at our peril. While we cannot endorse populist or ethnonationalist solutions, we can empathize with their discontent, understand the reasons for it, and make every effort to promote their flourishing. We can improve the conditions of everyone's lives through greater investment in rural infrastructure and human capital including improved education and better access to healthcare, drug rehabilitation, and job-retraining.

The other sources of discontent are harder to address. Earlier this year North Carolina's Lieutenant Governor gave a speech urging parents to stand up against school boards for "pushing these perverted agendas, to try to teach our children that they're really not boys or girls, or they're shoving this homosexuality garbage down their throats" (WITN Web Team 2021). His is the discontent that comes from seeing one's own moral views—views that were once widely shared—rapidly become a minority view and object of scorn. There is only so much one can do to reduce that kind of discontent. We can try to be more humane in how we criticize people for holding these kinds of views—we can try to be more understanding and forgiving of them as persons as they try to deal with their bewilderment and distress at a changing world—but since the Lieutenant Governor of North Carolina is a public official, comments like his cannot go uncriticized and unchallenged, and those of us who believe in pluralism ought to do all we can to see that people who hold views like his do not get re-elected.

Cancel Culture

We are currently in the midst of a public debate about *cancellation*—the social ostracism of people whose statements (past or present) we now deem objectionable. What role do the moral virtues of honesty, courage, benevolence and fairness and the intellectual virtue of phronesis play in this debate?

The growing social unacceptability of derogatory slurs that diminish the humanity and dignity of people on account of their race, ethnicity, religion, sexual preference, gender orientation, or disability status seems, all things considered, a good thing. The world is a better, kinder place when people think twice before inflammatory and hurtful language. It also seems fair and appropriate to let friends and acquaintances know we find these slurs offensive when they make use of them. In doing so, we are displaying the virtues of honesty and courage in service of benevolence. But—and here is the crucial "but"—it is also important we don't devalue our friend's and acquaintance's humanity, or globally label them bad or deficient in the process. The virtue of phronesis entails saying the right thing in the right way at the right time. Similarly, the Buddhist virtue of *right speech* calls for speech that is not only truthful, but also worded as kindly as possible, and spoken only when likely to do some good.

When I was growing up in the 1950s and early 1960s, all the young males I knew—myself included—employed racial, ethnic, sexist, or homophobic slurs in jokes they told members of their own peer group. I'm glad that's becoming increasingly unacceptable, but I don't feel a need to condemn myself, my family, or my friends for our past un-enlightenment. This is an area where cultural mores are rapidly evolving and we can afford to be generous in judging people for things said or done decades ago.

But what about public figures who are neither our friends nor acquaintances? Do the same rules apply? We always have a choice about whether to patronize businesses or entertainments when businessmen or movie stars make comments we find objectionable. Our judgements about such matters ought to be tempered by mitigating factors, however: How egregious was the comment? How long ago was it made? Is the person unapologetic? Is the person still engaging in behavior consistent with it?

Social consequences for offensive opinions also ought to be proportional to the offense. It's fair game to correct others—no one is entitled to a free pass from criticism—but no one should lose their livelihood if their offensive opinions are irrelevant to their professional roles. Finding the right balance between discouraging hate speech and allowing people the right to their opinions is a delicate task. Allowing people their offensive beliefs, however, does not mean privately owned or publicly traded media are obligated to provide them with a platform. The first amendment protects speech from government encroachment but doesn't guarantee a public forum.

The question of whether people ought to lose their jobs on account of their beliefs becomes trickier when they are the public face of a company. Companies must choose between defending their employee's rights to hold offensive opinions as private citizens and retaining the good will of their clients. These are cases that must be judged on a case-by-case basis as no single rule can cover all cases.

There is also the related question of our feelings about cultural artifacts that are created by people whose views or behavior we find offensive. A good deal of the world's culture was created by imperfect people who held views or engaged in conduct we now find reprehensible. If we cancelled all their contributions our culture would be greatly impoverished.

Sometimes we find we are able to separate a work of art from the artist's views or personal behavior and sometimes we can't. People may have trouble, for example, appreciating Wagner's operas, Gilbert and Sullivan's *Mikado*, Shakespeare's *Merchant of Venice* and *Othello*, Nabokov's *Lolita*, and Phillip

Roth's novels or Picasso's and Gauguin's paintings. Sometimes it takes an effort to appreciate what is great about these cultural artifacts while simultaneously recognizing they are the expressions of artists whose views or actions we (now) disapprove of. People have a right to choose whether or not to read or view material they deem offensive, but they shouldn't have the right to dictate how others should feel or what they read and view.

It's best to learn how to view works of art like these in their full context. We shouldn't cancel them from curricula, museums, or theaters, but should try to understand why they are worthy of appreciation (on some grounds) and problematic (on others). It really shouldn't be all that hard to make these kinds of judgements—after all, we do it all the time when we recognize the good and bad qualities of people we love.

I am grateful that, as an undergraduate at a college with a plurality of Jewish students, I was able to view a college film society presentation of Leni Riefenstahl's (1935) Nazi propaganda film *Triumph des Willens*. The film was worth viewing on three counts: it offered a way to understand Hitler's appeal to the German populace, it demonstrated the power of art as propaganda, and it was a masterful work of editing and cinematography. No one protested showing the film, because no reasonable person worried the film would convert us to Nazism. The college also rightly assumed we didn't need protection from material that might "traumatize" us or make us feel "unsafe," even though a fair number of students were children of Holocaust survivors. The university community treated us as if we were adults capable of making our own moral and aesthetic judgements—and that is the way my generation wanted to be treated.

Unfortunately, almost every day brings new examples of excessive zeal on the part of social justice proponents trying to police offensive speech. Just the other day, a respected geophysicist was scheduled to give a scientific talk at the Massachusetts Institute of Technology. MIT cancelled the talk because some students and faculty objected to the scientist's opposition to affirmative action. His opposition was based on his conviction that it was wrong to judge applicants as members of groups rather than as individuals. He wasn't against diversity, per se, but against a specific means of attaining it—the sort of thing reasonable people may disagree on. The chair of the geoscience program at Williams College supported MIT's cancellation. When asked whether it was a university's job to protect free speech, she was quoted as saying, "this idea of intellectual debate and rigor as the pinnacle of intellectualism comes from a world in which white men dominated" (Powell 2021).

As if free speech protected only White males! It's a pity when social justice advocates take the same antidemocratic, anti-free inquiry stance reactionaries do. It's a shame when reasonable political differences are assumed to be evidence of offensive racist views. It's unfortunate when political views one disagrees with preclude someone from speaking on a neutral topic they have genuine expertise on. While we have a responsibility to criticize bad ideas, we shouldn't be in the business of judging the overall worthwhileness of people. Democracy is in perilous shape, and its condition is made more perilous when liberals and progressives fail to uphold the principles of free inquiry.

Three Final Cautions

A liberal flourishing-based agenda cannot be implemented everywhere and all at once; it is a long-term historical project. Implementation requires altering a wide variety of social beliefs and norms—beliefs and norms which most people take for granted as the "way things have been since time immemorial" and so ought to remain. As a result, social progress is always halting and piecemeal.

The Fifteenth Amendment granted Black male suffrage a full half-century before the Nineteenth Amendment granted women's suffrage and almost a century-and-a-half before *Obergefell v. Hodges* mandated recognition of same-sex marriage. Could women's suffrage have been included in the Fifteenth Amendment? The issue was debated at the time—certainly Susan B. Anthony and Elizabeth Cady Stanton thought so—but while the moral answer is "it should have been," the historical answer was "not quite yet." The legislative votes were not yet there; the woman's movement was not yet strong enough; the general social understanding of women's roles hadn't yet evolved sufficiently. It is even more difficult to imagine *Obergefell v. Hodges* a century-and-a-half earlier. A good deal of social transformation had to occur first—changes to the predominant Victorian Christian moral code; the ways the abolitionist, suffragette, and anticolonial movements created new metaphors for human freedom and dignity; changes in how psychological science (which did not yet exist in 1870) would eventually come to view gender and sexuality; and changes in homosexuals' ability to safely organize and publicly advocate for themselves as a group.

This means that before the changes we desire can be implemented, the groundwork must first be laid, and the preconditions for those changes fought for, nurtured, and allowed to evolve. This is, understandably, a frustrating reality: we want to get from here to there immediately if not sooner. Unfortunately, there is never such an immediate route.

Second, the desire to achieve a new consensus on a flourishing-based ethics is in some ways reminiscent of previous efforts to "reform" human nature—efforts in which some elite strata hoped to awaken, improve, and transform "the people." This was the Confucian project in Warring States China, the clerical project during the Protestant Reformation, the Bolshevik project during the Russian Revolution, and the Evangelical project during the American temperance movement. These movements shared the belief that "the common person" was morally deficient and in need of "lifting up." Elites tried to work these transformations through sermonizing, scolding, criticizing, shaming, and ostracizing—and at times through the Gulag and guillotine. Current liberal attempts to reform average Americans and cleanse them from their sins of racism, sexism, homophobia, and transphobia bear a significant resemblance to these past crusades.

As much as elites may try, however, "the common people" stubbornly resist efforts at being coerced into "improvement." They don't want to be scolded, shamed, and preached to, to confess their sins, or be made into "better people." They just want to be left alone to live their lives without hectoring and interference. A good deal of right-wing populism reflects this kind of resistance and resentment over attempts to make them over into more "enlightened" people.

This doesn't mean reform is never successful. The temperance movement greatly reduced the average daily amount of alcohol Americans consumed. The Protestant Reformation successfully turned Northern Europeans into a more thrifty, sober, and hard-working people. These movements were, in essence, aspects of the longer-term project of *civilization*, of the turning of brawling, drunken brutes into people fit for polite society. We can think of this in Freudian (1962) terms as the repression and sublimation of aggression and libido, or in terms of nation states harnessing their citizenry to the engine of economic prosperity to maximize their geopolitical power, or in terms of just about everyone's wish for less crime and disorder. Civilization comes with a price, however, and one shouldn't be surprised when people resent elites intent on their betterment. This is an argument for adopting a more charitable approach to civilizational improvement with less scolding, shaming, and ostracism—more carrot than stick; more positive reinforcement than punishment; more "God loves you" than hellfire and brimstone.

Third, this is a good place to humbly acknowledge that there are never any perfect solutions to problems—every solution creates new (often unintended and unforeseen) problems. This is why the "settled" solutions of the past can almost always benefit from renewed inquiry in the present. While the internal combustion engine was an improvement over reliance on horses for transportation, it introduced new problems: the need for expensive infrastructure, traffic jams, motor vehicle casualties, and fossil fuel dependence. While antibiotics extended the human life span, they increased the incidence of chronic and acute diseases of old age.

The principle of "no perfect solutions" also applies to proposed solutions to present-day social inequities. Ceasing admissions testing for educational opportunities may help Blacks who, as a group, tend to do relatively poorly on such exams for historical and cultural reasons, but hurt Asian Americans who, as a group, tend to do relatively well on such exams, also for historical and cultural reasons. Allowing transgender women to compete on women's sports teams may allow transgender women opportunities formerly denied them, but also prevent some cisgender women from earning a chance to compete.

Every new social policy involves tradeoffs that may help some and harm others. This is not an argument against such policies, but only for an awareness that the voices of people potentially injured by such policies have the same right to be heard as their intended beneficiaries. The process of negotiating proposed changes so they end up seeming fair to (most) people is almost always slower, messier, and more contentious than one might like. This is the unfortunate price we pay for democracy, which is, as Winston Churchill (1947) famously noted, "the worst form of government except for all those other forms that have been tried."

Conclusions

I began this book outlining the conflict threatening to tear America apart: the emergent vision of America as an inclusive pluralistic, multicultural democracy, and the older vision of America as exclusively White, Christian, cisgender, and patriarchal. That older view is slowly dying, but still embraced, in part or in whole, by a significant number of Americans. The only way this older view can be successfully reimposed is through a disenfranchisement of minority voters and a rejection of democratic principles.

I then suggested a way forward through this conflict: a whole-hearted embrace of a pragmatic, pluralistic, flourishing-based ethics. Not everyone can embrace such an ethics, but perhaps enough of us can so that we can continue function as a society and make progress towards a flourishing future.

In the chapters that followed, I outlined the basis for such an ethics. I based it on a set of moral and intellectual virtues that are (almost) universally valued because they contribute to individual and collective flourishing. I culled this set of virtues from the commonalties between ancient Aristotelian, Buddhist, and Confucian ethics and the ethics of today's modern world religions and humanisms. It included the moral virtues of *courage, benevolence, conscientiousness, temperance, equanimity, truthfulness, and justice*, and the intellectual virtue of *phronesis* or *practical wisdom*. These were virtues that enabled people to pursue personally fulfilling and meaningful lives while recognizing their responsibilities to family, community, and the environment. They enabled people to find fulfillment in relationships, accomplishments, aesthetics, and meaning, through the attitudes of whole-heartedness, acceptance, and open inquiry, and through greater levels of personal integration.

This final chapter explored the implications of a pragmatic, pluralistic, flourishing-based ethics for public policy. It concluded that wealth should be valued for its ability to promote individual and collective flourishing and not as an end-in-itself. Corporations ought to honor their obligations to their employees, customers, community, and environment, and not just their shareholders. Governments need to measure their success by the flourishing of their citizenry and not (solely) by their gross national product. Current compensation practices overvalue managerial skills and undervalue caretaking. There should be greater educational and economic opportunities for people not inclined to a four-year college education. The vast inequality between the very rich and the rest is feeding and intensifying cultural conflict. Education should prepare children for flourishing and not just employability.

Foreign policy ought to be a tool for promoting flourishing at home and abroad. Just as we are learning to appreciate multiculturalism and pluralism at home, we must learn to accept it abroad. America has engaged in a series of wars in Vietnam and the Middle East that have done nothing to improve American well-being at home, slaughtered millions abroad, and squandered trillions that could have been spent on bettering people's lives. American foreign policy must come to terms with its strengths and limitations in a world in which it is no longer the sole superpower. Managing conflicts with rising nations like China and Iran will require phronesis —the careful calibration of risk and benefit to national well-being, taking all costs into account. This is an argument for balancing our prudential concerns with our ideals.

Finally, a pragmatic, pluralistic, flourishing-based ethics has implications for how we relate to each other at home. It stresses benevolence and fairness in interactions with those we disagree with, and the importance of listening, understanding, and appreciating our common humanity. While we wish to protect and extend democracy and oppose a return to an ethic of male, White, cis-gender or Christian privilege, we owe those we disagree with all the dignity, respect, and care we can muster. White and Christian ethnonationalism grow out of a loss or threat of loss to well-being among its adherents. Their well-being, too, falls within our circle of concern. We may have differing opinions about how to resolve those concerns, but their concerns must be heard and addressed.

We co-create culture in the individual and collective process of accepting, revising, and rejecting our inheritance from the past. We each have a personal and collective responsibility to help form and re-form the cultures we live in, and when it is our time to leave the stage, to pass the never-finished project of cultural formation on to our descendants.

Ethical questions are never about "me," but always about "us." Our lives should not be about simply "getting ahead," but about flourishing—and not just about our flourishing but creating a culture that supports everyone's flourishing. This is the message passed down to us by Aristotle, the Buddha, and Confucius. It is also the message of the Hebrew prophets and Christian fathers. It is our job to make these teachings relevant to our lives and pass them on to our children and grandchildren. This is the only way we can hope to fulfil the promise of democracy in a pluralistic world.

Philosopher John Dewey (2012) emphasized that democracy is not simply a set of formal institutions (checks and balances, the franchise) but more fundamentally an ethos—an idea about how community members can participate cooperatively to help maximize each other's unique potentials for flourishing. As such, democracy is an ideal that can be approached but never fully realized. Solutions that seem to advance the possibilities for democratic life in one generation can result in a new sets of problems that call for revised solutions in the next. Democracy is always, at best, a work in progress.

In addition, the state of a society at any given point in time is always the end-product of a lengthy history of institutional and cultural evolution. Dewey contended that societies can never be reconstituted *de novo* but are best advanced by pragmatic adjustments in already existing sets of relations. There is no way to get to utopia from here, but we can always do better, and the best ways forward are always empirically-based.

It is anyone's guess whether American democracy as a set of formal institutions can survive the present tide of *ressentiment*, misinformation, distrust, alienation, populism, authoritarianism, and tribal conflict. If it is to survive, it will be because enough of us cultivate the personal and civic virtues outlined in this book, are steadfast in our courage and commitment, and are guided by a benevolent heart.

Even if it falters, all will not be lost. As long as democracy persists as an ideal, what is lost can always be regained.

References

Abernathy, R. 1998. *And the walls came tumbling down: An autobiography*. New York: Harper & Row.
Allan, L. and E. Robinson. 1942. *The House I Live In*. London: Chappell and Company.
Allcott, H., L. Braghieri, S. Eichmeyer and M. Gentzkow. 2020. "The welfare effects of social media." *American Economic Review* 110(3): 629–676. https://bit.ly/3NocxsS
America first caucus policy platform. 2021. https://bit.ly/3Yrds2P
American Academy of Pediatrics. 2017. "Children's hospitals admissions for suicidal thoughts, actions double during past decade." https://bit.ly/3z1Usld
Ananat, E., G. Gruber, P. Levine and D. Staiger. 2009. *Abortion and Selection. National Bureau of Economic Research Working Paper* 12150. http://www.jstor.org/stable/25651322
Angle, S. 2013. "Is conscientiousness a virtue? Confucian answers." In *Virtue Ethics and Confucianism*, by S. Angle and M. Slote, 182–191. London: Routledge.
Anscombe, G.E.M. 1958. "Modern moral philosophy." *Philosophy* 33(124): 1–19.
Aristotle. 1973. "Nichomachean ethics," translated by W. D. Ross, In Introduction to Aristotle edited by R. McKeon. 2nd Edition. Chicago, IL: University of Chicago Press.
———. 1943. *Politics*. Translated by B. Jowitt. http://classics.mit.edu/Aristotle/politics.html
Badhwar, N. 2014. *Well-being: Happiness in a Worthwhile Life*. Oxford: Oxford University Press.
Ballard, J. 2020. "How Republicans and Democrats would feel if their child married across the political aisle." *YouGov America*. https://bit.ly/3pxuLPQ
Belkin, D. 2021. "A generation of American men give up on college: 'I just feel lost.'" *Wall Street Journal*, September 6. https://on.wsj.com/3pyvDny
Berlin, Isaiah. 1979. *Four Essays On Liberty*. Oxford: Oxford University Press.
Blatt, S. and R. Ford. 1994. *Therapeutic Change: An Object Relations Perspective*. New York: Plenum.
Blight, D. 2018. *Frederick Douglass: Prophet of Freedom*. New York: Simon & Schuster.
Bloom, P. 2013. *Just Babies: The Origins of Good and Evil*. New York: Crown.

Bhikkhu Bodhi, Trans. 2020. "Half the Holy Life." In *The connected discourses of the Buddha: A New Translation of the Sāyutta Nikāya*. Boulder, CO: Shambhala.

Bowles, S. and H. Gintis. 2011. *A Cooperative Species. Human Reciprocity and Its Evolution*. Princeton, NJ. Princeton University Press.

Brecht, B. 2003. *Poetry and Prose,* Edited by Reinhold Grimm. New York: Continuum.

Britannica, The Editors of Encyclopaedia. "Key Facts of the Vietnam War". *Encyclopedia Britannica*, 15 Oct. 2020, https://www.britannica.com/summary/Key-Facts-of-the-Vietnam-War. Accessed 8 August 2023.

Burge, R. 2021. "Why 'Evangelical' is becoming another word for 'Republican.'" New York Times, October 26. https://nyti.ms/3N2b7od

Chan, M. 2015. "White Christians now make up less than half of Americans." *Time*. https://bit.ly/3puagUg

Churchill, W. S. 1947. "Speech before the House of Commons," November 11, 1947." https://bit.ly/3v5UoKe

Cohn, M. 2022. "Do Americans support abortion rights? It depends on the state. " New York Times, May 4. https://nyti.ms/3L1SAXL

Cox, D. 2021. "After the ballots are counted: Conspiracies, political violence, and American exceptionalism." *Survey Center on American Life*. https://bit.ly/3JothiU

Csikszentmihalyi, M. 1990. *Flow: The Psychology of Optimal Experience*. New York: Harper & Row.

Darwin, J. 2008. *After Tamerlane: The Rise and Fall of Global Empires, 1400–2000*. London: Bloomsbury.

Dewey, J. 2005. *Art as Experience*. New York: TarcherPerigee.

———. 2008. "Creative Democracy—The Task Before Us." In *John Dewey: The Later Works*, Volume 14: 1939–1941, Essays, Reviews, and Miscellany, edited by J.A. Boydston, 224–230. Carbondale: Southern Illinois University Press.

———. 2012. *The Public and its Problems: An Essay in Political Inquiry*. University Park: Pennsylvania State University Press.

———. 2013. *A Common Faith*. New Haven, CT: Yale University Press.

Dhammapada (Buddharakkhita, trans.) 1996. https://bit.ly/3pw21XJ

Dhammapada, A translation (Thanisarro Bhikkhu, trans.) 2011. https://bit.ly/3eqTUFx

Dias, E. and R. Graham. 2022. "The growing religious fervor in the American right: 'This is a Jesus Movement.'" New York Times, April 11. https://nyti.ms/3KXeivD

Dyer, T. 1980. *Theodore Roosevelt and the Idea of Race*. Baton Rouge: Louisiana State University Press.

Eavis, P. 2022. "How Elon Musk helped lift the ceiling on C.E.O. pay." New York Times, , June 26. https://nyti.ms/3R1qSi3

Erikson, E. 1994. "Identity and the Life Cycle. New York: W.W. Norton.

Freud, S. 1962. *Civilization and Its Discontents.* Translated and edited by James Strachey. New York: W.W. Norton & Company.

Flanagan, O. 2014. *Moral Sprouts and Natural Teleologies: Twenty-First Century Moral Psychology Meets Classical Chinese Philosophy*. Milwaukee, WI: Marquette University Press.

References

Gardner, H. 2011. *Frames of Mind: The Theory of Multiple Intelligences*, 3rd edition. New York: Basic Books.

Gawande, A. 2013. "Slow ideas. Some innovations spread fast. How do you speed the ones that don't." *The New Yorker*, July 22. https://www.newyorker.com/magazine/2013/07/29/slow-ideas

Gendlin, E. 2018. *A Process Model*. Evanston, IL: Northwestern University Press.

General Social Survey. 2020. [Data Set]. https://bit.ly/3JmKFEr

Gingrich, N. 2021. "The crisis of American civilization." *Gingrich360*. https://bit.ly/3xYVA2e

Gladwell, M. 2008. *Outliers: The Story Of Success*. Boston, MA: Little, Brown, & Company.

Goldin, P. 2020. *The Art of Chinese Philosophy: Eight Classical Texts and How to Read Them*. Princetn, NJ: Princeton University Press.

Goleman, D. 1995. *Emotional Intelligence: Why it can matter more than IQ*. New York: Bantam.

Gottman, J. 1994. *Why Marriages Succeed or Fail: What You Can Learn From Breakthrough Research To Make Your Marriage Last*. New York: Simon & Schuster.

Guisinger, S. and S. Blatt. 1994. "Individuality and relatedness: Evolution of a fundamental dialectic." *American Psychologist* 49(2): 104–111. https://www.doi.org/10.1037/0003-066X.49.2.104

Haidt, J. and C. Joseph. 2008. "The moral mind: How five sets of innate intuitions guide the development of many culture-specific virtues, and perhaps even modules." In The Innate Mind: Foundations and the Future, edited by Peter Carruthers, Stephen Laurence and Steven Stich, 367–391. Oxford: Oxford University Press.

Half the Holy Life. 2020. In *The connected discourses of the Buddha: A New Translation of the Saṃyutta Nikāya*, (Bhikkhu Bodhi, trans.), 1524. Boulder, CO: Shambhala.

Halpern, S. 2018. "How Republicans became anti-choice." *The New York Review of Books*, November 8. https://www.nybooks.com/articles/2018/11/08/how-republicans-became-anti-choice/

Hayes, S., K. D. Strosahl and K. G. Wilson (2016). *Acceptance and Commitment Therapy: The Process and Practice of Mindful Change,* 2nd edition. New York: Guilford Press.

Hunter-Gault, C. and J. Kane. 2019. "Derek Black grew up as a white nationalist. Here's how he changed his mind." PBS Newshour, November 5. https://to.pbs.org/3OomszX

Jiang, T. 2021. *Origins of Moral-political Philosophy in Early China*. Oxford: Oxford University Press.

Jung, C. 1960. *On the Nature of the Psyche*. Princeton, NJ: Princeton University Press.

Kaczynski, T. 1998. "Excerpts from Unabomber's journal." *New York Times,* Section A, Page 18, April 29. https://www.nytimes.com/1998/04/29/us/excerpts-from-unabomber-s-journal.html

Lemoine, B. 2022. "Is LaMDA sentient—an interview." *Medium*, June 11. https://bit.ly/3xB99VDhttps://bit.ly/3qdRjZj

Linehan, M. 1993. *Cognitive-Behavioral Treatment of Borderline Personality Disorder*. New York: Guilford Press.

Luhur, W., T. Brown and A. Flores. 2019. "Public opinion of transgender rights in the United States." 2017 IPSOS International Survey Series. https://bit.ly/3erRAOq

Major, J., S. Queen, A. Meyer and H. Roth, trans. and eds. 2010. *The Huainanzi: A Guide to the Theory and Practice of Government in Early Han China*. New York: Columbia University Press.

Mencius. 2016. *Mencius: Translation, Commentary, and Notes*. Translated by R. Eno. https://bit.ly/32yPGJw

MacIntyre, A. 1981. *After Virtue: A Study In Moral Theory*. South Bend, IN: University of Notre Dame Press.

Maturana, H. and Varela, F. 1980. *Autopoiesis and Cognition: The Realization of the Living*. Dordrecht: D. Reidel.

Mosteller, A. 2021. "CEO vs. employee salaries at America's top companies." https://bit.ly/32Blq0n

Neihardt, J. 2014. *Black Elk speaks: The Complete Edition*. Lincoln: University of Nebraska Press.

Nicholson, D. 2019. "Is the cell really a machine?" *Journal of Theoretical Biology* 477(21): 108–126. https://www.doi.org/10.1016/j.jtbi.2019.06.002

Nussbaum, M. 2016. *Anger and Forgiveness: Resentment, Generosity, and Forgiveness*. Oxford: Oxford University Press.

Olendzki, A.. trans. 2005. *Skinny Gotami & the mustard seed* [Commentary to Therigatha 10.1], Access to Insight. https://bit.ly/3OL9Y5k

Oneybuchi Eke, M. 2010. *Intellectual History in Contemporary South Africa*. London: Palgrave MacMillan.

Outreach Magazine. 2018. "7 startling facts: An up close look at church attendance in America." *Outreach Magazine*. https://bit.ly/3z0Q7bD

Pew Research Center. 2019. "Attitudes on Same Sex Marriage." https://pewrsr.ch/3mCxci5

Piaget, J. and B. Inhelder. 1974. *The Child's Construction of Quantities*. London: Routledge and Kegan Paul.

Pirkei Avot (n.d.). Joshua Kul, trans. Sefaria. Retrieved 6/27/22. https://bit.ly/3xVnSuB

Powell, M. 2021. "M.I.T.'s choice of lecturer ignited criticism. So did its decision to cancel." *The New York Times,* October 20. https://bit.ly/43YXz4P

Rand, A. 1992 [1957]. *Atlas Shrugged*. 35th anniversary edition. Boston, MA: Dutton.

Rawls, J. 1993. *Political Liberalism*. New York: Columbia University Press.

Rockhill, W. W., trans. *Udànavarga: A Collection of Verses from the Buddhist Canon*. 1883. London: Trübner and Company.

Rorty, R. 1989. "The Last Intellectual in Europe: Orwell on Cruelty." In *Irony, Contingency, and Solidarity*, 169–188. Cambridge: Cambridge University Press.

———. 2021. *Pragmatism as Anti-Authoritarianism*. Boston, MA: Belknap Press of Harvard University Press.

Russell, D. 2009. *Practical Intelligence and the Virtues*. Oxford: Oxford University Press.

Śantideva. 1979. *Bodhisattvachayavatara*. Translated by S. Batchelor. Library of Tibetan Works and Archives. https://bit.ly/32vu29d

Sarokin, D. 2020. "CEO compensation in the US vs. the world." *Chron*. https://bit.ly/3u2tlid

Scott, D. 2013. *The Love That Made Mother Teresa*. Nashua, NH: Sophia Institute Press.

References

Seligman, Martin. 2011. *Flourish: a Visionary New Understanding of Happiness and Well-Being*. New York: Free Press.

St. Jean De Crèvecœur, J. H. 1904. *Letters from an American Farmer*. New York: Fox, Duffield & Company.

Shklar, J. 1982. "Putting Cruelty First." *Daedelus* 111(3): 17–28.

Saint Francis of Assisi (n.d.). "Canticle of the Sun." (Franciscan Friars Third Order Regular, trans.) https://bit.ly/3xVJwyZ

Spinoza, Benedict. 2005. *Ethics*. London: Penguin.

Stace, W. T. 1961. *Mysticism and Philosophy*. London: MacMillan and Company.

Steger M., T. Kashdan and O. Shigehiro. 2008. "Being good by doing good: Daily eudaimonic activity and well-being." *Journal of Research in Personality* 42: 22–42. https://www.doi.org/10.1016/j.jrp.2007.03.004

Taylor, Charles. 1992. Sources of The Self: The Making of Modern Identity. Boston, MA: Harvard University Press.

———. 2007. "A Secular Age." Boston, MA: The Belknap Press of Harvard University Press.

The analects of Confucius: An online teaching translation, translated by R. Eno. 2015. https://bit.ly/3z0RU0l

The great learning and the doctrine of the mean: An online teaching translation, translated by R. Eno. 2016. https://bit.ly/3pz7jSt

Thanissaro Bhikkhu, trans. 2004. "Karaniya Metta Sutta." *Access to Insight*. https://bit.ly/3QOhX3e

Thebault, R. and D. Rindler. 2021. "Shootings never stopped during the pandemic: 2020 was the deadliest gun violence year in decades." Washington Post, March 23. https://wapo.st/3z6Gat1

Tiberius, V. 2018. *Well-Being As Value Fulfillment: How We Can Help Each Other To Live Well*. Oxford: Oxford University Press.

Tractate Shabbat. 2017. *The William Davidson Edition of the Babylonian Talmud, Sefaria*. https://bit.ly/3ynIcWV

United States Census Bureau. 2015. "Gini Index of money income and equivalence-adjusted Income: 1967 to 2014." https://bit.ly/3mDUsMJ.

United States Federal Reserve. 2020. "Wealth by wealth percentile group." https://bit.ly/3ew6aol

University of Virginia Center for Politics. 2021. "New initiative explores deep, persistent divides between Biden and Trump voters." https://bit.ly/3mB6Ugo

Voelkel, J., J. Chu, M. Stagnaro, J. Mernyk, C. Redekopp, S. Pink, J. Druckman, D. Rand and R. Willer. 2021. "Interventions reducing affective polarization do not improve antidemocratic attitudes." *Open Science Foundation Preprints*. https://osf.io/7evmp/

Wang, W. 2020. "Marriages between Democrats and Republicans are extremely rare." *Institute for Family Studies*. https://bit.ly/3bmT9Pr

Watson Institute of International and Public Affairs, Brown University. 2021a. "Human cost of post-9/11 wars." https://watson.brown.edu/costsofwar/figures/2021/WarDeathToll

———. 2021b. "Costs of War: Economic costs." https://watson.brown.edu/costsofwar/costs/economic

Wells, G., J. Horowitz and D. Seetharaman. 2021. "Facebook knows Instagram is toxic for teen girls, company documents show." *The Washington Post*, September 14. https://on.wsj.com/3HfGt7F

Werner, H. 1957. "The concept of development from a comparative and organismic point of view." In *The Concept of Development*, edited by D. Harris, 125–148. Minneapolis: University of Minnesota Press.

White, R. 2016. *American Ulysses: The Life of Ulysses S. Grant*. New York: Random House.

WITN Web Team. 2021. Lt. Gov. Robinson defends homophobic comments, dismisses calls for resignation, WITN-TV, October 8. https://bit.ly/3FwVr96

Wolf, S. 1982. "Moral saints." *The Journal of Philosophy* 79(8): 419–439. https://www.doi.org/10.2307/2026228

Zangwill, Israel. 1909. *The Melting Pot, Project Guttenberg*. https://bit.ly/3mBGk6M

———. 1917. *The Melting Pot: A Drama in Four Acts*. New York: The Macmillan Company.

Index

A

Abolition 26–27
Abortion 156–159
Acceptance 117–124
Acceptance and Commitment Therapy (ACT) 123
Accomplishment 95–98
Aesthetics 98–101
Affective Polarization 161
Analects 37–38, 42–44, 51, 52, 137
Anscombe, G.E.M. 28
Arete 32
Aristotle 32–34, 39. 42, 43, 46, 48, 50, 55, 61, 64, 67, 68, 78, 83, 88, 89–90, 163–164
Atheism 6, 7, 18,
Autism 93

B

Badhwar, Neera 47
Benevolence 37–43, 50–54
Bentham, Jeremy 16, 19
Black Elk 135
Blatt, Sidney 139–140
Bloom, Paul 59
Bolshevik 28
Brahmaviharas 34
Brecht, Bertolt 154
Buddhism 34–36, 39, 43, 56, 102, 111, 133, 134

C

Cancel Culture 165–168
CEO compensation 141–142
Chengyu (four-character idioms) 68
Cognitive Dissonance 110
Conservative Christianity 4–14
Churchill, Winston 170
Compartmentalization 114
Conscientiousness 54–55
Confucianism 37–42, 43, 44
Confucius 37, 42, 43, 44, 46, 50, 51, 52, 61, 67, 126, 134, 136, 137, 144
Corporations 141–144
Courage 43, 47–50
Cruelty 51

D

de Crèvecœur, Hector 3
Dewey, John x, xiv, xv, 9, 100, 127, 137, 152, 172
Dialectical Behavioral Therapy (DBT) 123
Dobbs v. Jackson Women's Health Organization 158–159
Douglass, Frederick 2, 50

E

Economic Inequality 9, 12, 15, 65, 72, 142, 171
Education 101, 149–150
Enlightenment (Buddhist) 36

Equanimity 56–57
Eudaimonia 33, 34
Emotional Intelligence 69–70

F

Fairness 59–60
Fifteenth Amendment 168
Foreign Policy 145–149
Franklin, Benjamin 26
Friendship 34, 64, 82, 89, 90, 92, 93
Flourishing 33, 46–47, 81–130, 170–172
Flow 106

G

Gardner, Howard 69
Gawande, Atul 161–162
Gendlin, Eugene 73
Gini Coefficient 142
global warming 144–145
Golden Rule 14, 37, 38, 40, 51–52,126
Goleman, Daniel 69
Gottman, John 95
Great Learning 38
Griswold v. Connecticut 159

H

Haidt, Jonathan 44–45
Happiness 33, 34. 47, 53, 54, 56, 61, 83–86
Hadith 52
Hillel, Rabbi 51, 67, 126, 134
Hobbes, Thomas 53
Huainanzi 68
Hume, David 16

I

Immigration 1–3
Individualism x, 19, 35, 39, 88, 134, 137–143
Integration 113–117
interpersonal intelligence 69
Internalization of Values 25

J

Jiang, Tao x, 40
Jung, Carl 115
Justice 40, 43, 56, 59–61, 137

K

Kant, Immanuel 16, 19, 52, 126, 163
Kaczynski, Ted 93
Kisa Gotami 56–57

L

Lawrence v. Texas 159
LGBTQ+ Rights 5, 9, 112, 124,159
Linehan, Marsha 101, 123
Lovingkindness 34, 36, 42, 51, 134, 136,
Loving v. Virginia 159

M

Macintyre, Alasdair 15
Mahabharata 52, 67
Meaning 8–9, 107–113
Meditation 56, 102, 104, 105, 121, 136
Melting Pot 3–4
Mencius 39–41, 44, 51–53, 68, 134
Menmitsu no-kafu 102
Metaphysics 15, 17–18, 22, 34, 38, 41, 42, 45, 133
Metta 42, 135, 136
Mill, John Stuart 16
Mindfulness 75–76, 104–105, 136
Mohists 39
Montaigne, Michel de 51
Moral babies 59
Moral Foundations Theory 44–45, 50
Moral Sainthood, the problem of 63–65
Multiculturalism 4, 131, 171

N

Nature 112–113
Nietzsche, Fredrich 16
Nussbaum, Martha 61

O

Obergefell v. Hodges 132, 159, 168
Open Inquiry 76–77, 171

P

Paramitas 34
Peirce, Charles 163
Piaget, Jean 71, 139–140
Pluralism xviii, 6, 12–13, 18, 165, 171

Index

Phronesis 29, 30, 32, 34, 42, 57, 68, 70–78, 95, 146, 148, 149, 150, 165, 175
Prajña 35, 42, 78,

R
Rand, Ayn 141
Rawls, John 15
Reading the air 69
Relatedness 93, 101, 133–140, 164
Relationships 49, 70, 81–84, 86, 87–95
Rén 37–39, 40, 42, 50, 61, 136
Rorschach Test 140
Rorty, Richard 131–132, 152
Russell, David 29
Russia xv, 15, 28, 148–149, 169

S
Saint Francis 134–135
Śantideva 35–36, 67
Socrates 32, 59, 67, 155
Schweitzer, Albert 115, 136
Secularization 5–12, 16, 159
Seligman, Martin 86
Shklar, Judith 51
Slavery 1, 17, 26–28, 77, 132–133, 157, 158
Social Media 133, 150–151
Spinoza, Benedict 67, 95, 126
Sprout Theory (Mencius) 40

T
Taiwan xv, 147–148
Taylor, Charles 6, 65, 137, 138
Temperance 32, 34, 43, 46, 56, 61, 64, 69, 76, 91, 129
Tiberius, Valerie 124–126
Truthfulness 32, 34, 43, 45, 46, 58–59, 61, 62, 64, 71, 91, 98, 127

U
Ubuntu 136–137
Udanávarga 43
Ukraine 148–149

V
Values
Values Coherence 115
Value Conflicts (Personal vs. Community) 26–28
Virtue Cultivation 31, 38–39, 41–42, 61, 62–63
Virtue Ethics iv, xiv, 19, 22, 46, 65
Werner, Heinz 139

W
Women's Rights 5, 128, 132, 168
Women's Suffrage 2, 132, 168
Whole-heartedness 101–106, 129, 149, 171
Wisdom 29–30, 32, 35, 37, 42, 64, 67–79
Wolf, Susan 63

Z
Zangwill, Israel 3–4
Zen 102
Zhi 37, 39, 40, 42, 68
Zhuangzi 39, 6